About This Book

Why is this topic important?

A lot of instructional content is uninteresting or worse, and learning content delivered over the Internet or corporate networks is too often dreadfully boring, depersonalized, one-dimensional, generic, force-fed, lock-step, and prepackaged, with meaningless activities and assessments. Some say it's because that's what can be done. Nuh-uh. We can and must do better than that.

What can you achieve with this book?

Many books recommend teaching and learning strategies based on current learning research and theory but provide few examples of how to apply them in the real world. This book *shows* you concrete examples of people making learning better every day, in all kinds of settings, all over the world.

This book showcases ideas that make learning more fun and engaging. You will acquire great ideas that you can adopt or adapt for making your instructional materials appealing, getting out of the rut you are in, and peeking over the shoulders of some of the world's most creative instructors, instructional designers and developers, trainers, programmers, media developers, artists, and others. In fact, the ideas in this book will very likely spark new ideas of your own and make you better at creating effective instruction. How cool is that?

How is this book organized?

This book is organized into two sections and ten chapters:

Section 1: Learners, Activities, and Assessments

1. Ideas for Supporting Learners and Learning
2. Ideas for Making Collaboration Work
3. Ideas for Making Discussions Work
4. Ideas for Self-Directed and Asynchronous Activities
5. Ideas for Synchronous Activities
6. Ideas for Self-Check Activities and Assessments

Section 2: Instructional Design

7. Ideas for the Design and Development Process
8. Ideas for Navigation and Usability
9. Ideas for Creative Design
10. Ideas for Creative Media

Each chapter contains numerous individual ideas related to the topic of the chapter, and each idea contains screen captures and other information about the idea that will help you adopt or adapt it.

About Pfeiffer

Pfeiffer serves the professional development and hands-on resource needs of training and human resource practitioners and gives them products to do their jobs better. We deliver proven ideas and solutions from experts in HR development and HR management, and we offer effective and customizable tools to improve workplace performance. From novice to seasoned professional, Pfeiffer is the source you can trust to make yourself and your organization more successful.

Essential Knowledge Pfeiffer produces insightful, practical, and comprehensive materials on topics that matter the most to training and HR professionals. Our Essential Knowledge resources translate the expertise of seasoned professionals into practical, how-to guidance on critical workplace issues and problems. These resources are supported by case studies, worksheets, and job aids and are frequently supplemented with CD-ROMs, websites, and other means of making the content easier to read, understand, and use.

Essential Tools Pfeiffer's Essential Tools resources save time and expense by offering proven, ready-to-use materials—including exercises, activities, games, instruments, and assessments—for use during a training or team-learning event. These resources are frequently offered in looseleaf or CD-ROM format to facilitate copying and customization of the material.

Pfeiffer also recognizes the remarkable power of new technologies in expanding the reach and effectiveness of training. While e-hype has often created whizbang solutions in search of a problem, we are dedicated to bringing convenience and enhancements to proven training solutions. All our e-tools comply with rigorous functionality standards. The most appropriate technology wrapped around essential content yields the perfect solution for today's on-the-go trainers and human resource professionals.

Pfeiffer
www.pfeiffer.com   *Essential resources for training and HR professionals*

Pfeiffer™

The **Online Learning Idea Book**

95 Proven Ways to Enhance Technology-Based and Blended Learning

PATTI SHANK, EDITOR

John Wiley & Sons, Inc.

Published by Pfeiffer
An Imprint of Wiley
989 Market Street, San Francisco, CA 94103-1741
www.pfeiffer.com

For additional copies/bulk purchases of this book in the U.S. please contact 800-274-4434.

Pfeiffer books and products are available through most bookstores. To contact Pfeiffer directly call our Customer Care Department within the U.S. at 800-274-4434, outside the U.S. at 317-572-3985, fax 317-572-4002, or visit www.pfeiffer.com.

Pfeiffer also publishes its books in a variety of electronic formats. Some content that appears in print may not be available in electronic books.

Cataloging-in-Publication Data on file with the Library of Congress

ISBN-13: 978-0-7879-8168-6

Acquiring Editor: Matthew Davis
Director of Development: Kathleen Dolan Davies
Developmental Editor: Susan Rachmeler
Production Editor: Nina Kreiden
Editor: Alice Rowan
Manufacturing Supervisor: Becky Carreño
Editorial Assistant: Julie Rodriguez

Printed in the United States of America
Printing   10   9   8   7   6   5   4   3   2   1

For my dad, Bob Oringel,
who inspired me to believe in myself
and to put pen to paper. I miss you.

CONTENTS

Chapter 5
Ideas for Synchronous Activities

Chapter 6
Ideas for Self-Check Activities and Assessments

Chapter 5 **141**

Chapter 6 **177**

SECTION 2
Instructional Design   **209**

Adults are always asking little kids what they want to be when they grow up because they're looking for ideas.

—*Paula Poundstone (American Comic)*

'm nonlinear, which is probably why I love the Internet and the Six Degrees of Kevin Bacon (trivia game). Connections fascinate me. It's probably why hearing, coming up with, and sharing ideas is one of the things that makes me most happy. Kicking around ideas with other instructional designers, a subject-matter expert, and perhaps a graphic artist and some multimedia developers is so much fun it hardly seems like work. And when someone throws out an idea that someone else in the group improves upon, it feels like we just invented stick-on postage stamps or take-out food or something else we couldn't live without. Even bizarre and unusable ideas provide endless amusement. I'd have to add laughter to the list of things you can't have too much of. But I digress. . . .

This book grew out of a certainty that many people who build online instruction have some great ideas that others could adopt or adapt to make their online instructional materials better, and that the implementation of these ideas would initiate even more great ideas that could be shared, and so on. Connections.

The book started out as just an idea and I am extremely grateful that Matt Davis, the senior editor I work with at Pfeiffer, thought it should come to fruition. I didn't know whether enough people would share their ideas to make this book possible, but because there are so many great people in this field, I thought many of them would. And they did.

Patti Shank
December 2006

ACKNOWLEDGMENTS

To everyone who willingly and openly shared good ideas for this book and no doubt share their ideas every day, I offer my heartfelt thanks. The book exists because of your creativity and willingness to share. Folks like you make the world a better place and I'm so glad that our lives have intersected.

Ann Yakimovicz, Jackie Dobrovolny, Eric Replinger, and Katica Roy helped me think through what I was trying to accomplish and gave me advice while I got this project under way. Helen Macfarlane helped me secure some great media ideas. Joanne Wagner helped with the never-ending details needed to make the book a reality. I'm far too nonlinear to have done this without her help. Terry Morris, one of the contributors to the book, provided an extraordinary level of organizational help. The book is no doubt easier to use as a result.

My family dealt with more than occasional (ha!) crankiness after I spent too much time at my computer. My children, Jess and Andy, both good writers, regularly implored me not to embarrass them by making stupid writing mistakes like "abusing apostrophes" (as one contributor's idea calls them).

Thanks to you too for buying this book and for loving ideas.

INTRODUCTION

The use of technology for learning was once a new idea. The widespread use of computer networks, especially the Internet, made even greater uses of technology for learning inevitable. The Internet and computer networks afford opportunities for learning that folks who were openly skeptical only a few years ago are beginning to employ. They enable users to, for example,

- Share documents, help, and resources across time and space.

- Provide widely available and ongoing (rather than time-limited) instruction and support.

- Track instruction and learners.

- Increase access to learning experiences.

- Augment classroom-based learning with additional tools and resources.

These same networks bring endless junk mail, pop-up ads, information overload, viruses, techno-anxiety, information of dubious (or worse) value, and too often, boring, unengaging online instruction. It shouldn't be this way.

Learning takes time, contact with and input from others, realistic activities, and support. Many people have built instructional materials, online and offline, that are engaging and enjoyable, and you'll see many examples of these in this book. Many of these ideas are quite easy to adopt or adapt, and they are likely to prompt some great new ideas of your own (that we hope you'll share).

Purpose

The purpose of this book is to showcase proven ideas from some of the world's most creative instructors, instructional designers and developers, trainers, programmers, media developers, artists, and others that can be adopted or adapted to make learning more fun and engaging. They are meant to improve your skills and spark new ideas of your own.

Audience

If you picked up this book, chances are you are involved with using technology for learning in one way or another. This book will give you many dozens of ideas that can improve what you are doing or considering doing.

You may be someone who teaches online or creates instructional content. Or a multimedia developer. Or the head of distance learning. Or someone who only occasionally puts something online for classroom-based learners to use in or out of class. Or someone who never uses technology but wonders how you might.

Maybe you've been asked or want to put instructional materials online and need some good ideas. You might want to develop a course to sell or provide free tips on your favorite hobby. You may have been putting courses online for a while and are doing the same thing over and over. Perhaps you do professional development with teachers or faculty and want to give them some new ideas. You might be an online learner who wants to give your online instructor ideas on how to make the course more interesting (um, might want to wait until grades are posted) or an instructional designer who wants to improve your skills.

You may work in K–12, higher education, corporate training, or professional development, or on the moon. If you use or want to use technology for learning, this book is for you. It is filled with ideas that some of the world's most creative instructors, trainers, and instructional designers are willing to share.

How the Book Is Organized

The book is organized into two sections and ten chapters:

Section 1: Learners, Activities, and Assessments

1. Ideas for Supporting Learners and Learning

2. Ideas for Making Collaboration Work

3. Ideas for Making Discussions Work

4. Ideas for Self-Directed and Asynchronous Activities

5. Ideas for Synchronous Activities

6. Ideas for Self-Check Activities and Assessments

Section 2: Instructional Design

7. Ideas for the Design and Development Process

8. Ideas for Navigation and Usability

9. Ideas for Creative Design

10. Ideas for Creative Media

Each chapter contains numerous individual ideas related to the topic of the chapter.

How Each Idea Is Presented

Each idea contains screen captures and other information about the idea that will help you adopt or adapt it. Individual ideas are presented in the following format:

The Big Idea

What

A short description of the idea, so you'll know if you want to read it, and (in most cases) some screen captures, so you'll know what it looks like.

Why

A brief explanation of why the idea is valuable.

Use It!

How

A more detailed description of the idea, how it came about, how it was implemented, and tips for using it.

Adopt or Adapt

A few ideas to get you started thinking about how to use the idea yourself.

Attribution

The originators of the idea and their affiliation, location, and contact information.

Each idea was submitted by the person or persons identified at the end of the idea. Many contributors submitted their own ideas and some submitted them on behalf of a team of colleagues. A few of the ideas are my own. I also wrote the final write-up of each idea. Some or most of the words are from the original submission but, as editor, I took great liberties with wording, sequencing, titles, selecting screen captures, and adding or deleting content. The musings in the Adopt or Adapt sections are primarily my own. I changed spelling to American English (for consistency only) and attempted to make the voice somewhat consistent as well. I hope I represented each idea well.

How to Use the Book

Individual Use

The book was designed to be read in any order because each idea stands on its own. Open to any idea and read, or skim for screen captures that intrigue you. It's that easy. If you are looking for ideas on a specific topic, find the chapter that most closely matches that topic and skim through its ideas. Take notes in the margins. Many ideas could have been placed in more than one chapter, so skim the rest of the book too.

This is a fun book, so have fun.

Group Use

One great use for a book such as this is to use the ideas as jumping off points for learning and for generating new ideas. Brainstorming and discussion of ideas by interested groups of people can produce spectacular energy and results.

Instructional Design Courses

Use the ideas to enhance discussions of creativity, design, selecting instructional strategies, navigation, media and graphics, and other important instructional design topics. Discuss the applicability of various ideas to a variety of projects. Consider how the ideas would be implemented differently in classroom, blended, and online learning. Discuss how the ideas embody current research and thinking about learning. Use the ideas to brainstorm new ideas. Implement some of the ideas and evaluate the results.

Multimedia Authoring Courses

Prompt individuals or teams to build out and enhance the ideas and evaluate the results. Discuss the authoring and programming implications of the ideas and consider other methods for achieving similar results.

Teaching Methods Courses

Use the ideas as a springboard for considering the role of creativity in teaching. Discuss how to use the ideas in classroom and online teaching. Analyze the skills needed to implement the ideas. Consider how the ideas embody current research and thinking about learning. Use these ideas to brainstorm new ideas and share the best ones.

Faculty Workshops

Discuss the rationale for using these ideas and brainstorm how to use them in different content areas. Provide hands-on workshops on how to implement the ideas. Share the results of implementing the ideas. Have a contest to see who has the most creative implementation and new ideas. Give the book as a reward for creative online teaching.

User Groups

Discuss the programming implications for implementing each idea and brainstorm effective approaches. Brainstorm new ideas. Develop a way to share ideas with members of the group.

Learners, Activities, and Assessments

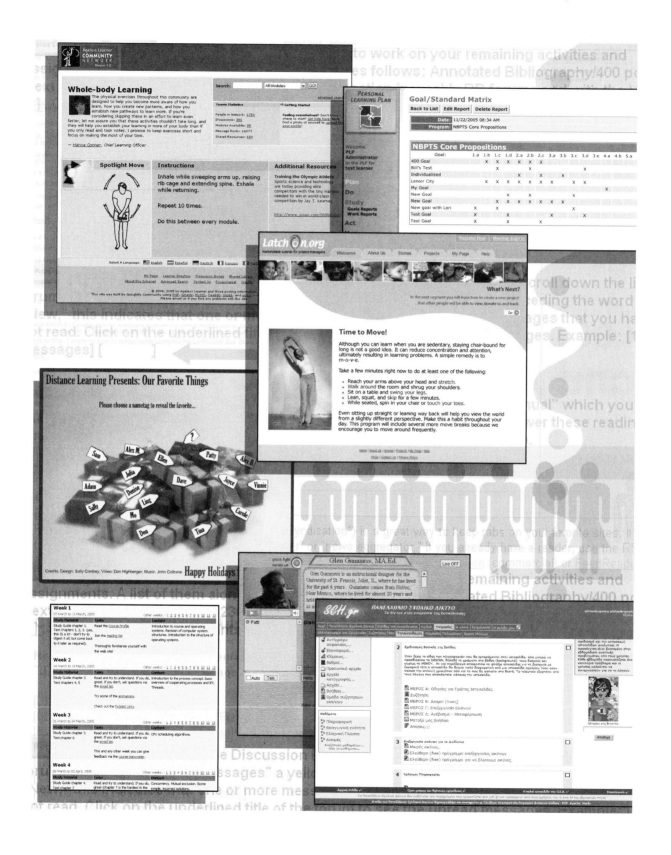

CHAPTER 1

Ideas for Supporting Learners and Learning

This chapter highlights ideas that support learners and improve the potential for desired results. These elements are often, sadly, forgotten but they can have a huge impact.

Organizations will sometimes spend tons of money building multimedia or buying a learning management system and then forget to support learners so they can learn. It is critical for designers, instructors, and organizations to consider how learners will know what's expected of them, become prepared, stay on task, and gain support when they need it (and they will need it). Many of these simple ideas take little time and money to implement but can have huge results.

Learning Agreements

The Big Idea

What

A learning agreement helps learners clarify, for themselves and for the instructor, how they will proceed before beginning a course. Clarity helps learners develop commitment at the front end.

Figure 1.1. Learning Agreement

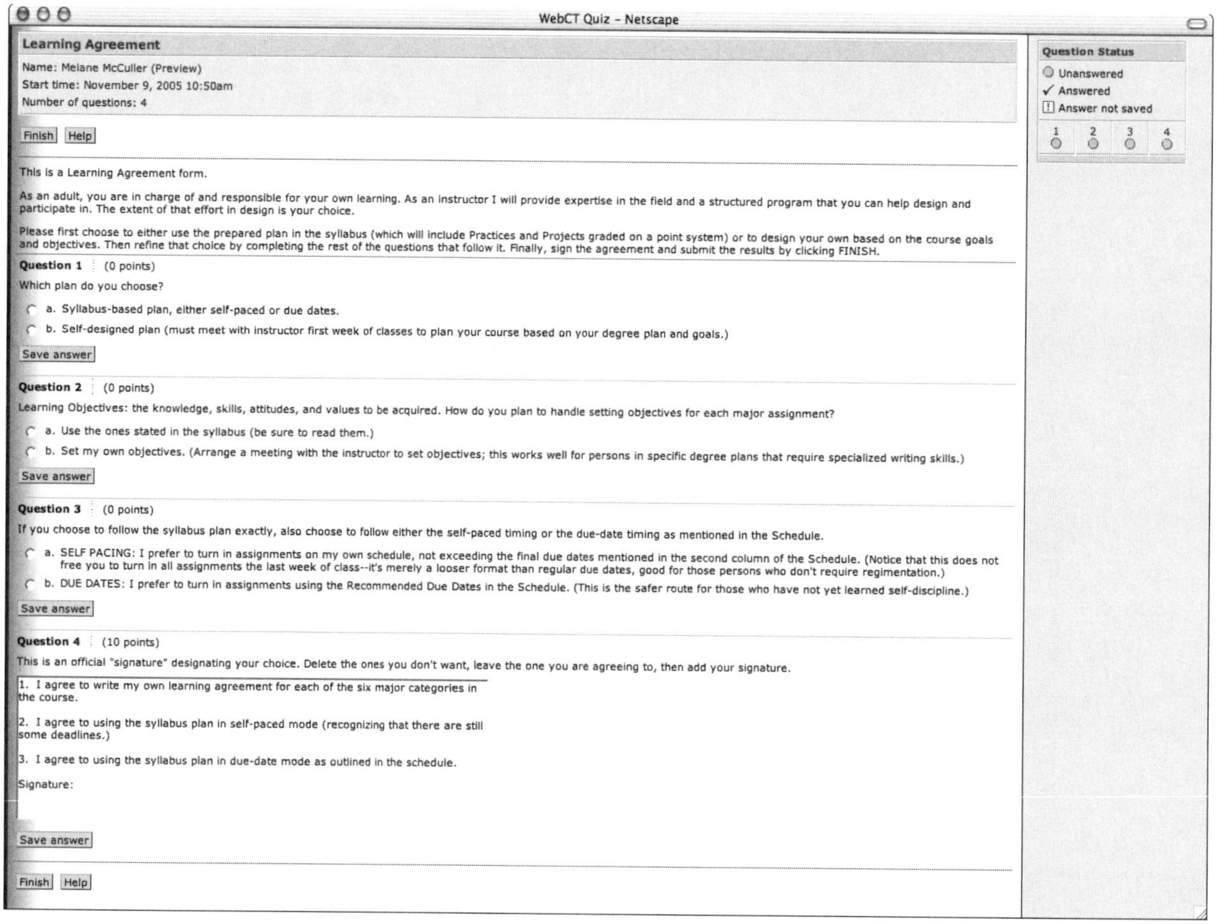

WebCT Quiz – Netscape

Learning Agreement

Name: Melane McCuller (Preview)
Start time: November 9, 2005 10:50am
Number of questions: 4

Finish Help

Question Status
Unanswered
Answered
Answer not saved
1 2 3 4

This is a Learning Agreement form.

As an adult, you are in charge of and responsible for your own learning. As an instructor I will provide expertise in the field and a structured program that you can help design and participate in. The extent of that effort in design is your choice.

Please first choose to either use the prepared plan in the syllabus (which will include Practices and Projects graded on a point system) or to design your own based on the course goals and objectives. Then refine that choice by completing the rest of the questions that follow it. Finally, sign the agreement and submit the results by clicking FINISH.

Question 1 (0 points)

Which plan do you choose?

a. Syllabus-based plan, either self-paced or due dates.
b. Self-designed plan (must meet with instructor first week of classes to plan your course based on your degree plan and goals.)

Save answer

Question 2 (0 points)

Learning Objectives: the knowledge, skills, attitudes, and values to be acquired. How do you plan to handle setting objectives for each major assignment?

a. Use the ones stated in the syllabus (be sure to read them.)
b. Set my own objectives. (Arrange a meeting with the instructor to set objectives; this works well for persons in specific degree plans that require specialized writing skills.)

Save answer

Question 3 (0 points)

If you choose to follow the syllabus plan exactly, also choose to follow either the self-paced timing or the due-date timing as mentioned in the Schedule.

a. SELF PACING: I prefer to turn in assignments on my own schedule, not exceeding the final due dates mentioned in the second column of the Schedule. (Notice that this does not free you to turn in all assignments the last week of class--it's merely a looser format than regular due dates, good for those persons who don't require regimentation.)
b. DUE DATES: I prefer to turn in assignments using the Recommended Due Dates in the Schedule. (This is the safer route for those who have not yet learned self-discipline.)

Save answer

Question 4 (10 points)

This is an official "signature" designating your choice. Delete the ones you don't want, leave the one you are agreeing to, then add your signature.

1. I agree to write my own learning agreement for each of the six major categories in the course.

2. I agree to using the syllabus plan in self-paced mode (recognizing that there are still some deadlines.)

3. I agree to using the syllabus plan in due-date mode as outlined in the schedule.

Signature:

Save answer

Finish Help

Source: Melane Z. McCuller, http://www.oit.sfasu.edu/faculty/mmcculler/ENG_273_502_McCullerS06.html

Why

Motivation and perseverance are likely to be increased when learners are asked to consider and then commit to how they will proceed.

Use It!

How

In Melane McCuller's *Scientific and Technical Writing* course, learners complete a Learning Agreement, in which they commit to a course of action to be followed throughout the semester. Learners have the option of largely determining their own course of action or going along with the plan developed by the instructor. They can choose from a range of options including strict due dates, partially self-paced due dates, emphasis on product, emphasis on process, and others.

After using this agreement for six semesters, McCuller reports that while most learners are content to accept the traditional approach, those who choose one of the optional plans seem to be more actively involved in their own learning process and are generally more successful in implementing self-disciplined strategies resulting in better learning outcomes. Even those who choose the syllabus with due dates expressed that having a choice made them feel more committed to maintaining consistent progress. McCuller suggests that instructors wanting to implement a similar process must be flexible, diligent in tracking learner progress, and prepared for a high level of interaction with learners.

McCuller implements learning agreements using the quiz function in WebCT, but this could also be implemented using other quiz or survey programs, a Web form and database, or via email.

Adopt or Adapt

This idea can be used effectively in any classroom, blended, or online course and, if used, should be implemented at the beginning of the learning experience. It could be used in self-paced learning, with the learning agreement sent to (and hopefully followed up by) the learner's manager. It would be beneficial to request that learners consider and commit to the effort and results they will provide.

This idea could also be implemented with an online survey tool such as Question Pro (http://www.questionpro.com) or Zoomerang (http://info.zoomerang.com) or by using a Web form, word processing document, or email.

Attribution

Submitted by Melane Z. McCuller, instructional media specialist, Office of Instructional Technology, Stephen F. Austin University, Nacogdoches, Texas, USA

Contact: mmcculler@sfasu.edu

URL: http://www.oit.sfasu.edu/faculty/mmcculler/ENG_273_502_McCullerS06.html

Prework Verification

The Big Idea

What

A simple Web form and database lets learners verify that they have completed the required prework prior to a learning event. A dynamically populated Web page (with the data coming from a live database) also shows course administrators who has completed the prework. In addition, this form can request important information about each of the participants so that the instructors can be prepared to meet the participants' needs.

Figure 1.2. Prework Form

Step 5: Let us know you have completed Steps 1-4 no later than October 6:

Since preparation of your laptop greatly impacts the value of the workshop, we need to know you have completed these steps. We'd also like a few pieces of additional information in order to make the workshop a success (this information will only be shared with workshop presenters). Please fill out the following form and click the Submit button. (If you have questions about pre-work or the workshop, post them in the discussion area.)

Name: _____ Email: _____

Primary job responsibility: [select one ▾] Primary work environment: [select one ▾]

Have you completed steps 1-4? yes ○ no ○

What 2 things do you need to get from this workshop? [_____]

Anything else we should know about you to help you get the most from this workshop? [_____]

[Submit]

Source: Learning Peaks, LLC

Figure 1.3. Prework Results

.canon.com	Instructional design	Corporate	Yes	1) Overview of Online Learning and Training Fundamentals 2) Instructional Design Overview	instruction as well looking forward to concepts and strat implemented
@irs.gov	Trainer	Government	Yes	Hands-on experience Knowledge	First-time user.
oe.gov	Other (explain)	Government	Yes	Practical experience in developing—quick and dirty. ;>	I have developed has been some tim initiative.
erault@novell.com	Trainer	Corporate	Yes	Identify new activities to make our online learning more interactive. Gain some practical experience creating this type of training using different tools.	I split my time betw and designing anc looking at gaining that will develop sl
.ngc.com	Instructor/ faculty	Corporate	Yes	Learn something about developing a web site and about putting information on the site. Plus . . . learn how to work the programs that you have suggested that we put on the lap-top. I know nothing about them . . . have never used them.	Please start with b never written in htr language. I'm a M computer user.

Source: Learning Peaks, LLC

Why

Confirming completion of prework compels learners to be accountable and allows instructors to intervene as needed with those who have not finished. Getting information about learners in advance helps instructors prepare to meet learner needs.

Use It!

How

Eric Replinger and Patti Shank taught a beginner's authoring workshop that required learners to undertake a fair amount of technical preparation prior to the course. Anyone attending unprepared would not be able to perform the activities and this would negatively impact the experience of other participants as well. To ensure that all participants had adequately prepared, Replinger and Shank developed a simple Web site with explicit preparation instructions and a discussion board so participants could ask questions or get help with preparation.

The last step of learner preparation was filling in a form that verified that all the steps had been completed and provided information about their specific needs. Form data were sent to a database. Replinger built a very simple results Web page that pulled all the data into a simple table so he and Shank could ensure that preparation was complete and understand learner needs. Development was done with Dreamweaver, PHP, and mySQL.

Adopt or Adapt

This idea could be adapted for any type of prework or follow-up for a classroom-based, blended, or online course. For example, a process like this could be used by learners before instruction to commit to the steps needed to complete the instruction or to confirm pre-reading, and afterwards to commit to follow-on activities or to confirm completion of action plan items. These measures could also be accomplished through emails or telephone calls.

Attribution

Submitted by Eric Replinger, Flambeau Productions, Inc., Centennial, Colorado, USA

Also involved: Patti Shank, president, Learning Peaks, LLC, Centennial, Colorado, USA

Study Schedule

The Big Idea

What

Online learners often experience reduced external motivation to stay on task, making it easy to fall behind and never recover. A study schedule and a weekly update can help learners stay accountable and on track.

Figure 1.4. Study Schedule

Week 1

07 March to 11 March, 2005   Other weeks: - 1 2 3 4 5 6 7 8 9 10 11 12

Study Material	Tasks	Content
Study Guide chapter 1. Text chapters 1, 2, 3. (yes, this IS a lot - don't try to digest it all, but come back to it later as required).	Read the Course Profile Join the mailing list Thoroughly familiarise yourself with the web site!	Introduction to course and operating systems. Revision of computer system structures. Introduction to the structure of operating systems.

Week 2

14 March to 18 March, 2005   Other weeks: - 1 2 3 4 5 6 7 8 9 10 11 12

Study Material	Tasks	Content
Study Guide chapter 2. Text chapters 4, 5	Read and try to understand. If you do, great. If you don't, ask questions via the email list. Try some of the animations. Check out the Related Links.	Introduction to the process concept. Basic overview of cooperating processes and IPC. Threads.

Week 3

21 March to 24 March, 2005   Other weeks: - 1 2 3 4 5 6 7 8 9 10 11 12

Study Material	Tasks	Content
Study Guide chapter 3. Text chapter 6	Read and try to understand. If you do, great. If you don't, ask questions via the email list. This and any other week you can give feedback via the course barometer.	CPU scheduling algorithms.

Week 4

29 March to 01 April, 2005   Other weeks: - 1 2 3 4 5 6 7 8 9 10 11 12

Study Material	Tasks	Content
Study Guide chapter 4. Text chapter 7	Read and try to understand. If you do, great (chapter 7 is the hardest in the	Concurrency. Mutual exclusion. Some simple, incorrect solutions.

Source: Tim Roberts, http://www.infocom.cqu.edu.au/Staff/Tim_Roberts/

Why

Helping learners remain accountable and on track improves their likelihood of success.

Use It!

How

The study schedule, which guides learners' weekly activities, is posted on the course Web site. This is a core component of all of Tim Roberts's courses. It describes the following components:

- Study materials and readings relevant to the week

- Tasks to be accomplished (with links)

- Content covered

Roberts sends an email at the end of each week to reinforce the items in the study schedule in a friendly manner, reminding learners what they should have completed during the week. For example:

Hi all,

Well, it's the end of week two already. So let me state where you should be if you're going to keep up and pass this course:

In the first two weeks you should have

1. Bought the textbook

2. Subscribed to this list

3. Read the course profile

4. Dedicated one or more blocks of time each week to coursework

5. Acquainted yourself with the Web site and read the details of the assessment items for this semester

6. Read the first two chapters in the Study Guide

7. Read the first five chapters of the textbook

An average learner will need to allow AT LEAST TEN HOURS PER WEEK to read and understand the material. Remember that if there are things in the list that you have any difficulty with, there are lots of help resources. In particular:

- PowerPoint slides

- Other texts available from the library

- Animations illustrating some of the concepts

- Other operating system resources on the Web

Most important of all, there is this discussion list, where you can ask questions about anything you don't understand. Please post questions about any of the course content. Otherwise, I will have to assume it has all been understood and hence must be easy, and I will set the exam based on this assumption. :-)

These messages reinforce the importance of keeping on track and reminding participants that they are part of a larger community whose members all face similar difficulties and challenges. Emails also deliberately remind learners of the resources available to help them learn and to encourage them to post questions and concerns.

Adopt or Adapt

The study schedule and reminder emails can be adapted easily. Although this approach is especially relevant to instructor-led online courses, it could be adapted for self-paced and ongoing classroom-based and blended courses that have readings and assignments. It could even be adapted for use with project teams.

Attribution

Submitted by Tim Roberts, Central Queensland University, Bundaberg, Queensland 4670, Australia

Contact: t.roberts@cqu.edu.au

URL: http://www.infocom.cqu.edu.au/Staff/Tim_Roberts/

Also involved: The whole CQU InfoCom Web Tech Team

Performance Tips

The Big Idea

What

Put yourselves in a learner's place and determine what help they will need. Then add performance tips to help learners gain direction with study strategies and course activities.

Figure 1.5. Performance Tip 1

Performance Tips Access the Discussion Board [vii] at least once a day. Scroll down the list of forums. If you see under "Messages" a yellow highlight over a number preceding the word "New," this indicates that one or more messages have been added – messages that you have not read. Click on the underlined title of the forum to see the unread messages. Example: [11 messages] [   ]

Source: Frank L. Christ

Figure 1.6. Performance Tip 2

Performance Tips Your catch-up week is a time to work on your remaining activities and assignments. A list of them along with point values follows: Annotated Bibliography/400 points Next Steps Paper/400 points, 230 points for interaction in weekly DB forums and with the V VS [x] , Open Book Exam/300 points BQRQ [xi] /75 points for a total of 1405 points.

Source: Frank L. Christ

Figure 1.7. Performance Tip 3

Performance Tips The Help Manual, "Course Reading Questions Help Manual" which you can find in the "Learning Support" section, is helpful for you to use as you answer these reading questions. Print it and store in your Course Binder for offline study and use.

Source: Frank L. Christ

Why

Helping learners thrive is a large part of our jobs. Using existing data about common problems or questions will help learners be more successful.

Use It!

How

Frank Christ integrates performance tips into his online courses through course announcements, emails to learners, and his weekly introductions to reading assignments. As he teaches the course, he compiles a master list of performance tips and then cuts and pastes from that list into the course as appropriate. He also asks learners to contribute performance tips to help other learners.

Adopt or Adapt

As a course is used by learners, data about problems and questions become available. In addition to fixing problems that trip up learners, it's helpful to anticipate common questions and ways to get off track and provide guidance. This could be done for any type of course, whether classroom-based, blended, or online.

Attribution

Submitted by Frank L. Christ, adjunct professor, Educational Leadership, Grambling State University; and visiting scholar, University of Texas-Austin, Sierra Vista, Texas, USA

Contact: flchris@cox.net

Move It

The Big Idea

What

Are we more than eyeballs? We are. Although we usually focus only on the computer portion of the online learning experience, a whole-body experience has definite merits. Consider encouraging learners to get out of that chair between lessons.

Figure 1.8. Movement Instructions in an Online Tutorial

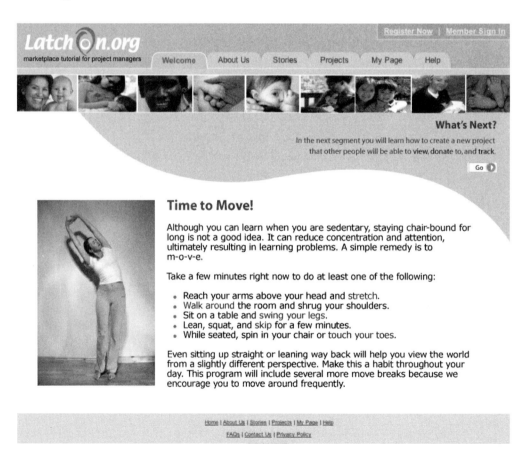

Source: Marcia L. Conner, http://www.agelesslearner.com

Figure 1.9. Movement Instructions in an Online Community

Whole-body Learning

The physical exercises throughout this community are designed to help you become more aware of how you learn, how you create new patterns, and how you establish new pathways to learn more. If you're considering skipping these in an effort to learn even faster, let me assure you that these activities shouldn't take long, and they will help you establish your learning in more of your body than if you only read and took notes. I promise to keep exercises short and focus on making the most of your time.

— *Marcia Conner*, *Chief Learning Officer*

Search: [   ] All Modules [▼] [GO!]

advanced search

Course Statistics

People in Network: 1753
Discussions: 386
Modules Available: 88
Message Posts: 16077
Shared Resources: 684

⇨ Getting Started

Feeling overwhelmed? Don't know where to start? Get help here! Next, find a photo of yourself to upload for your profile!

Spotlight Move

Instructions

Inhale while sweeping arms up, raising rib cage and extending spine. Exhale while returning.

Repeat 10 times.

Do this between every module.

Additional Resources

Training the Olympic Athlete Sports science and technology are today providing elite competitors with the tiny margins needed to win in world-class competition by Jay T. Kearney

http://www.sciam.com/0696issue/

Select A Language: 🏳 English 🏳 Español 🏳 Deutsch 🏳 Francais 🏳 Italiano About language...

My Page Learner Directory Discussion Groups Shared Library Help
About this Intranet Advanced Search Contact Us Privacy/Legal Credits Ageless Learner

© 2004, 2005 by Ageless Learner and those posting information.
This site was built by GoLightly Community using PHP, Smarty, MySQL, freeBSD, phpBB, and pLog. — version 1.007, 2005.07.22 17:53PDT
Please email us if you find any problems with the site.

Source: Marcia L. Conner, http://www.agelesslearner.com

Why

Sitting in a chair for long periods leads to lethargy, drowsiness, and decreased attention, which are not the best states for learning. A simple remedy is to encourage learners to *move.*

Use It!

How

Even though it's possible to learn while sedentary, staying chair bound for long isn't a good idea. Sitting for a long time takes its toll on your body. It can result in poor breathing, back trouble, poor eyesight, body fatigue, and a limited perspective. These problems can reduce concentration and attention, ultimately resulting in difficulty staying focused and learning. Something as simple as changing posture can energize and encourage the learning process.

A simple remedy is to encourage learners to get up, walk, swing their legs or arms, lean, kneel, squat, spin, or skip at different times throughout the day. Instructional designers and developers can incorporate a movement break between content modules.

Some ideas: Invite learners to stretch, juggle, jog in place, walk to get water, or spin in their chairs. Even sitting up straight or leaning way back will help learners view the world from a slightly different perspective. Have learners stand and turn one rotation to the left or right and then sit back down. Ask them to tap the length of one arm with one hand, then change arms, and then reach up and stretch. Or have them create a figure eight in the air in front of them, focusing on a thumb, then on the wall behind it and then back at their outstretched arm. Have them wiggle their toes and rotate their heads from side to side, shrug their shoulders, or march around the room.

Marcia Conner came up with this idea after working with countless groups of learners whose attention was wandering after trying harder and harder but never getting up from their desks. Researching the body-mind connection led her to see that even a little movement would help regain focus. She has included movement in large curricula, in callouts on Web pages, in accompanying handbooks for e-learning courses—wherever she can stick a few lines of text (and maybe a simple picture or two) that encourage people to get up from their chairs.

Adopt or Adapt

This idea can be used in any classroom, blended, or online program.

Attribution

Submitted by Marcia L. Conner, managing director, Ageless Learner, Staunton, Virginia, USA

Contact: info@agelesslearner.com

URL: http://www.agelesslearner.com

Confirm Exercise Instructions

The Big Idea

What

After giving instructions in a synchronous online classroom, ask a participant to reexplain the instructions to the group before sending them off to work in breakout rooms, to share applications, or to view Web sites.

Why

To avoid frustration and potential rework, learners need to be sure they know what to do. Instructors often think they're being perfectly clear, but learners tell us this isn't so.

Use It!

How

When giving exercise instructions in a synchronous online classroom, make sure people understand what you are asking of them. Post the instructions on a slide, then explain the instructions, then ask someone to repeat what they think you just said.

Jennifer Hofmann's Example

"Since you'll be working on your own for the next ten minutes and I won't be able to see if you are moving in the right direction, can one of you please repeat the instructions back so I can be certain I've clearly explained the exercise? Mary, would you like to explain *your* understanding of the exercises?"

Adopt or Adapt

This idea can be used in classroom-based, blended, or online courses where synchronous activities are occurring.

Attribution

Submitted by Jennifer Hofmann, synchronous learning expert, InSync Training, Branford, Connecticut, USA

Contact: Jennifer@insynctraining.com

URL: http://www.insynctraining.com

E-Portfolio

The Big Idea

What

Learners can plan, create, organize, and reflect on work samples using an online portfolio.

Figure 1.10. Personal Learning Plan Goal Achievement Matrix

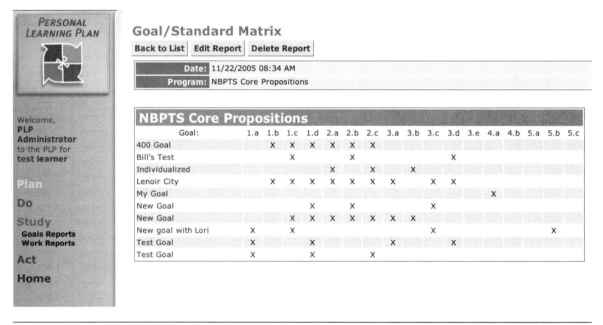

Source: David Gibson, http://www.curveshift.com

Why

Portfolios are becoming more and more popular as a means of demonstrating achievement of instructional outcomes and growth. E-portfolios allow this to occur online, making it easier for others to see the portfolio and provide input. E-portfolios can provide a place for learners to organize evidence of meeting instructional goals.

Use It!

How

E-portfolios often include the following elements:

- Coursework samples

- Artifacts from noncoursework (work or personal) activities

- Commentary about the portfolio items

More and more instructors ask learners to publish online course portfolios. Some universities are requiring online portfolios as a graduation requirement. The portfolio development process encourages learners to become more responsible for achieving educational goals. Learners benefit by

- Sharing work samples with instructors, peers, and potential employers

- Demonstrating mastery of skills beyond the classroom

- Reflecting on their learning

An electronic format allows learners to share work more easily.

The Personal Learning Plan is an e-portfolio application that can be used individually or as part of a team. The instructor gives learners the URL and the password so they can post their work and track achievement of their goals. Instructors, teaching assistants, and peers can provide online feedback.

Adopt or Adapt

Although they are most commonly used in a K–12 or higher education setting, portfolios could also be used to demonstrate progress and mastery in a training or coaching setting. They are especially useful where standards and professional outcomes are important benchmarks of achievement.

The portfolio products could be organized in a three-ring binder or electronic folder. If an electronic and publicly available version is desirable, a wiki or Web site could be used to describe and link to portfolio products.

Attribution

Submitted by David Gibson, founder, CurveShift, Stowe, Vermont, USA

Contact: David.Gibson@curveshift.com

URL: http://www.curveshift.com

Anonymous Weekly Survey

The Big Idea

What

Anonymous forms are used to solicit honest responses from learners. These responses can be summarized by the instructor, a learner, or a team.

Figure 1.11. Weekly Survey Form

Anonymous Weekly Survey

1. What questions or problems came up this week that will require further investigation (or, that you'd just like to know more about)?	
2. Are you experiencing any challenges with key course activities -- discussion, group work, and projects? What are your suggestions from improving these activities?	
3. Was the pace this week too fast, too slow, just right? What would you suggest as a way of changing the pace? e.g., cover the topics in less depth, restrict discussion, change project/s, etc.	
4. Why did I ask you to complete this week's activities? What was the purpose of each activity?	
5. What did you learn from the activities completed this week?	
6. What activity was the most useful for you this week? Why?	
7. What activity was the least useful for you this week? Why? How would you improve it?	
8. Other comments, concerns, issues?	

Submit Query

Source: Joanna C. Dunlap

Why

An anonymous survey lets learners provide timely feedback to the instructor that can be acted on immediately. Waiting until the end of a course to ask learners what needs to change doesn't allow the instructor to make needed changes for current learners.

Use It!

How

Online instructors need to create environments in which learners feel safe to express themselves, share their ideas, and ask questions; otherwise, learner concerns can escalate into significant problems. It is important to provide a variety of ways for learners to communicate with the instructor. An anonymous weekly survey lets learners ask questions and voice concerns.

To gather information that can lead to appropriate enhancements, provide learners with specific questions to answer, such as those shown in Figure 1.11. Once you receive learners' responses, it is imperative to respond in public with points of clarification, modified plans of action, and appreciation. Besides helping learners feel more connected to the course and instructor, this activity can encourage learners to reflect on their achievement, learning processes, and progress toward learning goals as well as recognize how the course is supporting or derailing their efforts.

As an alternative to the instructor responding, individual learners or teams can take responsibility for summarizing and responding to each week's survey responses. An interesting outcome of this is that it requires learners to think about their comments from the instructor's perspective and consider why the course is set up as it is. It can give them a newfound appreciation for the level of commitment it takes to create successful online learning opportunities. It can also be a particularly enlightening experience for learners who are preparing to be online educators, because they get to experience firsthand the reflective process behind making instructional strategy decisions and then defending or modifying them as appropriate.

Finally, the valuable information shared during these exchanges can be turned into a frequently asked questions (FAQ) document to benefit the class participants, both currently and in the future.

Joanna Dunlap explains that this approach addresses her need to anticipate and proactively address learners' questions and potential problems as the course progresses, as opposed to waiting for end-of-semester evaluations. She wants learners to have a clear voice in the process and outcome of their experience throughout the course. She also wants to improve her skills as a teacher and realizes that honest, constructive feedback from learners will help her to do so.

An anonymous Web form, instead of email, allows learners more freedom to share concerns they might otherwise not disclose. These forms send the data to Dunlap's email address.

Adopt or Adapt

This technique would work well for any classroom-based, blended, or online course. A survey tool such as Question Pro (http://www.questionpro.com) or Zoomerang (http://info.zoomerang.com) would also work for this purpose, as would email, but as already noted, the latter would not be anonymous. This approach could also work in ongoing classroom-based courses, using either electronic or paper forms.

Attribution

Submitted by Joanna C. Dunlap, assistant professor, School of Education and Human Development, University of Colorado at Denver and Health Sciences, Denver, Colorado, USA

Contact: Joni.Dunlap@cudenver.edu

Personal Wishes

The Big Idea

What

Use media to send holiday or other greetings to learners.

Figure 1.12. Web Card

Source: Distance Learning, Regis University, School for Professional Studies,
http://support.regis.edu/holiday_card05/holiday_card05.html

Figure 1.13. Ellen's Video Message

Source: Distance Learning, Regis University, School for Professional Studies, http://support.regis.edu/holiday_card05/holiday_card05.html

Why

Graphics and audio and video messages can help people at a distance connect with people they have not met in person and feel part of the greater community.

Use It!

How

Regis University's School for Professional Studies, which includes the group responsible for distance learning, developed a holiday greeting that used graphics, audio, and video to wish learners, faculty, and others involved in the school a happy holiday. The greeting provides personal video messages from each staff member.

Adopt or Adapt

Media-based welcome messages, birthday greetings, and faculty course introductions can help learners connect with people involved in course development and implementation, including designers, faculty, multimedia developers, tech support people, registrars, and others. This approach could provide a warm touch from training developers too.

Attribution

Submitted by Ellen Waterman, director of distance learning, Regis University, School for Professional Studies, Denver, Colorado, USA

URL: http://support.regis.edu/holiday_card05/holiday_card05.html

Also involved: Sally Cordrey, multimedia specialist, Regis University, School for Professional Studies, Denver, Colorado, USA

Really Simple Syndication Feeds

The Big Idea

What

Provide critical information to employees and customers with a Really Simple Syndication (RSS) feed so they can get critical information quickly.

Figure 1.14. RSS Feed

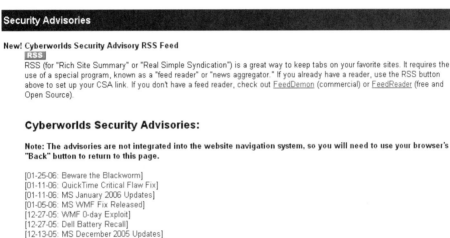

Source: Jack Johnson, http://www.cyberworlds.com

Why

RSS feeds can be more effective than email as a way to provide critical information.

Use It!

How

RSS is an XML format for sharing content items. Once information about each content item is in RSS format, an aggregator can check the RSS feed for changes and display new items. RSS is now used for many purposes, including news headlines, bug reports, and periodic updates. On Web pages, the XML used to link to the RSS feeds is found by clicking on the universal RSS icon. `RSS`

One of the services that Cyberworlds, an information technology consulting firm, provides its clients is the Cyberworlds Security Advisory. When Cyberworlds becomes aware of a security issue that clients may need to know about, it publishes an advisory on its Web site and sends out an email notification. Because email is becoming a less reliable way to communicate critical information (because of email spam filters and so on), Cyberworlds now provides an RSS feed so clients can get needed information in a more reliable manner.

Adopt or Adapt

Learn about RSS (a good place to start would be http://weblogged .com/wp-content/uploads/2006/05/RSSFAQ4.pdf) and consider using this technology to get critical information to employees and customers.

Attribution

Submitted by Jack Johnson, president, Cyberworlds, Beloit, Wisconsin, USA

Contact: info@cyberworlds.com

URL: http://www.cyberworlds.com

Contingency Plans

The Big Idea

What

Have in place contingency plans in case of technology failures or other typical technology-based learning problems, and have others who are involved in the process develop them too.

Figure 1.15. Contingency Planning Activity for Instructors, Facilitators, and Administrators

Program Component	Situation	Contingency Plan
Participants	Several participants monopolize the question-and-answer segments, keeping others from contributing.	
Guest Expert(s)	An interviewee, who was scheduled to be at the instructor's site, calls 15 minutes before the session to say she has car trouble and will not be able to make the session.	
Site	The Site Coordinator calls in ill shortly before the program is to begin.	
Activities	You have planned a group interaction at each site. Because of extenuating circumstances, one of the sites has only one person.	

Source: Rosemary Lehman, http://www.uwex.edu/ics/design

Why

Some people say there are only two types of technology-based learning events—those that have encountered glitches and those that will! Glitches and problems happen and back-up plans make them easier to deal with.

Use It!

How

Rosemary Lehman's team develops activities and plans for use in the event of video or audio failure or both (sometimes even instigated by the instructors to illustrate technology failure) during live online learning events. A colored envelope with an activity inside is included in class materials for each site to "open in case of emergency." Instructions on how to complete the activity are included. The content of the activity can be either general or specific to the session. Activity results can be used as discussion points when reconnection is made, at the following session, or for discussion about contingencies.

Developing contingency plans is a good activity to do "on purpose" when training instructors, facilitators, and administrators how to handle glitches and problems.

Adapt or Adapt

This idea can be adapted for use in any learning environment. Have contingency activities available and have instructors, facilitators, and administrators develop contingency plans for the most common problems. Show examples of plans that others have successfully implemented. This would also be a good activity to use when training classroom trainers (for example, how to handle rude participants, use of cell phones during instruction, and so on).

Attribution

Submitted by Rosemary Lehman, senior outreach/distance education specialist and manager, Instructional Design Team, Instructional Communications Systems, University of Wisconsin-Extension, Madison, USA

Contact: lehman@ics.uwex.edu

URL: http://www.uwex.edu/ics/design

Also involved: Richard A. Berg, instructional design/distance education specialist, and Bruce E. Dewey, outreach/distance education specialist, both from the Instructional Design Team, Instructional Communications Systems, University of Wisconsin-Extension, Madison, Wisconsin, USA

Virtual Office Hours

The Big Idea

What

Virtual office hours with text chat and real-time video and audio conferencing allows instructors and learners to interact easily in real time.

Figure 1.16. Virtual Office Hours

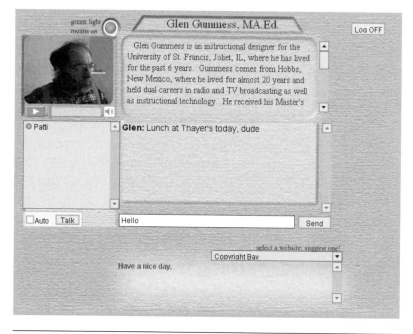

Source: Glen Gummess, http://www.stfrancis.edu/cid/gummess

Why

Learners and instructors can easily communicate at a distance, improving the sense of connection.

Use It!

How

Glen Gummess created a virtual office hours application using Flash to build the interface and the Flash Communication Server to build the application. It allows text-based chat, audio- and videoconferencing, and instructor controls for changing passwords, erasing chat messages, and dropping the learner, if needed.

The application is easily customized for each instructor by changing one line of ActionScript code. Deployment takes a few minutes after a request is received. Users need only have basic skills in accessing the Web page to use this application. A less experienced user may use just the text chat, but with an additional webcam, microphone, and minimum broadband connection, the whole range of videoconferencing possibilities are within reach.

This idea requires a Web server of sufficient size and speed to host Flash Communication Server, which establishes the paths for communication between client computers and streaming video and audio. The Flash Communication Server is a relatively inexpensive streaming technology that Gummess says is quite challenging to learn. The developer must be competent at writing both client-side and server-side ActionScript. Gummess cautions that it's also critical to make the finished application easy to use. "In fact, usability is so important that to disregard the issue is to invite serious technical and administrative support ramifications." Once developed, the application should be instantly usable for the online novice instructor and learner, with very little support required.

The idea grew out of a need expressed by nursing college professors who wanted to afford learners a rich interpersonal experience. Gummess developed a pilot and then mass-produced it after successful testing with instructors.

Adopt or Adapt

Although the development technology may be daunting for some, once developed it is easy to implement and use. Other Web conferencing applications could be used for the same purpose.

Attribution

Submitted by Glen Gummess, instructional designer, University of St. Francis, Joliet, Illinois, USA

Contact: ggummess@stfrancis.edu

URL: http://www.stfrancis.edu/cid/gummess

Chatbots

The Big Idea

What

Chatbots (also known as chatterbots or talk bots) can help prepare online learners, initiate conversation, respond to questions, and break the ice.

Figure 1.17. PhiliPa

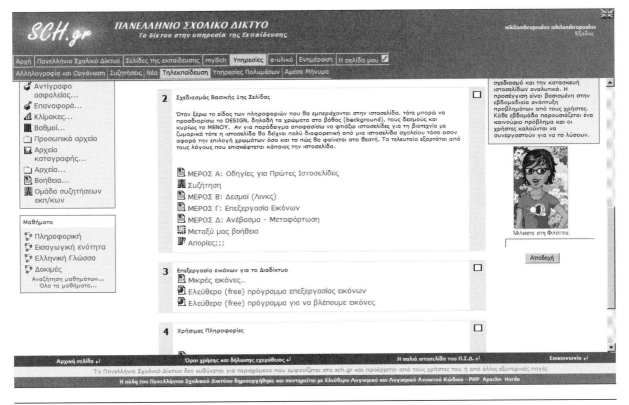

Source: Niki Lambropoulos, http://nikilambropoulos.org

Why

This is a relatively new technology with a great deal of promise for supporting online learners. Although it's not in widespread use yet in learning, it's being used more and more to encourage online sales (see http://www.oddcast.com/sitepal for an example). This technology may soon be used to help online learners feel more connected.

Use It!

How

Chatbots are computer-generated, simulated "people" that can conduct a conversation with a human being using text or audio. Niki Lambropoulos's research suggests that chatbots can provide needed information and break the ice. This helps learners get started and stay engaged.

Lambropoulos's chatbot, PhiliPa (which can be seen at http://e-mmersion .net), can appear above discussion forums, ready to answer learners' questions. PhiliPa informs and also questions learners about course elements, their aims and objectives, assignments and submission details, how to get connected and use the course management system, how to learn online (such as study habits and time management), and how to communicate with communication tutors, developers, and so on. The instructor can program new information into the chatbot based on what is happening during the course (emails, content of the discussion forum, and so on). For example, if the instructor sees that learners are having problems with finding resources, he or she can program the chatbot to answer questions about resources (and recommend that learners see what the chatbot has to say).

PhiliPa is programmed with PHP (PHP Hypertext Preprocessor) and AIML (Artificial Intelligence Markup Language) using Ajax technology for instant messaging.

Adopt or Adapt

Although this is a relatively new technology and not yet in widespread use, it has a great deal of promise for augmenting online instruction. Enter "chatbots" into your favorite search engine to learn more, or start with the Wikipedia description (http://en.wikipedia.org/wiki/Chatbot) for a good introduction. I've been hearing people talk about Flash-based chatbots too.

Attribution

Submitted by Niki Lambropoulos, Centre of Interactive Systems Engineering, London South Bank University, United Kingdom

Contact: niki@lambropoulos.org

URL: http://nikilambropoulos.org

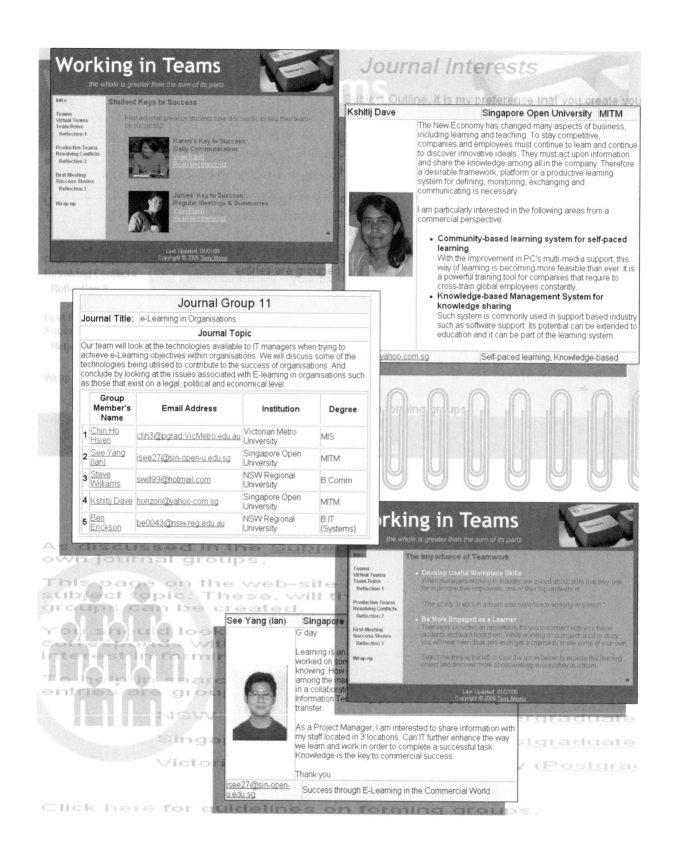

Working in Teams
the whole is greater than the sum of its parts

Intro

Teams
Virtual Teams
Team Roles
Reflection 1

Productive Teams
Resolving Conflicts
Reflection 2

First Meeting
Success Stories
Reflection 3

Wrap-up

Student Keys to Success

Find out what previous students have discovered to help their teams be successful.

Karen's Key to Success:
Daily Communication
View Flash
Read text transcript

James' Key to Success:
Regular Meetings & Summaries
View Flash
Read text transcript

Last Updated: 01/01/05
Copyright © 2005 Terry Morris

Journal Interests

| Kshitij Dave | Singapore Open University | MITM |

The New Economy has changed many aspects of business, including learning and teaching. To stay competitive, companies and employees must continue to learn and continue to discover innovative ideals. They must act upon information and share the knowledge among all in the company. Therefore a desirable framework, platform or a productive learning system for defining, monitoring, exchanging and communicating is necessary.

I am particularly interested in the following areas from a commercial perspective.

- **Community-based learning system for self-paced learning**
  With the improvement in PC's multi-media support, this way of learning is becoming more feasible than ever. It is a powerful training tool for companies that require to cross-train global employees constantly.
- **Knowledge-based Management System for knowledge sharing**
  Such system is commonly used in support based industry such as software support. Its potential can be extended to education and it can be part of the learning system.

| yahoo.com.sg | Self-paced learning, Knowledge-based |

Journal Group 11

| Journal Title: | e-Learning in Organisations |

Journal Topic

Our team will look at the technologies available to IT managers when trying to achieve e-Learning objectives within organisations. We will discuss some of the technologies being utilised to contribute to the success of organisations. And conclude by looking at the issues associated with E-learning in organisations such as those that exist on a legal, political and economical level.

	Group Member's Name	Email Address	Institution	Degree
1	Chin Ho Hsien	chh3@pgrad.VicMetro.edu.au	Victorian Metro University	MIS
2	See Yang (Ian)	isee27@sin-open-u.edu.sg	Singapore Open University	MITM
3	Steve Williams	swill99@hotmail.com	NSW Regional University	B.Comm
4	Kshitij Dave	horizon@yahoo.com.sg	Singapore Open University	MITM
5	Ben Erickson	be0043@nsw-reg.edu.au	NSW Regional University	B.IT (Systems)

Working in Teams
the whole is greater than the sum of its parts

Intro

Teams
Virtual Teams
Team Roles
Reflection 1

Productive Teams
Resolving Conflicts
Reflection 2

First Meeting
Success Stories
Reflection 3

Wrap-up

The Importance of Teamwork

- **Develop Useful Workplace Skills**
  When managers working in industry are asked about skills that they look for in prospective employees, one of their top answers is:

  "The ability to work in a team and experience working in a team."

- **Be More Engaged as a Learner**
  Teamwork provides an opportunity for you to connect with your fellow students and learn from them. While working on a project or case study, you will hear new ideas and even get a chance to share some of your own.

  Select the links at the left or click the arrow below to explore this learning object and discover more about working successfully in a team.

Last Updated: 01/01/05
Copyright © 2005 Terry Morris

| See Yang (Ian) | Singapore |

G'day

Learning is an...
worked on som...
knowing. How...
among the me...
in a collaborati...
Information Te...
transfer.

As a Project Manager, I am interested to share information with my staff located in 3 locations. Can IT further enhance the way we learn and work in order to complete a successful task. Knowledge is the key to commercial success.

Thank you

| isee27@sin-open-u.edu.sg | Success through E-Learning in the Commercial World |

Ideas for Making Collaboration Work

Prominent learning researchers and theorists describe the importance of social interaction for learning, and many say that this type of interaction is critical to learning. Many online learning environments would be far more effective and meaningful if social interaction elements were more fully integrated. Collaboration, having learners work together toward specific results (such as analyzing a scenario, building a decision matrix, and so on), is an important form of social interaction. If you have ever planned an event or made decisions with a working group, you know that collaboration can be problematic and frustrating if it is not implemented well. Collaborating online is harder still. This chapter presents ideas that can help make online collaboration work better.

People who build online courses often don't consider collaborative activities, but they should, for the reasons noted. The ideas offered here can help them prepare learners and gain better results from collaborative activities.

Group Formation

The Big Idea

What

In online instructor-led courses, learners often know little about one another, and forming groups by self-selection, however desirable, is difficult. A simple and effective process to facilitate group formation on the basis of common interests makes group formation easier and more fruitful.

Figure 2.1. Journal Group Formation Instructions

Journal Interests

As discussed in the Subject Outline, it is my preference that you create your own journal groups.

This page on the web-site is for you to publish your personal interests in the subject topic. These, will then become the basis from which your journal groups can be created.

You should look through the entries and, when you find one which corresponds with your own interests, send an email to that person stating your interest in forming a group.

To help in searching for students from other classes, the Journal Interest entries are grouped as follows. Click for access to that class of students.

NSW Regional University (Undergraduate)

Singapore Open University (Postgraduate)

Victorian Metropolitan University (Postgraduate)

Click here for guidelines on forming groups.

Source: Michael K. Lawrence-Slater

Figure 2.2. Journal Group Postings

See Yang (Ian)	Singapore Open University	MITM
	G'day Learning is an essential part of daily life. We learned when we worked on something. We accumulate knowledge without knowing. How can we share and impart individual knowledge among the members of an organization? Can we achieve this in a collaborative manner with the current technology. Can Information Technology (IT) helps in speeding up knowledge transfer. As a Project Manager, I am interested to share information with my staff located in 3 locations. Can IT further enhance the way we learn and work in order to complete a successful task. Knowledge is the key to commercial success. Thank you	
isee27@sin-open-u.edu.sg	Success through E-Learning in the Commercial World	

Kshitij Dave	Singapore Open University	MITM
	The New Economy has changed many aspects of business, including learning and teaching. To stay competitive, companies and employees must continue to learn and continue to discover innovative ideals. They must act upon information and share the knowledge among all in the company. Therefore a desirable framework, platform or a productive learning system for defining, monitoring, exchanging and communicating is necessary. I am particularly interested in the following areas from a commercial perspective. • **Community-based learning system for self-paced learning** With the improvement in PC's multi-media support, this way of learning is becoming more feasible than ever. It is a powerful training tool for companies that require to cross-train global employees constantly. • **Knowledge-based Management System for knowledge sharing** Such system is commonly used in support based industry such as software support. Its potential can be extended to education and it can be part of the learning system.	
horizon@yahoo.com.sg	Self-paced learning, Knowledge-based	

Source: Michael K. Lawrence-Slater

Figure 2.3. Final Journal Group

Journal Group 11			
Journal Title: e-Learning in Organisations			
Journal Topic			
Our team will look at the technologies available to IT managers when trying to achieve e-Learning objectives within organisations. We will discuss some of the technologies being utilised to contribute to the success of organisations. And conclude by looking at the issues associated with E-learning in organisations such as those that exist on a legal, political and economical level.			

	Group Member's Name	Email Address	Institution	Degree
1	Chin Ho Hsien	chh3@pgrad.VicMetro.edu.au	Victorian Metro University	MIS
2	See Yang (Ian)	isee27@sin-open-u.edu.sg	Singapore Open University	MITM
3	Steve Williams	swill99@hotmail.com	NSW Regional University	B.Comm
4	Kshitij Dave	horizon@yahoo.com.sg	Singapore Open University	MITM
5	Ben Erickson	be0043@nsw-reg.edu.au	NSW Regional University	B.IT (Systems)

Source: Michael K. Lawrence-Slater

Why

Forming groups can create problems for online instructors and learners; the process presented here can reduce angst and improve group results as well as how learners feel about group work.

Use It!

How

In online courses, participants often start out knowing nothing about one another, so it's quite difficult to form groups based on any commonalities. The process discussed here allows learners to find out about each other and form meaningful groups. Learners first post information about themselves and then use others' information to find commonalities and form groups.

The screen captures in Figures 2.1 through 2.3 (altered to protect identities) show how Michael Lawrence-Slater uses this process to help learners form groups to collaboratively review journal articles. Learners post the topics they are most interested in so they can form groups with those who share their interests. Learners post their information into HTML forms. This could also be done using discussion forums.

Adopt or Adapt

This idea can be adopted easily in online or blended courses and could be adapted for classroom-based courses by having people post (online or on the wall) information and interests. Depending on the collaborative task, learners could post or share different types of information that would help with group formation for that task. For example, some tasks may benefit from a team with heterogeneous interests or skills while other tasks would benefit from a more homogenous composition.

Attribution

Submitted by Michael K. Lawrence-Slater, postgraduate research fellow, Faculty of Education and Social Work, University of Sydney, New South Wales, Australia

Contact: mls@ieee.org

Prep for Collaborative Work

The Big Idea

What

A short Web-based module, Working in Teams, helps prepare learners for successful collaborative activities.

Figure 2.4. Working in Teams Module

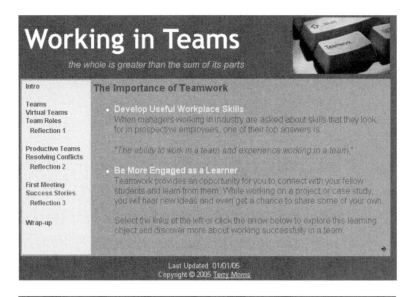

Source: Terry Morris, http://terrymorris.net

Figure 2.5. Being a Productive and Positive Team Member

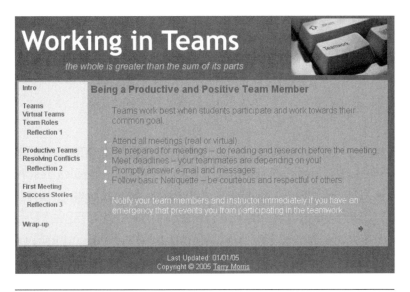

Source: Terry Morris, http://terrymorris.net

Figure 2.6. Success Stories

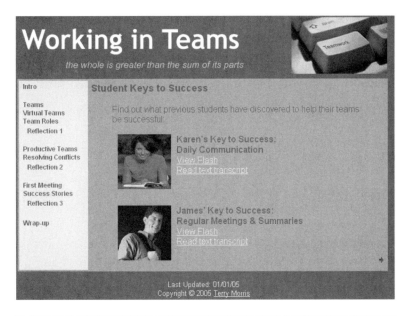

Source: Terry Morris, http://terrymorris.net

Why

Activities that improve understanding about collaboration can improve learning and reduce frustration.

Use It!

How

Before beginning group projects, learners should learn about collaborative work concepts, including virtual teams, team roles, resolving conflicts, and how teams work. It's also helpful to hear stories of successful team experiences and think about how to make the experience work well.

Terry Morris has been including team activities in her online courses for years and has found that many learners are not well prepared for group activities. She developed this module to help them have a more productive and positive team experience. The success stories are based on real experiences. Her college-age children, James and Karen Felke, recorded the voices for the stories.

Adopt or Adapt

The Working in Teams module is freely available on the Web (see the URL in the Attribution section). Anyone can access and use it, or develop a similar module of their own.

Attribution

Submitted by Terry Morris, associate professor, William Rainey Harper College, Palatine, Illinois, USA

Contact: tmorris@harpercollege.edu

URL: http://terrymorris.net/teamwork

Team Agreement Template

The Big Idea
What

We often ask learners to work in teams, but teams can be very dysfunctional. To help teams work more efficiently and effectively, learners can create a team agreement that outlines how team members are going to work together and clarifies assumptions, constraints, and goals.

Why

Teams can be an effective learning mechanism or they can be dysfunctional and interfere with learning. A team agreement gives learners the opportunity to deal with likely differences and conflicts up front. It also helps them identify warning signs and solutions to potential problems.

Use It!
How

Jackie Dobrovolny provides a team agreement template to learners, who customize the template to their unique needs, requirements, and goals. The last section of each team agreement contains each team member's answers to three reflection questions, which ask learners to assess the process of writing the team agreement and their role on the team. This collaborative activity is a critical first step to good teamwork.

The team agreement template is a Microsoft Word document. Learners typically discuss the template within the team and then work together to customize it for the group. They email it to the instructor, who reviews it and uses Track Changes or Comments to provide feedback.

Dobrovolny feels strongly about the importance of helping learners be successful and believes we set them up to fail if we do not help them progress through the five stages of team development—forming, storming, norming, performing, and mourning (adapted from Tuckman, 1965).

Jackie Dobrovolny's Team Agreement Template

Maximum total points = 100

Basic Guidelines

- Due date: third week of class

- One to three pages, single-spaced

- Thoughtful, well written, concise

- Professional (grammatically correct, no typos, professional appearance). *Please run spell check before sending it to me!*

- Send your team agreement to me as an email attachment. The name of the file you send must use the following convention: first names of everyone on your team, for example, ted_mary_joan_bob_team.doc.

Organize the agreement into six sections:

1. *Team members:* Names of the people on your team.

2. *Goal and purpose of the team:* The goal and purpose of your team is to provide a forum for learning from one another. What else?

3. *Team work management*

    - How will you manage the work of this team?

    - We will have time during class each week to review one another's work but do you want to review the work of your teammates before class each week?

    - Do you want to meet outside of class or is email adequate for your reviews?

    - Who is the leader of your team? Do you want to select one person to be the leader for the entire semester or do you want to rotate the leadership responsibilities?

    - What are the responsibilities of the leader?

4. *Problems*

- How will you handle the inevitable situation when a team member does not complete his or her work by the agreed-upon date?

- How long will you tolerate lack of input from a team member?

- At what point will you contact me and ask me to meet with the team?

- Be sure to give yourselves a guideline for when to revise this agreement if you find it is not working for you.

- Consider the stages of team development and how your team will work in each stage. Review the following sites to learn more about the five stages of team development:

    http://www.strategosinc.com/work_team_3.htm

    http://www.goer.state.ny.us/train/onlinelearning/FTMS/400s1.html

    http://web.mit.edu/hr/oed/learn/teams/art_stages.html

5. *Other team work issues:* Use this section to define, describe, or explain how you want to handle other important team work issues.

- How you provide feedback to your teammates is very important. Saying "I really like what you did" is nice but is not very helpful in terms of improving the document. Similarly, saying something like "This section is confusing" is also not very helpful. The ideal feedback is specific and includes recommendations for improvement. It also is "owned" by the reviewer, that is, it is easier to receive feedback if the reviewer owns the opinion and uses *I* rather than *you*. For example, in the following feedback the reviewer owns the feedback and is probably not insulting the receiver: "I was confused by the colors you selected. I could not find a justification for those colors and they did not seem to align with the gestalt of the site. That is, given that this is a site about American history, I think the color scheme should be red, white, and blue rather than purple and yellow."

- How are you going to track different versions of the same document? Are you going to use a numbering system and are you going to use that convention in the name of the document and in the subject line of your email messages?

- What is the backup plan for your final products? That is, who is responsible for the final version of each document and who is responsible for the backup of each final product? It is critical to have at least one backup for each final product and for the backup document to be the responsibility of someone other than the person responsible for the original document.

6. *Reflection paragraphs:* Each team member should answer each of the following three reflection questions.

   - What did you learn from writing this team agreement?

   - How does the process we used for writing this team agreement compare to other team agreements you have developed?

   - What concerns or questions do you have about your team or your team agreement?

Evaluation

The full 100 points will be given if your team agreement follows the basic guidelines outlined here.

Revisions and Improvements

If your team agreement does not meet the basic guidelines, I will return it to you with a tentative score. If you want to improve your score, you can revise it and return it to me. If you revise your paper, please use the Word Track Changes feature and revise the original document. Change the file name to team members' names.team2.doc—for example, bob.mary.louise.sam.team2.doc

Adopt or Adapt

> This idea can be used in any classroom, blended, or online course that utilizes teamwork. It is especially important when the required outcome of the team's collaboration has moderate or higher stakes, such as an impact on grades. Dobrovolny uses this approach along with the team assessment described in the next idea. Both can be customized to any learning situation.

Attribution

Submitted by Jackie Dobrovolny, Triple Play, Aurora, Colorado, USA

Contact: jdoffice1@comcast.net

Reference

Tuckman, B. (1965). Developmental sequence in small groups. *Psychological Bulletin, 63,* 384–399.

Team Assessment

The Big Idea

What

Teams need opportunities to assess the effectiveness of the agreements they have developed (see the previous idea for a team agreement template) and team members need a way to assess individual effectiveness.

Why

Team assessments help team members improve their participation skills, which in turn helps the team become a successful educational experience.

Use It!

How

Jackie Dobrovolny requires each team member to provide anonymous feedback to each of his or her teammates twice during the semester. The instructor compiles the data, sharing data about specific team members only with the individual and sharing answers about the state of the team with the entire team. Team members complete these assessments either online or on paper.

Dobrovolny typically has learners assess their team twice during a sixteen-week semester. Team Assessment 1 takes place around week six and Team Assessment 2 takes place around week fourteen or fifteen. This schedule allows learners adequate time to modify or improve their team performance.

Jackie Dobrovolny's Team Assessment 1

1. In what stage of team development do you think your team is currently operating?

    a. Forming

    b. Storming

    c. Norming

    d. Performing

    e. Mourning

Comments:

2. I think our team is working well together.

    a. Strongly agree

    b. Agree

    c. Sometimes yes, sometimes no

    d. Occasionally

    e. Never

Comments:

For questions 3, 4, and 5, write in the name of a different teammate for each question and then answer the question about the degree to which that person has helped you. If you have more than three teammates, copy and paste the question below questions 3, 4, and 5 and label it 6, 7, and so on.

You will receive the full fifty points if everyone on your team strongly agrees or agrees that your feedback is helpful. For each person on your team who says your feedback is sometimes, occasionally, or never helpful, you lose five points.

3. Name of the team member being assessed:

This person's feedback is always very helpful in terms of improving my visuals and my design justifications.

    a. Strongly agree

    b. Agree

    c. Sometimes yes, sometimes no

    d. Occasionally

    e. Never

Comments about this person's feedback and suggestions for how this person could be more helpful to you:

4. Name of the team member being assessed:

This person's feedback is always very helpful in terms of improving my visuals and my design justifications.

    a. Strongly agree

    b. Agree

    c. Sometimes yes, sometimes no

    d. Occasionally

    e. Never

Comments about this person's feedback and suggestions for how this person could be more helpful to you:

5. Name of the team member being assessed:

This person's feedback is always very helpful in terms of improving my visuals and my design justifications.

    a. Strongly agree

    b. Agree

c. Sometimes yes, sometimes no

d. Occasionally

e. Never

Comments about this person's feedback and suggestions for how this person could be more helpful to you:

Your name:

Date:

Jackie Dobrovolny's Team Assessment 2

1. In what stage of team development do you think your team is currently operating?

    a. Forming

    b. Storming

    c. Norming

    d. Performing

    e. Mourning

Comments:

2. I think our team is working well together.

    a. Strongly agree

    b. Agree

    c. Sometimes yes, sometimes no

    d. Occasionally

    e. Never

Comments:

For questions 3, 4, and 5, write in the name of a different teammate for each question and then write in the best thing about this person's feedback to you during this class. If you have more than three teammates, copy and paste the question again below questions 3, 4, and 5 and label it 6, 7, and so on.

You can cite a specific instance or describe this person's general approach. The goal is for you to identify the feedback this person gave you that helped you the most.

You will receive the full fifty points for this assessment if you and your teammates answer each question. As with the first team assessment, I will send you the feedback from your teammates. Be sure to sign and date your assessment.

3. Name of the team member being assessed:

Comments on the most useful or helpful feedback this person gave you during this class:

4. Name of the team member being assessed:

Comments on the most useful or helpful feedback this person gave you during this class:

5. Name of the team member being assessed:

Comments on the most useful or helpful feedback this person gave you during this class:

Your name:

Date:

Adopt or Adapt

This idea can be used in any classroom, blended, or online course that utilizes teamwork. Dobrovolny uses this form with the Team Agreement Template described in the previous idea. Both ideas can be customized to any learning situation. Dobrovolny has also used both with volunteer committees.

Attribution

Submitted by Jackie Dobrovolny, Triple Play, Aurora, Colorado, USA

Contact: jdoffice1@comcast.net

Rules of Engagement Agreement

The Big Idea

What

> Group activities can be hindered by poor group communication and un-equal sharing of obligations. These activities can be enhanced by having groups develop a rules of engagement agreement.

Figure 2.7. Joanne C. Dunlap's Prompts for Agreement

Teamwork Questionnaire

Each team needs to respond collaboratively (which means all team members are in agreement with the response) to the following questions:

1. Purpose of teams: Define the role and purpose of your team (and the teamwork completed) during the course. What value does the team offer, if any?

2. Individual learning goals vs. team requirements: What are each team member's individual learning goals for the course, and how will the team make sure that everyone achieves those goals? (Teams need to be responsible for every team member's learning, not just completing products together.)

3. Project leadership: Who will provide leadership during each phase of the project? Will leadership rotate? What are leaders responsible for (e.g., Does a leader need to fill in the gaps if other team members do not follow through? Does a leader need to send reminders to team members regarding products and timelines?)?

4. Independent and/or collaborative work: Do members of your team prefer to work on their own? If so, how will they coordinate their individual contributions so that they "go together" in both form and style? Or do members of your team prefer to work collaboratively, perhaps in joint work sessions during which work can be coordinated?

5. Weekly communication patterns and format: Discuss the issue of asynchronous vs. synchronous—strength, weakness, reason for both—as part of this process so you have a plan of action for working together. Will you communicate asynchronously or set up a synchronous time each week to connect?

Figure 2.7. Joanne C. Dunlap's Prompts for Agreement, Cont'd

6. Workload: What agreements has your team developed regarding workload? Will team members assume equal portions of the work each week, or do you anticipate contributions varying over the semester? If the latter, how will you ensure that this is fair?

7. Review and feedback: What expectations have been established regarding thoughtful, regular critique of team members' work? How will you provide feedback when you feel someone's work needs to be revised? When you are receiving feedback, how can you remain open to new ways of thinking and doing?

8. Addressing problems: How will your team communicate about problems that emerge, and develop solutions? (Unanticipated emergent problems; work not done on time/not what was agreed to/not sufficient quality or quantity; meetings are missed; etc.)

9. Commitment to quality: Describe the commitment team members are making and the quality of work you are aiming for.

10. Evaluating process: How and when will you evaluate your team process/collaboration in terms of what is working, not working, needs adjustment, and so on?

11. How, when, and why to ask for mediation: Specifically define under what conditions you will ask for mediation from Dave and Joni.

Source: Joanna C. Dunlap

Figure 2.8. Joanne C. Dunlap's Example Team Agreement

Team E Agreement

1. Will you have a leader who keeps the team on track during team assignments?

   After a preliminary review of the projects, Team E has decided that it is best to have a different team leader for each of the weeks that have a team assignment. The team leader will be assigned a week in advance on the basis of personal schedules at that time.

2. How do you prefer to work?

   After reviewing individual work schedules, we have decided to assign a team leader a week in advance so that he/she can organize and assign tasks to be completed by the

(Continued)

Figure 2.8. Joanne C. Dunlap's Example Team Agreement, Cont'd

weekend before the due date. This will provide an adequate amount of time for completion and review by our teammates. The team leader will assign a preliminary due date prior to the actual due date for all to adhere to. This offers flexibility to each team member to work on his/her task, yet holds him/her accountable to successful completion of his or her task by the due date.

3. Do you agree to provide timely, substantive feedback?

We all agree that it is important to provide feedback that is positive. This benefits the team and provides open communication. It is important to critique constructively . . . the team wants to creat a superior product.

4. How will you handle a team member who does not do what he/she has agreed to do?

The team is composed of professionals and we expect if an individual has a problem (technical or personal) hindering him or her from performing the assigned task, the team will be notified ASAP so the team can assist in the completion of that task. The team may advise, inform, break the task into smaller and more manageable parts, or assign it to another team member. The team leader will be the focal point for managing these activities. At that point the team will also negotiate how the team member's assignment score should be affected.

Source: Joanna C. Dunlap

Why

A team contract helps group members determine how they will work together to achieve the desired results, and documents their commitments to one another.

Use It!

How

Involving learners in group projects is a popular instructional strategy in online courses because

- Group work can help counter the isolation some online learners feel because they are physically removed from the institution, their peers, and their instructor.

- Exposing learners to multiple perspectives can open their eyes to diverse ideas.

- Learners can more readily achieve desired results with support.

- The quality of individual learner work can be enhanced through collaboration.

- Group projects can help instructors manage their workload because instead of evaluating twenty-five individual learner projects they may evaluate only five group projects.

Lack of support for group projects may erode positive outcomes and lead to groups that are dysfunctional or learners who feel that the assessment process is inequitable. To minimize obstacles to effective group work, teams can establish a formal agreement describing how they will work together. A rules of engagement team contract may be especially important for learners who have had negative experiences in which they had to cover for team members who did not contribute.

In the contract, each team specifies the following:

- Who will post deliverables?

- Who will lead the group during various projects?

- How will they communicate with one another? How often? Will they set interim deadlines?

- How will work be distributed?

- What is the preferred work style?

- What are the consequences of not getting work done?

- What are the known problems?

Learners can use this agreement with the Team Review Form (the next idea) to assess one another's contributions to group projects.

Joanna Dunlap explains that this strategy addresses her need to make sure she and the learners have a chance to realize the benefits of group projects by minimizing the problems associated with unstructured group activities. It also gives the learners responsibility for determining how they will work together and empowers them to establish their own rules and consequences.

Adopt or Adapt

This approach is perfect for classroom-based, blended, and online courses that utilize group work and could also be used in noninstructional group situations, such as committees or project teams.

Attribution

Submitted by Joanna C. Dunlap, assistant professor, School of Education and Human Development, University of Colorado at Denver and Health Sciences, Denver, Colorado, USA

Contact: Joni.Dunlap@cudenver.edu

Team Review Form

The Big Idea

What

Group results are hindered when team members do not fulfill their obligations. A team review form provides information to help team members know where they stand in meeting team commitments, which can augment group process and results.

Figure 2.9. Team Review Form

For each item, select the score you believe best reflects that person's efforts and contributions.

If the person:

- Always demonstrates the quality, you would give a score of 5.
- Frequently demonstrates the quality, you would give a score of 4.
- Sometimes demonstrates the quality, you would give a score of 3.
- Seldom demonstrates the quality, you would give a score of 2.
- Never demonstrates the quality, you would give a score of 1.

Your Name:					
Team Member Reviewed:					
1. Is willing to frequently share ideas and resources.	5	4	3	2	1
2. Accepts responsibilities for tasks determined by the group.	5	4	3	2	1
3. Respects differences of opinion and background.	5	4	3	2	1
4. Is willing to negotiate and make compromises.	5	4	3	2	1
5. Provides leadership and support by taking an active role in initiating ideas and actions.	5	4	3	2	1
6. Respects decisions of others.	5	4	3	2	1
7. Provides positive feedback on team members' accomplishments.	5	4	3	2	1

(Continued)

Figure 2.9. Team Review Form, Cont'd

For each item, select the score you believe best reflects that person's efforts and contributions.

If the person:

- Always demonstrates the quality, you would give a score of 5.
- Frequently demonstrates the quality, you would give a score of 4.
- Sometimes demonstrates the quality, you would give a score of 3.
- Seldom demonstrates the quality, you would give a score of 2.
- Never demonstrates the quality, you would give a score of 1.

8. Is willing to work with others for the purpose of group success.	5	4	3	2	1
9. Online communication is friendly in tone.	5	4	3	2	1
10. Keeps in close contact with team members for the purpose of maintaining team cohesion and collaboration.	5	4	3	2	1
11. Produces high-quality work.	5	4	3	2	1
12. Meets team deadlines.	5	4	3	2	1
13. Comments (Please provide your teammate with positive and constructive feedback.):					

Source: Joanna C. Dunlap

Why

A team review form allows learners to provide feedback to one another about how well they are meeting commitments.

Use It!

How

Learners use the Team Review Form to assess each group member's contribution (including their own contribution) on group projects. These assessments can have ramifications, such as 20 percent score reduction for individuals who receive less than fifty points from more than one team member. This feedback empowers learners to have a say in the point distribution on group projects. The review process also functions as an incentive for all group members to meet expectations (see the previous idea for a Rules of Engagement Agreement that can be used to document what is expected). It also provides the instructor with the following helpful insights and data for supplying feedback and support to individual group members and to the group as a whole:

- The Team Review Form summarizes the project work and the content of private group discussions.

- It alerts the instructor to specific group and group member problems. This allows the instructor to address the issues quickly and efficiently.

When given the means and opportunity, learners provide thoughtful and detailed feedback to group members and are honest about their own contributions. The reviews also provide the instructor with useful comments to be included in feedback to individual learners. Joanna Dunlap explains that this strategy addresses her need to make sure that she and the learners have a good chance of realizing the benefits of group projects.

Dunlap uses a Web form that sends the data to her email.

Adopt or Adapt

This idea would work well for classroom-based, blended, and online courses that utilize group work and could also be used in noninstructional group situations, such as committees or project teams. The process could also be accomplished using email, word-processed documents, or an online survey application.

Attribution

Submitted by Joanna C. Dunlap, assistant professor, School of Education and Human Development, University of Colorado at Denver and Health Sciences, Denver, Colorado, USA

Contact: Joni.Dunlap@cudenver.edu

Give karma point -

Michelle - It's not that I have additional info. for your posting, I j along providing hard evidence to back up your thoughts.

When you mentioned the idea of having a student sending their new perspective of online learning for me. The idea of sending th about some of the various products that students could create.
⊕ Respond

We have to keep reminding ours

Karma point for Michelle - wow

Criteria for Karma Points

Here is how we will assign our allotment of karma points for each discussion:

- 0 points: Though you may have introduced an interesting idea or contributed to the discourse, it is not original enough, or is somehow unclear.
- 1 point: You provide a succinct, interesting, original, and well-documented argument or idea, or provide a useful link or pertinent fact.
- 2 points: Your contribution is creative and original, and compellingly argues a very clear point. You support your contribution with evidence.
- 3 points: An exceptional contribution to the discourse, one that really opens eyes and encourages a lively discussion/debate. Exemplary in all respects.

Ways to Improve Chances of Receiving Karma Points

- Choose provocative subject lines to make our postings stand out.
- Present our own perspectives.
- Write clearly.
- Construct an argument. Provide evidence, present a rationale that supports our positions, and reference the opinions of others, linking to supplementary evidence when appropriate.
- Open up debate by remembering that the best response is one that gets people thinking, and that makes them want to reply.
- Learn from others who have posted before us by reading through the posts and referring to appropriate posts in our own.

Rules for Assigning Karma Points

Only award karma points to those who have contributed significantly to the discussion – vote trading is unacceptable. Award karma points based on the quality of the message, irrespective of the content of the message – vote for exceptional messages even if you do not necessarily agree with the ideas presented.

CHAPTER 3

Ideas for Making Discussions Work

T his chapter showcases ideas that make online discussions productive and successful. Although social interaction has numerous benefits for learners and learning, and this type of social interaction can be incredibly powerful, learners report numerous problems with discussion forums, including information overload from having to dig through large amounts of postings, and the large percentage of posting content that is off topic or irrelevant.

Instructors who teach online often use online discussions so everyone can share ideas, reflect on learning, and get and provide help. Discussions in asynchronous online courses help learners feel they aren't alone while learning. These ideas can improve online discussions so they are better vehicles for learning.

Discussion Message Protocols

The Big Idea

What

Message protocols for guiding discussion messages help learners make better use of the discussion tool and reduce frustration.

Why

Message protocols help learners write clear and useful messages, which encourages learner participation and collaboration in the discussion while decreasing anxiety and frustration.

Use It!

How

Barb Edwards's online course is case and discussion based. Before the message protocols were established, there were many problematic postings that led to frustration and reduced interest in reading messages. Plus, learners do not necessarily begin with the first message but may start anywhere, and context is needed to facilitate understanding without reading all the messages that were posted earlier. Through observation and surveys, a list of protocols was developed to contribute to useful messages and effective conversation.

The protocols promote clear and effective communication and avoidance of anything that is likely to detract from the conversation or slow it down. Therefore, message protocols establish a proper message format and set a standard for the expected content.

The protocols are a part of the larger course guide. At first the instructor may need to send private emails to remind individuals to use the protocols consistently and post messages to the class so they know the importance of using the message guide and adhering to a message content standard.

Barb Edwards's Message Protocols

We want to avoid anything that detracts or slows down the conversation. When drafting your message, keep the following in mind:

1. KISS—keep it short and simple. Long messages discourage interaction. Use HTML code sparingly to keep the message simple and to save time composing the message. Avoid the HTML editor as it adds excessive code that hinders the flow of conversation. Also, too much HTML code can result in the message not displaying on the screen or printing properly.

2. To reply, use the quote feature (not reply) and then edit the previous message to leave a short part of it to set the context for your reply. If each message has a context, the discussion efficiency tools like *compile* and *view thread* allow you to glance through the messages together rather than opening one message at a time. It also facilitates viewing unread messages in a topic rather than having all messages viewed. Be sure to leave the message number and the sender's name so that it is referenced for WebCT. Delete parts of the message that are not relevant or that are lengthy. By leaving the > notation in the previous message, others will be able to distinguish the previous message from your reply and will recognize that the text without the > notation is the new message.

3. Check grammar and spelling. If you are a poor speller or typist, draft messages in Word before copying into a WebCT message. Some may prefer to set up a Word file for each seminar anyway to maintain study notes.

4. Use a subject line that is *short, descriptive,* and *distinctive* so as not to confuse the class. For example, if a message's subject line in seminar 8 reads simply "seminar 8," it provides no clue as to content. A subject line that reads "product costs" at least tells us what the message is about.

5. Maintain a thread. In WebCT, threads keep messages about the same subject together, which makes it easy to follow the conversation. So change the subject line only if the conversation has changed.

6. Format the message. Use lists and spaces between paragraphs to make the message easy to read and respond to. Use word wrap to ensure that the message can be read on the screen without having to scroll sideways. Avoid the WebCT HTML editor because it results in too much code in a message and makes it difficult to reply using a context.

7. Reference other messages. In conversation, we might say, "Jack advised that. . . ." In WebCT you can write, "Jack advised in message 356 that. . . ." You can find message 356 by choosing to view the messages in a topic as unthreaded.

8. Minimize file attachments. At the discretion of the instructor, but generally unless the instructor has requested it, keep file attachments to a minimum because the conversation stops while the file is downloaded. It can also be difficult to respond to a message that has only a file attachment and no text. If a file is attached, be sure to explain briefly in the message what the attachment contains to facilitate the conversation. Also, don't forget to click on *attach file* after browsing for your file.

9. Think value-added. To reduce anxiety about the number of messages, ensure that your message adds value to the discussion. Messages that are appropriate face-to-face yet do not add value to online discussions include the common courtesies of saying "Thanks" and "You're welcome." In an online course, everyone does not need to read these. When replying you may reply to the sender or to the discussion topic, so use *reply to the sender privately* when appropriate so that the number of non-value-added messages is kept to a minimum.

10. Add links. WebCT messages require the full link (that is, http://) or the link will not be live. Reference your research just as you would in a written paper. For example, use quotation marks for direct quotes and cite sources as appropriate. Also test the link by previewing your message.

11. To test links, formatting, and spelling, preview the message before posting it.

Adopt or Adapt

These protocols were developed for the WebCT environment. Other course management software has its own discussion tools, so the list can be adapted to other course management systems easily. It would also be useful to provide these types of protocols when using a stand-alone discussion board such as WebCrossing (http://www.webcrossing.com) or phpbb (http://www.phpbb.com).

Attribution

Submitted by Barb Edwards, senior lecturer, Simon Fraser University, Burnaby, British Columbia, Canada

Contact: bjedwards@sfu.ca

Evaluate Your Contribution

The Big Idea

What

Let learners evaluate their own course contributions using an online quiz or survey tool.

Why

This approach allows learners to reflect on their contributions and reduces or eliminates the instructor's need to evaluate learners' postings subjectively.

Use It!

How

When teaching instructor-led distance courses, one of the most difficult tasks for instructors is to evaluate learners' course contributions. Lynn Kelting-Gibson used inspiration gained in a WebCT quiz workshop to help her solve this problem. She developed a simple three-question, five-point self-evaluation using the quiz tool that prompts online learners to evaluate their discussion postings. This evaluation was developed in the WebCT quiz tool because it was available and is self-correcting, simple to use, and self-reporting.

Example of Lynn Kelting-Gibson's Self-Evaluation

Question 1 (2 points) Did I thoughtfully respond at least once to the question or questions in this week's activities?

- a. Yes. (2 points or 100 percent correct)
- b. Somewhat. (1 point or 50 percent correct)
- c. No. (0 points or 0 percent correct)

Question 2 (2 points) Did I post at least two meaningful and constructive responses to other participants' messages?

    a. Yes. (2 points or 100 percent correct)

    b. I posted one response. (1 point or 50 percent correct)

    c. No. (0 points or 0 percent correct)

Question 3 (1 point) Did I read others' discussions?

    a. Yes, most of them. (1 point or 100 percent correct)

    b. I read some of them. (.5 point or 50 percent correct)

    c. I read very few or none at all. (0 points or 0 percent correct)

Adopt or Adapt

This type of self-evaluation quiz could easily be adapted with different questions or implemented using other online quiz tools or even email. It could be adapted to evaluate one's own contribution to a team effort or product results.

Attribution

Submitted by Lynn Kelting-Gibson, online instructor, Northern Plains Transition to Teaching, Montana State University, Bozeman, Montana, USA

Contact: lynnk@montana.edu

Karma Points for Contributions

The Big Idea

What

Karma points let learners evaluate the quality of discussion contributions. The idea behind karma points is that learners, rather than a moderator or instructor, should evaluate others' postings and recognize the most valuable contributions.

Figure 3.1. Karma Points Criteria

Criteria for Karma Points

Here is how we will assign our allotment of karma points for each discussion:

- 0 points: Though you may have introduced an interesting idea or contributed to the discourse, it is not original enough, or is somehow unclear.
- 1 point: You provide a succinct, interesting, original, and well-documented argument or idea, or provide a useful link or pertinent fact.
- 2 points: Your contribution is creative and original, and compellingly argues a very clear point. You support your contribution with evidence.
- 3 points: An exceptional contribution to the discourse, one that really opens eyes and encourages a lively discussion/debate. Exemplary in all respects.

Ways to Improve Chances of Receiving Karma Points

- Choose provocative subject lines to make our postings stand out.
- Present our own perspectives.
- Write clearly.
- Construct an argument. Provide evidence, present a rationale that supports our positions, and reference the opinions of others, linking to supplementary evidence when appropriate.
- Open up debate by remembering that the best response is one that gets people thinking, and that makes them want to reply.
- Learn from others who have posted before us by reading through the posts and referring to appropriate posts in our own.

Rules for Assigning Karma Points

Only award karma points to those who have contributed significantly to the discussion – vote trading is unacceptable. Award karma points based on the quality of the message, irrespective of the content of the message – vote for exceptional messages even if you do not necessarily agree with the ideas presented.

Source: Joanna C. Dunlap

Figure 3.2. Awarded Karma Points

Give karma point -

Michelle - It's not that I have additional info. for your posting, I j along providing hard evidence to back up your thoughts.

When you mentioned the idea of having a student sending their new perspective of online learning for me. The idea of sending th about some of the various products that students could create.
⊕ Respond

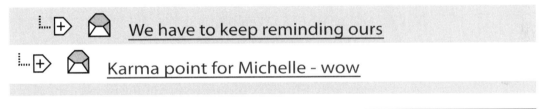

We have to keep reminding ours

Karma point for Michelle - wow

Source: Joanna C. Dunlap

Why

Karma points encourage learners to offer more valuable contributions and recognize the effort required.

Use It!

How

To make karma points work in an online course, the instructor gives each learner a certain number of karma points (for example, three) that she or he can assign to valued discussion contributions within a certain timeframe (for example, by week's end). Because learners are evaluating each other's contributions, it is important to encourage them first to establish criteria and then to apply that criteria to their assessments and their own contributions. For example, karma point criteria may include sharing original ideas, writing clearly, presenting a coherent argument, providing evidence to support an argument, "listening" to others and incorporating their ideas and perspectives, and so on.

When learners award karma points, they can simply write "karma point" in the subject line of their forum response, making it easy for the instructor to determine which learners have received karma points.

This approach improves the quality of contributions because learners are more reflective and thoughtful about their postings and responses. One interesting note is that karma points are awarded even if learners share opposing views (for example, as shown in Figure 3.2, Michael disagrees with Michelle's perspective but still acknowledges the posting's value to the overall discussion).

Karma points help learners participate more in the discussion because learners have taken over part or all of the evaluation role. The karma points learners accumulate for their contributions can be used to determine a score for class participation.

Joanna Dunlap explains that this strategy addresses her desire to give learners a voice in determining valuable contributions and to encourage participation without requiring learners to post a certain number of discussion responses each week. She also wanted a strategy that would allow her to be an equal participant in the discussion (rather than the judge of the discussion) and help learners appreciate the effort required to be active members of an online community.

She describes an online course in which she used karma points. "A few weeks before the end of the course, my daughter decided to be born five weeks early. I wanted to complete the course but needed to scale back on some of the activities, specifically my monitoring of the last couple of weeks of online discussion. I informed the learners that they were welcome to continue the discussions but need not assign karma points because I would no longer be monitoring. I thought for sure they would discontinue all discussion and focus on completing their final projects. To my amazement, they continued the discussion until the end of the course and continued to acknowledge each other's contributions by awarding karma points! They clearly believed that there was value in the process and, in fact, told me so in the end-of-course evaluations."

Adopt or Adapt

This idea is perfect for use in courses with online discussions but could also be adapted for noninstructional online discussions. It can also be adapted for other electronic communications media and for use in classroom-based instruction.

Attribution

Submitted by Joanna C. Dunlap, assistant professor, School of Education and Human Development, University of Colorado at Denver and Health Sciences, Denver, Colorado, USA

Contact: Joni.Dunlap@cudenver.edu

Acronym and Emoticon Help

The Big Idea

What

Where electronic communications are used in courses, everyone may not know commonly used acronyms and emoticons. Help everyone learn them!

Why

This activity will help learners who are new to using chat, email, and discussion forums not feel lost and stay focused on content.

Use It!

How

Acronyms have always been a problem in training sessions. Learners are struggling to learn new content and a new vocabulary at the same time. The introduction of electronic communications has compounded the problem. Acronyms can now be abbreviations of business terms (for example, LTC might mean "long-term care") or abbreviations of conversational phrases (for example, BRB might mean "be right back"). Getting caught up in this new vocabulary can be enough to distract and frustrate learners.

At the beginning of a course, provide a list of ten acronyms and their definitions. Provide opportunities for learners to practice using them. For example, in a synchronous online course, as learners log in, ask them to chat with one another and find out as much as they can about other learners while they practice using as many acronyms as possible. Provide a cheat sheet of acronyms. Provide a reward (perhaps a certificate made up of acronyms) for the best use of acronyms.

Jennifer Hofmann's Emoticons and Acronyms Cheat Sheet

Emoticons Emoticons (emotional icons) are used to compensate for the inability to convey voice inflections, facial expressions, and bodily gestures in written communication. Some emoticons are better known as "smileys." Emoticons can be very effective toward avoiding misinterpretation of the writer's intentions. While there are no standard definitions for the following emoticons, I have supplied typical meanings. Most emoticons will look like a face (eyes, nose, and mouth) when rotated ninety degrees clockwise.

:) or :-)	Expresses happiness, sarcasm, or joke
:(or :-(	Expresses unhappiness
:] or :-]	Expresses jovial happiness
:[or :-[	Expresses despondent unhappiness
:D or :-D	Expresses jovial happiness
:I or :-I	Expresses indifference
:-/ or :-<\\>	Indicates undecided, confused, or skeptical; also :/ or :<\\>
:Q or :-Q	Expresses confusion
:S or :-S	Expresses incoherence or loss of words
:@ or :-@	Expresses shock or screaming
:O or :-O	Indicates surprise, yelling, or realization of an error ("uh oh!")

Acronyms

AAMOF	As a matter of fact
BBFN	Bye-bye for now

BFN	Bye for now
BTW	By the way
BYKT	But you knew that
CMIIW	Correct me if I'm wrong
EOL	End of lecture
FAQ	Frequently asked question(s)
FITB	Fill in the blank
FWIW	For what it's worth
FYI	For your information
HTH	Hope this helps
IAC	In any case
IAE	In any event
IMCO	In my considered opinion
IMHO	In my humble opinion
IMNSHO	In my not so humble opinion
IMO	In my opinion
IOW	In other words
LOL	Lots of luck or laughing out loud
MHOTY	My hat's off to you
NRN	No reply necessary
OIC	Oh, I see
OTOH	On the other hand
ROF	Rolling on the floor

ROFL	Rolling on the floor laughing
ROTFL	Rolling on the floor laughing
RSN	Real soon now
SITD	Still in the dark
TIA	Thanks in advance
TIC	Tongue in cheek
TTYL	Talk to you later
TYVM	Thank you very much
WYSIWYG	What you see is what you get
<G>	Grinning
<J>	Joking
<L>	Laughing
<S>	Smiling
<Y>	Yawning

Adopt or Adapt

This idea is useful for any online course that utilizes electronic communications. It could be adapted with business acronyms and technical jargon.

Attribution

Submitted by Jennifer Hofmann, synchronous learning expert, InSync Training, Branford, Connecticut, USA

Contact: Jennifer@insynctraining.com

URL: http://www.insynctraining.com

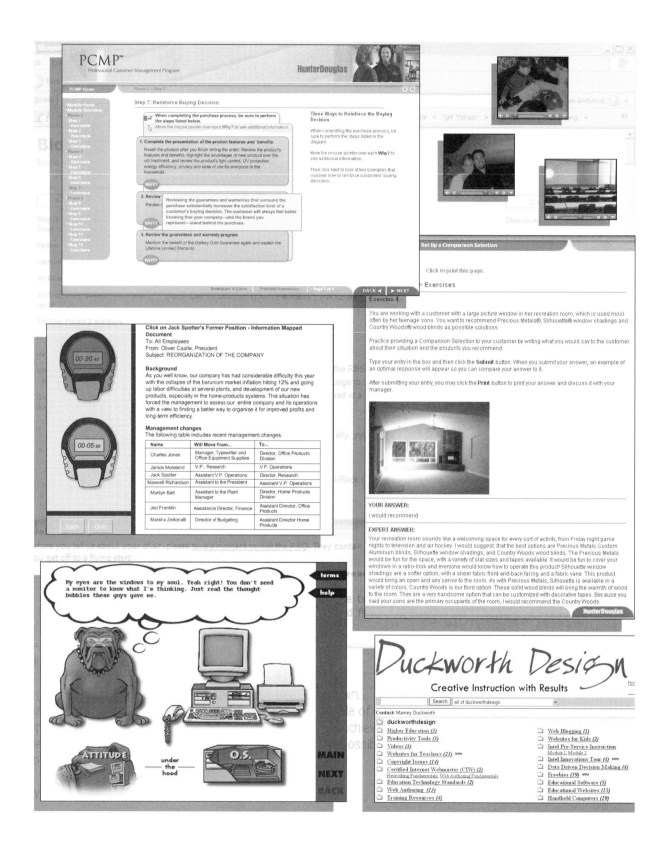

Ideas for Self-Directed and Asynchronous Activities

This chapter offers ideas for self-directed and asynchronous activities. Some of the ideas are meant to be used by learners learning on their own with no planned interaction with others. Others are more appropriate for being completed on one's own as part of a learning environment that involves interaction with others.

Many people assume that self-directed and asynchronous activities are bound to be boring, one-dimensional, lockstep, or unengaging. There's no reason they need to be except lack of imagination. That's not you, right? (Or it shouldn't be after looking through this chapter and others.)

Table Organizers

The Big Idea

What

Simple but effective graphic organizers can be built using the table functionality of a word processing program.

Why

Graphic organizers promote comprehension and retention (Vacca & Vacca, 2005) and can be used to build effective study guides.

Use It!

How

The organizers described here can be easily created by learners using the table functionality of popular word processing programs.

H-Chart

An H-Chart is similar in function to a Venn diagram and is used to compare and contrast two items. The example in Figure 4.1 asks learners in a teacher education course to compare and contrast the key points of the learning theories of two key theorists.

Figure 4.1. H-Chart

An H-Chart is similar in function to a Venn Diagram and is used to compare and contrast two items. The sample below asks teacher education students to compare and contrast two major theorists, Vygotsky and Piaget, after reading the appropriate chapter in their textbook.

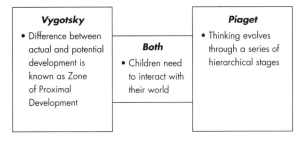

Source: Sarah Cecire, http://homepage.mac.com/cecires

Sorting

Closed and open sorting activities are good for reinforcing understanding of concepts. In a closed sort, the instructor provides the categories and the items to be sorted. In an open sort, the instructor provides the items to be sorted and learners determine the categories or the instructor provides the categories and learners provide the items that fit the categories. Learners can be asked to write a paragraph explaining or justifying why they sorted the items the way they did, to help the instructor understand the learner's reasoning. The example of a closed sort in Figure 4.2 asks learners in a teacher education course to sort a series of statements into philosophical approaches to reading.

Figure 4.2. Sorting

Philosophical Approaches to Teaching Reading Sort

Copy the statements below the chart and paste them under the approach that they illustrate. Note: The columns will not necessarily be even!

Top Down	Interactive	Bottom Up
Mistakes in oral reading should be ignored unless they change the sense of the passage.	Teach phonics and then teach students to apply this skill to real reading.	Oral reading should be accurate.

Source: Sarah Cecire, http://homepage.mac.com/cecires

Frames

Frames (also called chart diagrams or matrix diagrams) are useful for condensing and organizing data about the traits of multiple items. When a frame is completed, learners have a concise summary of a unit of instruction. Frames can be used in any subject area but are especially useful in the sciences. Completed frames make wonderful study guides for exams. The example frame in Figure 4.3 asks learners in a comparative religions class to determine how each religion views the issues posed in the first column.

Figure 4.3. Frames

Complete the frame by describing how each of the religions view the questions listed in the first column.

	Buddhism	*Hinduism*	*Islam*	*Judaism*
Nature of the Divine				
Problem of Evil				
Problem of Suffering				
Issues of Justice/Ethics				
Righteousness (Right Doing)				
Rewards for Justice/Righteousness				
Afterlife and Its Nature				

Source: Sarah Cecire, http://homepage.mac.com/cecires

Semantic Feature Analysis

Semantic feature analysis uses a grid to examine the similarities and differences among a group of items, people, events, concepts, and so on. Learners consider each item in the top row of the table and determine if the item has the feature listed in the first column of the table. They put a *Y* in the box if the feature is present, an *N* if the feature is not present, and an *S* if the feature is sometimes present. The example in Figure 4.4 asks learners in a teacher education course to compare major approaches to teaching reading.

Figure 4.4. Semantic Feature Analysis

Major Approaches to Teaching Reading

Place a "Y" in the square if the approach in the top row has the feature listed in the left column most of the time. Put an "N" in the square if the approach in the top row does not usually have the feature. Put an "S" in the square if the approach has the feature some of the time.

	Basal	**Literature Based**	**Individualized**	**Language Experience**	**Guided Reading**
Book Based					
Writing Based					
Self-selection of materials					
Individualized					
Strong emphasis on decoding					
Primarily for beginning readers					
Primarily for remedial readers					

Source: Sarah Cecire, http://homepage.mac.com/cecires

Sarah Cecire has used these graphic organizers in her teacher education courses to increase what learners understand as a result of textbook reading.

Adopt or Adapt

Graphic organizers can be applied to most content areas and, when completed, make wonderful study guides. One interesting adaptation is to have learners collaboratively build such organizers.

Attribution

Submitted by Sarah Cecire, associate professor, Bluffton University, Bluffton, Ohio, USA

Contact: cecires@bluffton.edu

URL: http://homepage.mac.com/cecires

Red Dog

The Big Idea

What

A humorous and interactive activity shows how the parts of a computer are like the parts of a dog.

Figure 4.5. Red Dog

Source: Dawn Adams Miller

Figure 4.6. Red Dog, Rollover Eyes

Source: Dawn Adams Miller

Why

Humorous analogies can engage learners and help them see how something unknown is like something they already know.

Use It!

How

This instruction was created to help non-computer-literate users better understand how a computer works. It shows how something known—a dog—and something unknown—a computer—are related. This analogy is humorous so learners will find the learning activity engaging.

The learner rolls the mouse over a part of Red Dog and the corresponding part of the computer lights up. For example, rolling the mouse over Red Dog's eyes makes the computer monitor light up, and text and audio explain how Red Dog's eyes and the computer monitor are alike.

The instruction was originally built using Macromedia Director but Macromedia Flash would be a good alternative today.

Adopt or Adapt

A humorous analogy can be an effective way to explain concepts and reduce anxiety at the same time.

Attribution

Submitted by Dawn Adams Miller, instructional designer, Charlotte, North Carolina, USA

Contact: dawnladams@hotmail.com

Enter, Compare, Print, and Discuss

The Big Idea

What

One often valuable activity is to ask learners to enter an answer and then compare it to an expert answer. A valuable additional functionality is the ability to print both answers easily so the learner can bring it to his or her manager or trainer for discussion. Printing the actual course page often doesn't work because the answer text can be somewhat hidden in form fields.

Figure 4.7. Input My Answer and See Expert's Answer

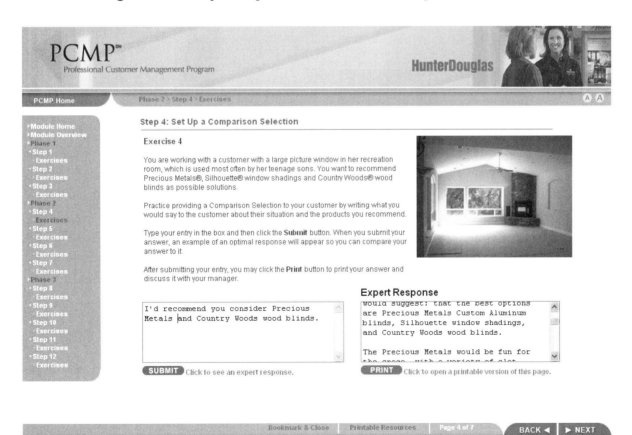

Source: Patti Shank, http://www.learningpeaks.com

Figure 4.8. Print My Answer and Expert's Answer

PCMP Selling: Step 4: Set Up a Comparison Selection

PRINT   Click to print this page.

Phase 2 > Step 4 > Exercises

Exercise 4

You are working with a customer with a large picture window in her recreation room, which is used most often by her teenage sons. You want to recommend Precious Metals®, Silhouette® window shadings and Country Woods® wood blinds as possible solutions.

Practice providing a Comparison Selection to your customer by writing what you would say to the customer about their situation and the products you recommend.

Type your entry in the box and then click the **Submit** button. When you submit your answer, an example of an optimal response will appear so you can compare your answer to it.

After submitting your entry, you may click the **Print** button to print your answer and discuss it with your manager.

YOUR ANSWER:

I would recommend

EXPERT ANSWER:

Your recreation room sounds like a welcoming space for every sort of activity; from Friday night game nights to television and air hockey. I would suggest that the best options are Precious Metals Custom Aluminum blinds, Silhouette window shadings, and Country Woods wood blinds. The Precious Metals would be fun for the space, with a variety of slat sizes and tapes available. It would be fun to cover your windows in a retro-look and everyone would know how to operate this product! Silhouette window shadings are a softer option, with a sheer fabric front-and-back facing and a fabric vane. This product would bring an open and airy sense to the room. As with Precious Metals, Silhouette is available in a variety of colors. Country Woods is our third option. These solid wood blinds will bring the warmth of wood to the room. They are a very handsome option that can be customized with decorative tapes. Because you said your sons are the primary occupants of the room, I would recommend the Country Woods.

HunterDouglas

Source: Patti Shank, http://www.learningpeaks.com

Why

Discussing important learning concepts with a manager or trainer adds impact and realism. Pulling learning from the screen into real life has many valuable learning benefits.

Use It!

How

Patti Shank's team wanted to make sure that key points could be easily discussed with a manager or trainer. They built in easy printing of these answers so the process would be facilitated. JavaScript (show/hide layer functionality) and Dynamic HTML are used to hide the expert's answer until a response is provided. JavaScript is used to pull the answers from the forms and display them in full on a printable page. Style sheets are used to format the printable page.

Adopt or Adapt

This idea could be adopted as is or adapted to facilitate easy printing of other course-based activities to share with a mentor or manager. This functionality could also be taken even further and used to send a copy of key activity answers to others automatically via email.

Attribution

Submitted by Patti Shank, president, Learning Peaks, LLC, Centennial, Colorado, USA

Contact: info@learningpeaks.com

URL: http://www.learningpeaks.com

Also involved: Kunal Thakkar, project manager, Instancy, Inc., Cary, North Carolina, USA; and Donna Keeler, director of training, Alliance Training Programs, Hunter Douglas, Broomfield, Colorado, USA

Tell Me Why

The Big Idea

What

When explaining a process that learners should follow, it's helpful to anticipate their concerns or questions (see the Learner Stories idea in Chapter Seven for more about how to do this) and provide short answers. Rollovers are a very simple way to do this. The learner puts the mouse over one area of the screen and additional information is revealed.

Figure 4.9. Why Rollovers

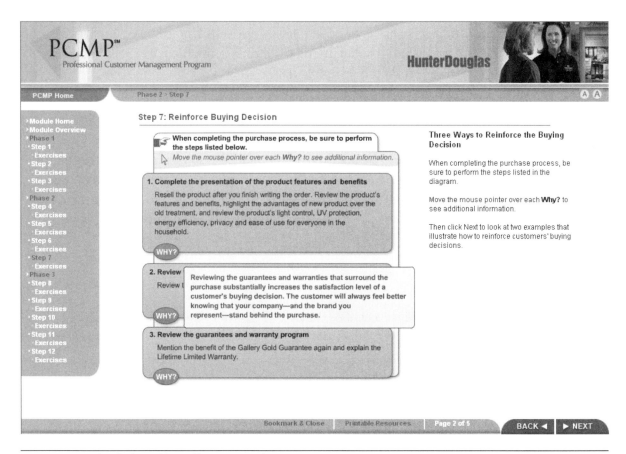

Source: Patti Shank, http://www.learningpeaks.com

Why

Because there's rarely a real person to ask questions of, self-directed learning can leave learners puzzled or curious. In addition, learners may want or need additional information in order to determine how the content applies. It is often valuable to provide ways to dig deeper for more information without cluttering the screen.

Use It!

How

Patti Shank's team developed a sales training module that described a variety of processes. Rollovers gave additional information about the steps and answered questions the designers expected learners to have. Previously, Patti used *Why* links (which opened a new window—not such a great idea these days because of usability and pop-up blockers) in university courses she taught and learners told her they were useful and fun. Using rollovers instead of links doesn't prompt pop-up blockers.

The rollovers were developed with Flash but could also be developed in Dreamweaver or by writing the HTML and JavaScript code. Flash rollovers can be created using XML content or ActionScript. In Dreamweaver, rollovers can be created using layers with the Show-Hide Layer behavior or by creating additional windows or pop-ups using the Open Browser Window behavior or Popup Message behavior, which opens a new browser window or pop-up window when the user clicks on a link.

Adopt or Adapt

Rollovers can be used to answer expected questions, add tidbits of information, provide contact information, or even add a bit of humor (use judiciously!).

Attribution

Submitted by Patti Shank, president, Learning Peaks, LLC, Centennial, Colorado, USA

Contact: info@learningpeaks.com

URL: http://www.learningpeaks.com

Also involved: Kunal Thakkar, project manager, Instancy, Inc., Cary, North Carolina, USA; and Donna Keeler, director of training, Alliance Training Programs, Hunter Douglas, Broomfield, Colorado, USA

Time Me

The Big Idea

What

A simple Flash animation of a timer helps learners experience the difference between the before state and the after state.

Figure 4.10. Timer, Nonmapped Document

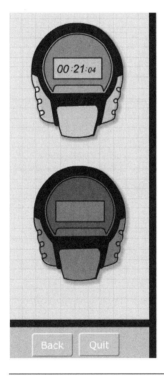

Click on Janice Moreland's New Position - Typical Business Document
To: All Employees
From: Oliver Castle, President
Subject: Company Reorganization

As you well know, our company has had considerable difficulty this year with the collapse of the barunium market inflation hitting 12% and going up labor difficulties at several plants, and development of our new products, especially in the home-products systems. This situation has forced the management to assess our entire company and its operations with a view to finding a better way to organize it for improved profits and long-term efficiency.

Some of our departments have been growing and shrinking without much rhyme or reason, and before this occasion we had not made the effort to take a really hard look at what were doing. Instead, we were patching things here and there with the aim of eliminating duplication when we could and pulling together groups that belong together functionally.

Now we are announcing a major reorganization to take effect on January 18. We will announce the details on January 12, such as when the desks will be moved and when the new managers will hold meetings with various employees to whom the information is pertinent. We will also, at that time distribute a complete schedule setting forth who will be working fro whom. In the meantime, we are announcing the following changes to the managers in charge of the affected divisions and departments can prepare for the reorganization.

Charles Jones will assume duties as Director of the new Office Products Division, leaving his present post of Manger of the Typewriter and Office Equipment Supplies. Janice Moreland will move from Vice President for Research to Vice President for Operations. Jack Spotter will be the new head of the Research Department, moving from his position as assistant Vice President for Operations. Marilyn Belt will become Director of the new Home

Source: Lisa Thompson, http://www.communicare.com

Figure 4.11. Timer, Same Document, Mapped

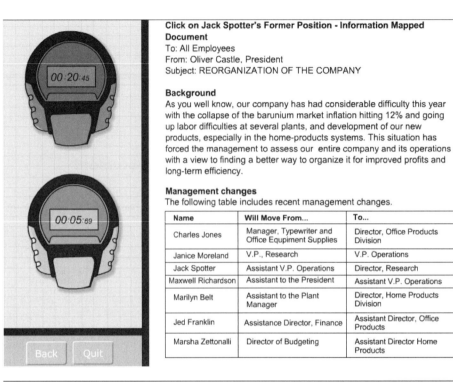

Click on Jack Spotter's Former Position - Information Mapped Document
To: All Employees
From: Oliver Castle, President
Subject: REORGANIZATION OF THE COMPANY

Background
As you well know, our company has had considerable difficulty this year with the collapse of the barunium market inflation hitting 12% and going up labor difficulties at several plants, and development of our new products, especially in the home-products systems. This situation has forced the management to assess our entire company and its operations with a view to finding a better way to organize it for improved profits and long-term efficiency.

Management changes
The following table includes recent management changes.

Name	Will Move From...	To...
Charles Jones	Manager, Typewriter and Office Equpiment Supplies	Director, Office Products Division
Janice Moreland	V.P., Research	V.P. Operations
Jack Spotter	Assistant V.P. Operations	Director, Research
Maxwell Richardson	Assistant to the President	Assistant V.P. Operations
Marilyn Belt	Assistant to the Plant Manager	Director, Home Products Division
Jed Franklin	Assistance Director, Finance	Assistant Director, Office Products
Marsha Zettonalli	Director of Budgeting	Assistant Director Home Products

Source: Lisa Thompson, http://www.communicare.com

Why

The animation makes the differences between before and after exceedingly clear. Sometimes a very simple animation can make a huge difference.

Use It!

How

A simple timer animation allows the learner to experience how long it takes to find specific information in the same document before and after applying a specific type of structuring and formatting. The learner starts the first timer (which begins counting the seconds) and then clicks on specific information in the first document, which stops the timer. Then the learner starts the second timer (which begins counting the seconds) and clicks on specific information in the second (structured and formatted) document, which stops the timer. The final time shown on both timers shows dramatically how much faster it is to find information in the second document.

The animation was developed using Flash.

Adopt or Adapt

A timer animation could be adapted for any activity where showing how long an activity takes is important. In the idea shown here, a timer animation is used twice to compare how long multiple activities take.

Attribution

Submitted by Lisa Thompson, manager of marketing, Communicare, Inc., Toronto, Ontario, Canada

Contact: info@communicare.com

URL: http://www.communicare.com/flash_timer.html

Also involved: Information Mapping, Inc., Waltham, Massachusetts, USA

Digital Stories

The Big Idea

What

Digital storytelling—using digital media such as video and audio to tell a story—can be used to increase personal connections at the beginning of online courses.

Figure 4.12. Scenes from Patrick Lowenthal's Digital Story

Source: Patrick Lowenthal, http://www.patricklowenthal.com

Why

Seeing and hearing learners' stories affords associations and provides a foundation for deeper social interactions.

Use It!

How

Digital stories are first-person narratives told using digital media. The Center for Digital Storytelling (www.storycenter.org) pioneered the concept more than ten years ago. However, it has only been in the past few years that educators have begun to use such stories as a pedagogical tool.

Patrick Lowenthal created his own digital story and has learners create them in courses he teaches. He is especially interested in the impact these stories have on teacher presence and isolation, which can be major problems in asynchronous online courses. Lowenthal recommends Adobe Premier or Premier Elements, Microsoft Photo Story or PowerPoint, Flash, Apple iMovie or iPhoto, or Windows MovieMaker as tools for building digital stories.

Adopt or Adapt

Digital stories use emerging technology to bring sharing, case studies, best practices, and challenges to a new level. They can also be used as reflective tools, allowing learners to show and tell what they have learned and the impact that learning has had.

Attribution

Submitted by Patrick Lowenthal, assistant professor, Regis University, Denver, Colorado, USA

Contact: plowenth@regis.edu

URL: http://www.patricklowenthal.com/PatrickLowenthalDV.mov

Also involved: Joanna C. Dunlap, assistant professor, School of Education and Human Development, University of Colorado at Denver and Health Sciences, Denver, Colorado, USA

Share Bookmarks

The Big Idea

What

An online bookmark tool allows instructors and learners to share bookmarks easily.

Figure 4.13. Bookmarks to Share

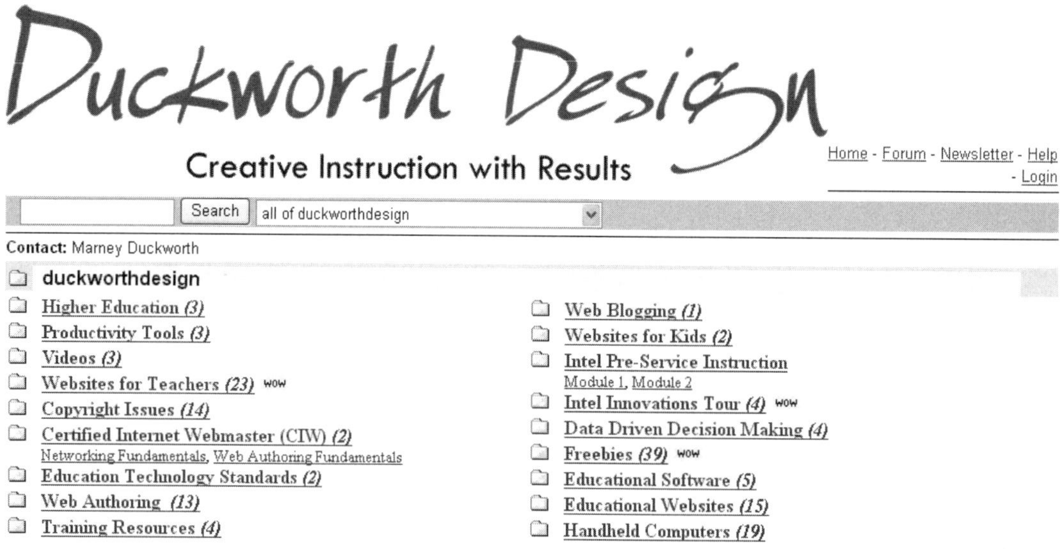

Source: Marney Duckworth, http://www.duckworthdesign.com

Why

Putting bookmarks online makes them easy to share during training sessions or meetings, and facilitates use when traveling because they are accessible on the Web from anywhere. Online bookmarks also help facilitate research and collaboration.

Use It!

How

When Marney Duckworth conducts trainings, it is often important to share or use links to Web sites throughout her sessions. A colleague showed her iKeepBookmarks.com as a way to manage Web links for personal use and she found this to be a perfect tool for solving her bookmarks problem in training sessions. She uses the tool for sharing bookmarks with learners in her university classes as well and has shared it with other educators who also find it useful.

iKeepBookmarks.com is also valuable when conducting research and collaborating with others. Using the search area of the tool allows users to search thousands of other iKeepBookmarks accounts in order to see others' favorite bookmarks on a given topic (which can save time searching for and evaluating URLs from scratch). Educators have found this tool extremely helpful when searching for content-specific resources.

Users can set up their personal accounts so that other users can upload links without administrative login access. Duckworth has found this feature to be effective when working collaboratively. Other users are able to share online resources with Duckworth without her having to login and post the links.

Duckworth says that iKeepBookmarks.com is easy to use but suggests reading the information contained in the help area before beginning.

Adopt or Adapt

Professionals in any industry, especially those who travel and train others, can easily organize and share bookmarks. Social bookmarking, an online activity that allows users to save and categorize (using tags) a personal collection of bookmarks and share them with others or save others' bookmarks to their personal collection, has become a very hot trend. There are now tons of online bookmarking applications and

Delicious (http://del.icio.us) is one of the most popular. This idea can also be adapted for sharing other digital items such as photos (see Flickr at http://www.flickr.com).

Attribution

Submitted by Marney Duckworth, instructional designer, Duckworth Design, Centennial, Colorado, USA

Contact: Marney@duckworthdesign.com

URL: http://www.duckworthdesign.com

Also involved: Brian Rice, president, Software Designs Development Corporation (creator of iKeepBookmarks.com), Darien, Illinois, USA

Tell Me About Yourself

The Big Idea

What

Gaining personal information from learners at the outset of a course helps online instructors better understand and connect with learners.

Why

Instructors who know about learners can personalize the learners' experience.

Use It!

How

A personal introduction helps the instructor connect with course participants. It helps learners feel that the instructor really wants to know about them and that they are not just a number. The instructor can also use this information to personalize communications. For example, when sending an email, the instructor could inquire about family or hobbies. Instructors can reply to each introduction with relevant personal information about themselves to make the exchange of personal information two-way.

Barb Edwards began using this idea to learn more about each learner. Because there were no in-person meetings, she chose questions that would elicit responses about the learner's personality or life and thus help her gain some understanding of each person's life. For example, recent classes have had a mixture of learners with and without family responsibilities. Some learners shared happy or painful events.

Edwards asks learners to provide the following information in an email as one of the first course assignments. The amount of disclosure is completely up to the learner.

Barb Edwards's Example Template

Name:

Describe two principles, key people, or events that have shaped who you are and that guide you in your decisions.

My career goal is. . . .

My work experience has been. . . .

My learning objective for this course is. . . .

Other personal information I wish to share (include family, hobbies, recent travels, any other information you wish to share). . . .

Previously Edwards has included questions about the two books the learner would want if stranded on a deserted island. Variations of this include asking the learner to list his or her two favorite books or movies and why. Philosophical questions can be used as well. These questions can also be used as a springboard to foster non-course-related interactions in another discussion forum (such as a "course café," a purposely off-topic discussion forum where learners can talk about movies, recipes, vacations, current events, and more). This helps learners connect on a more personal level and keeps these kinds of postings from cluttering up on-topic course forums.

Adopt or Adapt

The questions can be easily adapted for a specific course or program. For example, a doctoral course might ask about topics of interest and dissertation plans. An undergraduate course might ask about favorite courses, previous experience using technology, and so on. This idea is easily adaptable to include any topic.

Attribution

Submitted by Barb Edwards, senior lecturer, Simon Fraser University, Burnaby, British Columbia, Canada

Contact: bjedwards@sfu.ca

An Expert View

The Big Idea

What

Learner access to content experts can be facilitated in order to add additional insights, resources, and answers to questions.

Figure 4.14. Ask the Expert Link and Emails

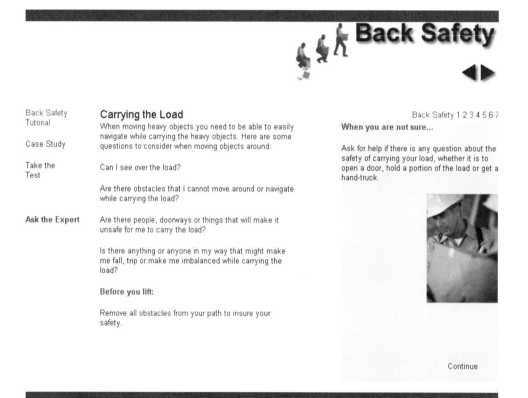

Source: Becky Haugen, http://designtosuccess.com

Why

Experts add practical, real-life knowledge of the domain and can provide additional insights, resources, and help.

Use It!

How

The instructor can arrange experts to be available during the course to respond to learners' questions. Experts can be rotated as topics change. The expert can be available for insights, tips, applied knowledge of the topic, and additional resources (such as suggested books and Web sites). Many professionals are happy to share their expertise and answer questions.

This idea could be accomplished by giving the expert access to the discussion forum or by providing his or her email address or a Web form that sends questions to the expert via email.

It might be valuable to have all questions go through one person who could send email at specific times and then post answers for the entire class. The instructor and expert would need to set up minimum expectations (answer turnaround, quantity of questions, and so on) to be shared with learners so everyone knows what to expect. Sharing the expert's photo and bio beforehand would also be beneficial.

Adopt or Adapt

This approach can be applied in both synchronous and asynchronous learning environments.

Attribution

Submitted by Becky Haugen, consultant, Learning Technology and Web Learning, Design to Success, Lyons, Colorado, USA

URL: http://designtosuccess.com

Email the Author

The Big Idea

What

> After carefully reading and analyzing individual journal articles, learners can formulate thoughtful follow-up questions about the content or implications of the article and email these to the author.

Figure 4.15. Email to Author

Dear Dr. Burt,

My name is Amy Buoni and I am a student majoring in Special Education at Ohio Dominican University in Columbus, Ohio.

I recently read the study conducted by you and your colleagues entitled "Aging in Adults with Down Syndrome: Report from a Longitudinal Study" in a 1995 issue of the *American Journal on Mental Retardation*. I found the article very interesting and would like to take the opportunity to ask you a couple of questions I have about the study.

1. What effect do you think progressive dementia has on aging adults with Down syndrome?

2. What is your opinion about age-related differences in the level of task difficulty? Do you feel that age-related differences are more likely to be evident on concrete simple stimuli, or on more complex tasks?

3. What would you change if you conducted this study again?

I would greatly appreciate it if you would take the time to answer these questions so I can share your insights with my classmates. Thank you for your time!

Sincerely,
Amy Buoni

Source: Jill C. Dardig

Figure 4.16. Response from Author

Ms. Buoni:

Here are answers to your questions about our aging study.

1. Regarding the effect that progressive dementia has on aging adults with Down syndrome: Our data suggest that there are different types of patterns in adults with Down syndrome. For example, one adult lost language skills first, and had behavior problems. In contrast, another adult had memory problems first, and few reported behavior problems.

   Of course, in order to be considered dementia, they must have documented declines in memory and other cognitive functions, in addition to emotional/ motivational changes (watch for Aylward et al. in the *Journal of Intellectual Disability Research*). It is very sad to see an adult with Down syndrome get demented. In the most advanced stages, they have severe memory problems and lose their typical behaviors (e.g., calling Mom every day). In early stages, they can become depressed and agitated. Familes are affected, but usually devoted to caring for their member with Down syndrome and dementia.

2. Regarding age-related differences: Of course, one must first consider differences related to level of intellectual functioning, which probably is a larger effect than any age differences. We do not know at this time if age-related differences are greater on more complex tasks, but I would hypothesize that they would be. In addition, older adults tend to be less motivated to perform lab tests needed to assess skills.

3. Regarding changes in the study: I would enroll older adults with Down syndrome if I could find them (they are hard to enroll, given that they often don't have a living relative, and are often not able to give consent on their own).

Thank you for your questions. Watch for a book on dementia coming out edited by Janicki and Dalton.

Diana Burt

Source: Jill C. Dardig

Why

Formulating questions and communicating with journal authors awakens curiosity about and deepens understanding of the topic. It also helps the topic come alive.

Use It!

How

Each learner is assigned an individual journal article to analyze and summarize. He or she formulates three questions not answered by the article, prepares a brief but thoughtful letter that asks these questions, and sends this letter via email to the author. If the author's email address is not listed in the article, the learner searches the Internet for the author's address, usually starting the search with a check of the author's college, university, or organization home page. In the case of multiple authors, the learner emails the senior author first, and then the others if there is no response. Each learner works on a different article so that no author gets more than one email.

Jill Dardig feels that few undergraduate learners exhibit higher level, in-depth questioning skills about the material they are reading or express curiosity about the implications of what they have read. This activity facilitates a more intimate examination of and interaction with material; it also teaches learners that authors investigate various topics but may not have all the answers, and demonstrates that many authors are willing to engage in a discussion about their subject areas with interested and well-prepared college learners.

Most learners who complete this activity formulate higher level questions and the majority receive email responses from their authors. One author phoned the learner for a lengthy discussion. Some responses arrived the same day and some were very detailed and insightful. All responses were shared and discussed in class. Learners were excited that they had communicated with experts from all over the world.

This is a simple and engaging way to use technology to enrich learners' understanding and appreciation of research materials.

Adopt or Adapt

This activity could be used in any higher education course where journal articles are used and the instructor wants learners to delve further. It could even be used in the K–12 setting in classes where learners read journal, magazine, or newspaper articles, and it could be adapted to corporate or government training sessions where participants read trade journals and other publications.

Attribution

Submitted by Jill C. Dardig, professor, Ohio Dominican University, Columbus, Ohio, USA

Contact: dardigj@ohiodominican.edu

MiniQuest

The Big Idea

What

A MiniQuest is an activity that uses a scenario, a task, and a product to promote inquiry and higher-order thinking skills as learners explore instructor-selected Web sites.

Why

This inquiry learning activity promotes critical thinking and knowledge construction.

Use It!

How

A MiniQuest is a Web-based assignment that guides learners to find factual information and then use critical thinking skills to produce a product. Steps for developing a MiniQuest are as follows:

1. *Scenario:* Write a scenario that establishes a context for the exercise. The scenario should place the learners in an authentic role similar to that of a professional in the discipline under study. The scenario establishes the "essential question" under study. It should require critical thinking and a decision or course of action.

2. *Task:* Write a task that is highly structured and directs learners to specific Web sites. Present learners with questions designed to help them find factual knowledge necessary to answer the essential question.

3. *Product:* Describe the product that the learners are to produce. The product should match the role given in the scenario and represent an answer to the essential question. Possible products include the following:

   a. Essay

   b. Plan of action

   c. Electronic presentation

This idea comes from Internet Innovations, Incorporated (http://www.biopoint.com). The format is open ended and can be adapted to any level and any discipline. Sarah Cecire has used the idea extensively in her teacher education courses at both the undergraduate and graduate levels.

A MiniQuest can be created using any word processing program where hyperlinks can be inserted. MiniQuests can also be created in an HTML editor. The completed assignment can be distributed to learners on paper or the Web.

Sarah Cecire's Example: Comparing the NEA to the AFT MiniQuest

The National Education Association (NEA) and the American Federation of Teachers (AFT) are two national organizations that represent the general interests of the teaching profession. It is important that you, as a future educator, understand the services these organizations offer to their members.

Scenario You have just graduated from college with a degree in education. During your final semester you applied for several positions in different locations. After two successful interviews you received two offers from two school districts. The salary and benefits are about the same and you feel you could be happy living in either community. As you researched the districts you noted that one was represented by the NEA and the other by the AFT. You decide to investigate the two organizations to determine which better reflects your personal philosophy of education. You feel that you will be happier working for a district where the professional organization reflects your personal beliefs about teaching and the profession.

The Task

To help you determine which organization reflects your personal belief system, read pages 39 to 41 of your text, *Teaching Today,* and go to the Web sites of the two major professional organizations for teachers and examine the material.

As you explore the Web sites, look for the answers to the following questions.

- How does the organization view teachers? (See text and review Web sites.)

    At http://www.aft.org/about explore the *About AFT* links.

    At http://www.nea.org/aboutnea explore the *About NEA* links.

- What services do the organizations provide for their members?

    At http://www.aft.org explore the various links on the page.

    At http://www.nea.org explore the links in the left frame.

- What issues does the organization support? What are its views on the issues?

    At http://www.unionvoice.org/legislativeaction/home.html explore the links on the Legislative Action Center page.

    At http://www.aft.org/topics explore the links on the Hot Topics page.

    At http://www.nea.org/lac explore the links on Legislative Action Center page.

    At http://www.nea.org/topics/index.html explore the links on the Education Issues page.

The Product Create a Venn diagram or a T-chart to summarize and illustrate the similarities and differences between the two organizations. On the basis of this comparison, write a one-page reflection stating which organization you would prefer to join, and why.

Adopt or Adapt

> This idea can be adapted to any level or discipline with an appropriate scenario, relevant Web sites, task, and product to be produced.

Attribution

Submitted by Sarah Cecire, associate professor, Bluffton University, Bluffton, Ohio, USA

Contact: cecires@bluffton.edu

URL: http://homepage.mac.com/cecires

Blog It

The Big Idea

What

Weblogs (blogs) can be excellent tools for learner reflections and sharing. Some blogs allow others to post questions and comments too.

Figure 4.17. Learner's Blog

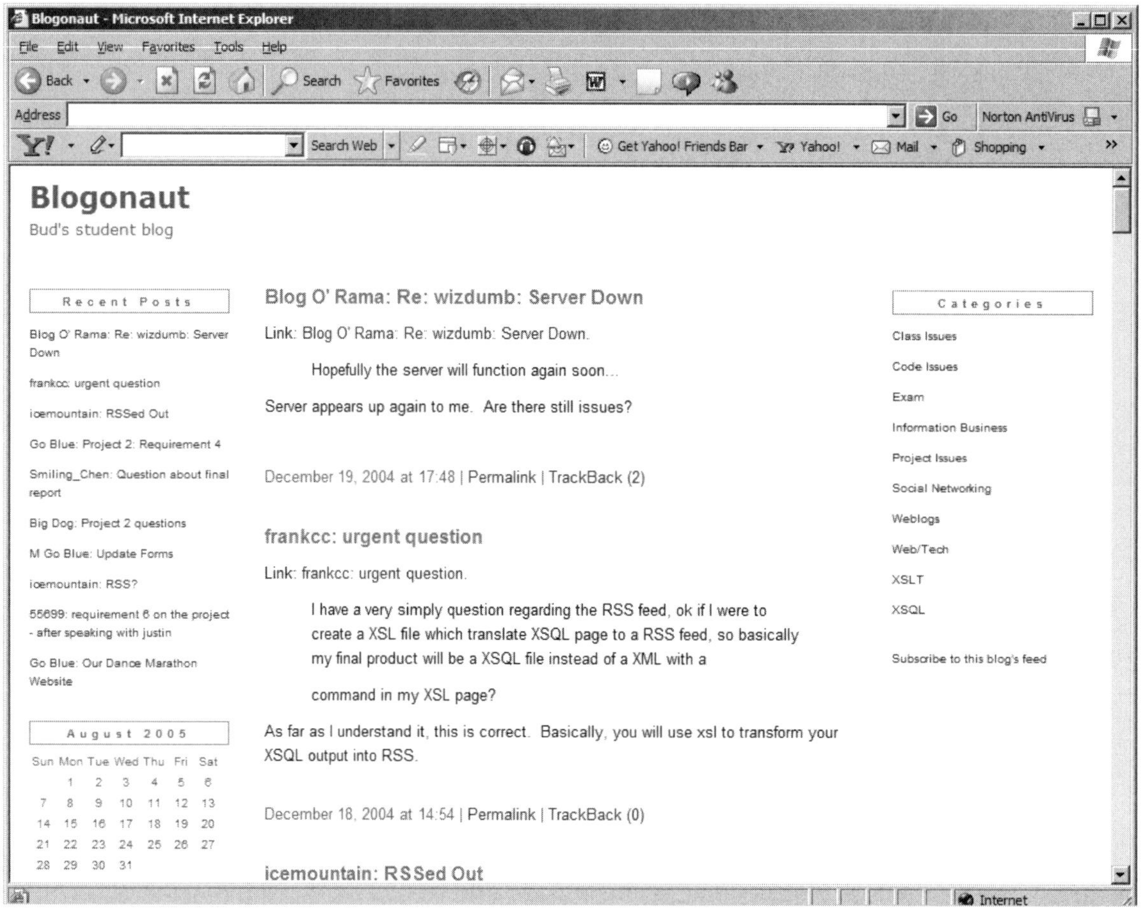

Source: Becky Haugen, http://designtosuccess.com

Why

Keeping a record of thoughts, understandings, insights, and resources augments learning for the blog author and those who read it.

Use It!

How

Learners can begin and maintain a blog to keep track of their learning experiences, new understandings, changing perceptions, and valuable resources. This process can help learners integrate new knowledge, develop insights, and keep a record of academic or professional growth. Blogs can also be used as collaborative tools for sharing information, links, and content.

Installation and setup of blogging applications is simple and many of the applications are open source. Hosted and free blogging applications like http://www.bloglines.com or http://www.blogger.com can also be used.

Demonstration of the software would be required to help all learners understand how to use the tool. Determination of the ground rules for using and posting should be established in advance.

Adopt or Adapt

Blogs can be incorporated into any K–12, higher education, or corporate learning environment. They would be best deployed for a long-term learning program but could potentially be used in short-term ones as well.

Attribution

Submitted by Becky Haugen, consultant, learning technology and Web learning, Design to Success, Lyons, Colorado, USA

URL: http://designtosuccess.com

Also involved: Faison (Bud) Gibson, founder and principal, The Community Engine, Ann Arbor, Michigan, USA, email: bud@thecommunityengine.com, http://thecommunityengine.com/home/archives/2005/03/a_learning_blog.html

My Chair

The Big Idea

What

This icebreaker is a great community-building exercise with room for tons of poetic license. It allows learners to tell others about themselves without giving a literal description of themselves.

Figure 4.18. The Chair Prompt

Welcome to the Attic ⌧

Before you tell us about your chair, please take a moment to visit the FAQ. They contain important information on how these discussions work and will help you get off to a flying start!

- Door's Open! Please . . . grab a chair (720 messages—439 unread)

   This is the general lobby area for everyone to get comfortable. It's a place to grab a hot (virtual) drink, put your slippers on and find out what we do here.

Source: Shula Klinger, http://words.ucourses.com

Figure 4.19. Klinger's Chair

Hi everyone—thank you all for the gracious welcome :-)

I guess the time has come to talk about my own chair again. . . . It's an office chair covered in orange vinyl. The back is nice and tall and the arms swoop around either side of me. The seat is nice and low and the whole thing tips backwards . . . very comfortable but also somewhat mischievous. Anyone is welcome to sit in it when I'm not here, but be warned! It tips so far back that it's actually possible to roll out of it—backwards! Trust me . . . I found out the wrong way.

Welcome to the Attic's second year, everyone!

Source: Shula Klinger, http://words.ucourses.com

Why

This idea allows learners to share personal information in creative ways while building a sense of community.

Use It!

How

Shula Klinger asks learners to post a description of the chair they would bring to this "space" if they could bring a chair perfectly designed for them. The chair can be as wild and extraordinary as the writer wishes. She has done this activity with learners in grades 8 through 12 and with adult learners, with equal success.

This exercise stimulates the development of a shared story. For example, if one learner says that her chair includes a drink machine, others can help themselves to a soda pop at any time. If it has a rocket pack, course participants can embark on long journeys around the globe at a moment's notice.

Because everyone's story is equally valid, the exercise helps build mutual respect and acceptance, as well as adding humor and mystery to a mostly silent environment. Online discussions can be very dry when they are focused entirely on the curriculum. Threads can be hard to follow without mental images of other learners and no shared class time. This is a creative way to build a virtual classroom in everyone's imagination. Anything we can imagine is there: we can build new furniture, share food, introduce pets, warm up a room, or change the climate in the time it takes to type a sentence. Visual images are a great way to engage participants and stimulate recall for different kinds of learners. For those who think in images, it helps to picture a set of class notes on a rosewood table, to the left of the fireplace, rather than as an email attachment from my instructor on—which day was that?

Klinger developed and moderated a forum for teens called The Attic, for learners at her former school (http://www.gvdes.ca) who love reading and writing and want to share their passions with others. She created The Attic as a way to get to know learners better, since all of the learners are at a distance. The activity was developed as a way to show that nobody had to describe their actual person, and to emphasize hospitality and welcoming. When established members became used to this ritual, they welcomed newcomers with a gentle prod, "Have you posted your chair yet?" She didn't have to say a word.

This activity won the Best Icebreaker Contest at the KnowTips online conference (http://knowtips.ca).

Adopt or Adapt

Instructors can customize this activity to reflect the discipline they are studying. It needn't be a description of a chair—just something that gives the learners something to visualize and develop. You could describe a lab (chemistry), a landscape (geography), a molecule (biology), or a new life form (science fiction writing). It could be adapted for any online community, instructional or not.

Attribution

Submitted by Shula Klinger, online education consultant, Richmond, British Columbia, Canada

Contact: shuflute@telus.net

URL: http://words.ucourses.com

Also involved: Cindy Gauthier, Greater Vancouver Distance Education School, Vancouver, British Columbia, Canada; Learner members of the Attic; and Frances Long, conference organizer, KnowTips, Vancouver, British Columbia, Canada

Easy Peer Editing

The Big Idea

What

Using a simple table created in Microsoft Word and Word's Track Changes features, learners can easily exchange writing in a way that allows for easy peer editing and commentary, and instructor comments.

Figure 4.20. Peer and Instructor Comments

Writer	Editor	Instructor	
Even worse than the strain on your wallet are the physical consequence of smoking. (Start with more of an introduction) Everybody knows that smoking is bad, but it goes deeper than that. Smoking above all causes lung cancer, and if not found early enough is fatal. In women, it also can cause cervical and breast cancer. In fact, smoking has been linked to heart disease, stroke, and cancer of the lungs, larynx, mouth, bladder, pancreas, and kidneys. Tobacco smoke also has more than fourthousand toxic chemicals. The statistics are astounding. Smoking kills one in ten people globally. someone dies from smoking every eight seconds. every cigarette takes five minutes off your	As you mention this paragraph mentions a lot about the physical consequences of smoking. You mention a lot of different diseases and some stats on death. I think you could choose a couple of the diseases and talk more about them. Most people already about what smoking causes. But you could go further and explain exactly what they do to a person's body, maybe get stats on that particular disease. So instead of just listing the different things it can do, take some of them, and discuss them.	These are good suggestions from the Editor. Specific detail and vivid pictures of real people make an impact.	Deleted: Like Deleted: , Deleted: is Deleted: in addition to lung cancer Deleted: following: Deleted: – Deleted: Also, Deleted: Finally,

Source: Richard Regan, http://faculty.fairfield.edu/rjregan

Why

Learners benefit by sharing their work and gaining thoughtful feedback.

Use It!

How

Richard Regan creates groups of four or five learners who work as peer editors of one another's work. Each writer (working in Microsoft Word) creates a table with three columns. The columns are headed WRITER, EDITOR, and INSTRUCTOR.

Step 1: The WRITER enters his or her essay in the first column, typing or pasting in an existing document.

Step 2: The EDITOR receives the document containing the essay as an email attachment, using the email function in a course management system or via conventional email. The EDITOR reviews the essay by using Track Changes in the WRITER column and writing comments in the EDITOR column.

Step 3: Two variants:

1. The WRITER receives the edited version with changes and comments and revises the original essay. The whole exchange is then sent to the INSTRUCTOR.

2. The INSTRUCTOR receives the edited version and writes his or her comments in the INSTRUCTOR column. The document is then sent to the WRITER for the next round of revisions.

Regan invented this process for a Composition course to help learners gain experience writing and editing others' writing. He has found the process to work exceptionally well.

Adopt or Adapt

This technique can be used by any instructor in any course where written assignments are critical. It can be adapted for classroom-based or online learning and for noninstructional use such as collaborative document writing.

Attribution

Submitted by Richard Regan, assistant professor of English, English Department, Fairfield University, Fairfield, Connecticut, USA

Contact: rjregan@mail.fairfield.edu

URL: http://faculty.fairfield.edu/rjregan

Introducing Critical Evaluation

The Big Idea

What

> Use a nonthreatening introductory activity to help learners use the com-
> munication technology, explore the topic, and begin to evaluate others'
> work critically.

Figure 4.21. Critical Evaluation Letter

Sarah R. Steele
September 13, 2007
Evidence-Based Medicine

Editor Letter

Dear Editor of *The American Journal of Medicine:*

I am writing in response to the article "Problems in the 'Evidence' of Evidence-Based Medicine," volume 103(6), December 1997, pp. 529–535.

By definition EBM is the integration of the best clinically relevant research evidence with clinical expertise and patient values. It was suggested by the article that EBM does not take all of these factors into account. It should be noted that EBM emphasizes first evaluating the evidence critically and then applying it in a way that is appropriate to the situation, while at the same time addressing the unique needs of the individual patient. There is no doubt that it is important to refrain from making generalizations to all patients. It is necessary to take into consideration each patient's own unique experiences and needs in order to effectively treat them. However, EBM does in fact emphasize the importance of the individual patient.

In contradiction to the article, EBM is not solely based upon meta-analyses and randomized control trials. Instead EBM integrates several different types of literature sources including overviews, practice guidelines, and decision-analyses, as well as cost effective-ness analyses.

Source: Anita Duhl Glicken

Why

This idea helps learners begin to master the pragmatics of online communication, creates an expectation that difference of opinion should be respected, and lets the instructor assess writing skills.

Use It!

How

This exercise helps learners become comfortable with using the communications technology for posting and providing feedback to others. In addition, attitudes toward the topic are explored in a nonthreatening manner through critical evaluation of published work. This activity models the importance and value of critical evaluation, allowing learners to build critical evaluation skills, and lays the groundwork for future exercises where learners are required to offer constructive criticism of their classmates' work. It also provides the instructor with an informal needs assessment on learners' writing skills and their knowledge of and attitudes toward the topic.

In teaching a new and at times controversial subject, it is often desirable to create an environment where learners' attitudes about the topic are openly identified. Anita Glicken created this exercise in which learners critically evaluate a published work using their own opinion and experience. This exercise simulates what they will be doing throughout the course (evaluating clinical evidence).

The activity is implemented using Blackboard through the discussion forum. Any online application that allows for discussion postings and responses could also work.

Adopt or Adapt

This idea could be adapted for use in any classroom, blended, or online course where critical evaluation is desirable.

Attribution

Submitted by Anita Duhl Glicken, professor of pediatrics, Child Health Associate/Physician's Assistant Program, University of Colorado, Denver, and Health Sciences Center, Aurora, Colorado, USA

Contact: Anita.Glicken@uchsc.edu

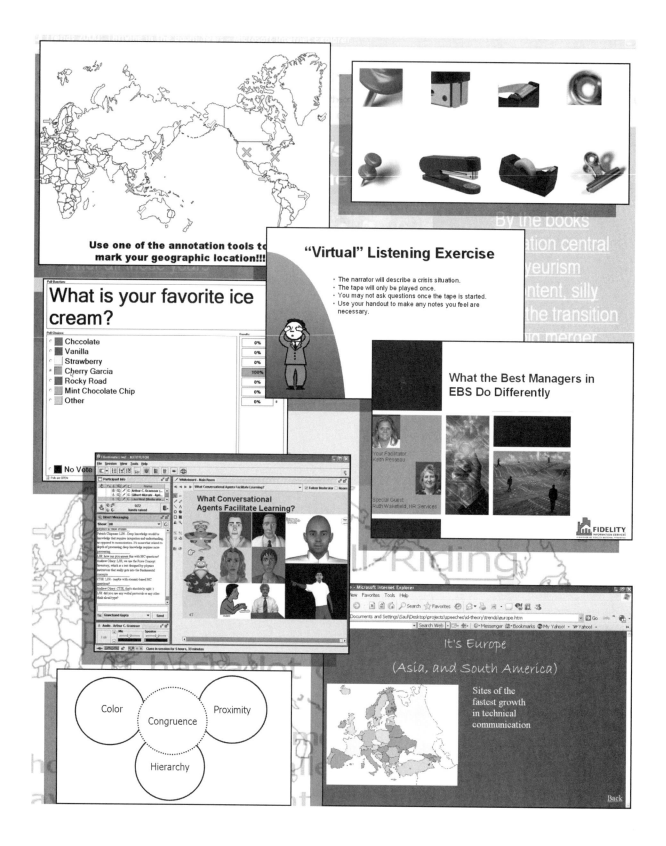

CHAPTER 5

Ideas for Synchronous Activities

This chapter provides ideas for activities that work well in synchronous learning environments such as Web conferencing and video conferencing. Synchronous tools and technologies are often used for taking the classroom "on the road," but it's far too easy to not use these tools creatively and thoughtfully. Some facilitators or instructors merely move their lectures online, which is almost guaranteed to be a virtual snoozefest. Others try to do the same activities they do in person but find these don't always work as expected because needed adaptations are missing.

Using synchronous tools and technologies well almost always involves well-thought-out activities and interactions with others. This chapter has plenty of both!

Chat Moderator

The Big Idea

What

In a synchronous online classroom, have a knowledgeable assistant moderate the text chat during a synchronous session to increase interaction and learning.

Figure 5.1. Assisted Text Chat in a Synchronous Classroom

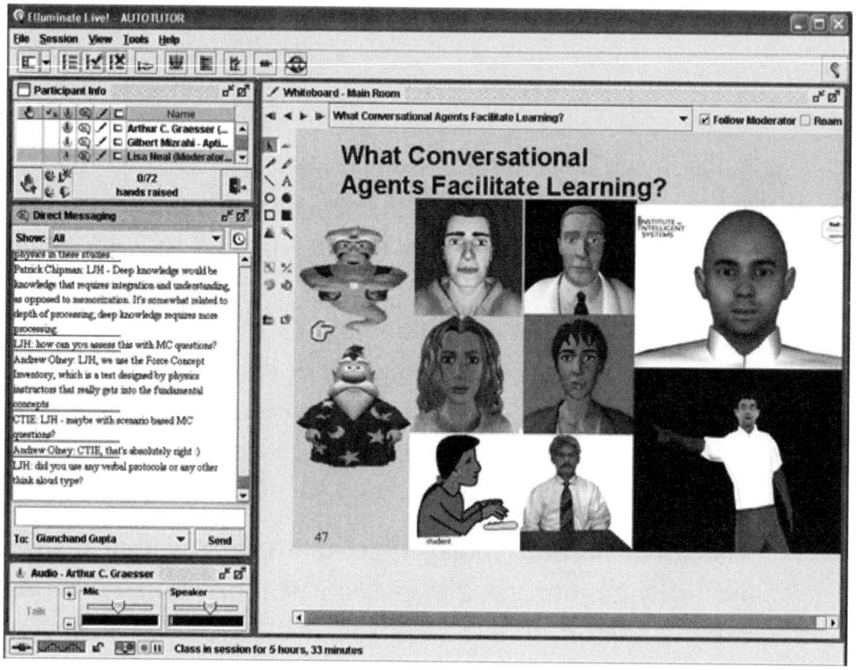

Source: Lisa Neal, http://www.eLearnMag.org

Why

Unmoderated chats can become a free-for-all and learners can easily become frustrated or tuned out.

Use It!

How

During synchronous sessions, no matter which technology is being used, a text chat has the advantage of immediacy—everyone can ask a question or make a comment when they have one. However, because most presenters can't read the chat and respond while they are also presenting, a knowledgeable assistant can moderate the text chat and answer questions and address comments as well as forward really important questions and issues to the presenter. Not only is this satisfying for the person asking the question, but it also increases learning and engagement for all participants. A lively chat also decreases the likelihood that participants will engage in additional noninstructional activities like checking and responding to their email concurrently with attending the synchronous session.

The screen capture in Figure 5.1. shows the Elluminate Live! e-learning system used by Art Graesser at the University of Memphis. The two chat moderators are his graduate students, Andrew Olney and Patrick Chipman. Lisa Neal is the facilitator, and the person kicking off the session is Tom Ward, executive officer of the Cognitive Science Society. The seminars were sponsored by the Office of Naval Research.

Adopt or Adapt

This idea is tailor-made for synchronous online classrooms. It may also be useful in other instructional situations that utilize a text chat.

Attribution

Submitted by Lisa Neal, editor-in-chief, eLearn Magazine, Lexington, Massachusetts, USA

Contact: lisa@acm.org

URL: http://www.eLearnMag.org

Come (Back) Early

The Big Idea

What

Start synchronous online learning session segments with some sort of brain teaser and reward the person who completes it first. The earlier learners log in and come back from breaks, the more time they will have to work on solving the puzzle.

Figure 5.2. Brain Teaser 1

Identify these extreme close ups of office supplies.

Source: Keith Resseau

Figure 5.3. Brain Teaser 2

Unscramble each word to reveal the quip and its author.

"Teavhwre uyo rae, eb a odog neo."

Mhaaabr Nnlloci

Source: Keith Resseau

(The answers to both of these teasers can be found at the end of this idea. Don't peek!)

Why

This exercise gets learners to log on early and come back from breaks on time.

Use It!

How

Even though precourse communications stress that learners need to log in to the synchronous online classroom a few minutes before class starts, they rarely do. Having learners log in early allows time to troubleshoot technical difficulties before the class starts. Instructors lose valuable time at the beginning of each class and after each break waiting for learners to get logged in and ready to start the synchronous portions of class. Learners who do log in early inevitably get frustrated waiting for class to start.

Ten minutes before the start of a class (and three minutes before the appointed time to be back from a break), put a brain teaser up on the display screen of the synchronous online classroom. The first person to send the answer (using the chat function) wins. Small online gift certificates can be used as prizes.

It is important to choose brain teasers that are fairly difficult to solve and to make sure the answers can't be looked up online. Trivia questions are too easy if the learner can do an online search and come up with the correct answer.

Adopt or Adapt

Brain teasers used in the face-to-face classroom can be easily adapted to the virtual classroom.

Attribution

Submitted by Keith Resseau, manager, Learning Technology, Fidelity Information Services, Jacksonville, Florida, USA

Contact: mary.keith.resseau@fnf.com

Figure 5.4. Brain Teaser 1 Answer

Source: Keith Resseau

Figure 5.5. Brain Teaser 2 Answer

Unscramble each word to reveal the quip and its author

"Teavhwre uyo rae, eb a odog neo."

Mhaaabr Nnlloci

"Whatever you are, be a good one."

Abraham Lincoln

Source: Keith Resseau

Low-Tech Listening Exercise

The Big Idea

What

Learners can listen to a simulated recording of a situation, as part of a soft skills simulation, during a synchronous online learning session.

Figure 5.6. Directions for Simulation Activity

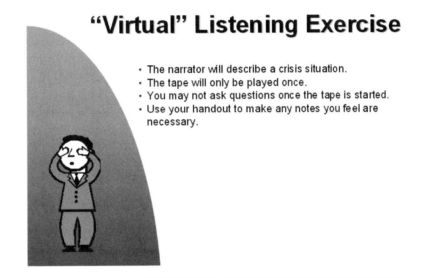

"Virtual" Listening Exercise

- The narrator will describe a crisis situation.
- The tape will only be played once.
- You may not ask questions once the tape is started.
- Use your handout to make any notes you feel are necessary.

Source: Keith Resseau

Why

A well-recorded audio simulation allows learners to get cues from and react to a realistic situation.

Use It!

How

Fidelity Information Services wanted to adapt a three-day, soft skills course for synchronous online delivery. They were concerned about adapting a listening skills exercise that had been used with great success in the face-to-face classroom. In the exercise, learners listen to a recording of a crisis situation, as related by a narrator, complete with realistic sound effects. Learners can take notes but cannot ask questions or request that the recording be played again. The class is then divided into teams to determine the best course of action.

Fidelity Information Services considered having the recording re-recorded digitally but had neither the technology nor permission from the author to do this. Putting the file online also meant that learners could access and replay the file at will, which was against the rules of the exercise. They considered having the trainer read a script of the crisis simulation but decided it wouldn't be as effective without the inflections of the professional narrator and the sound effects that re-create the feeling of the crisis situation.

The best solution turned out to be the cheapest, lowest-tech, and easiest of anything considered. While the learners were logged in to the synchronous classroom (connected by bridge line for audio), the trainer played the tape into his phone using the same tape player and speakers used in the face-to-face class. Audio distortion was not a problem—the sound came through loud and clear. The trainer then broke the class into small groups, gave each group its own bridge line number, and had them work virtually to solve the crisis.

The online activity actually better simulated the real work environment of the learners, who often problem solve over the phone.

Adopt or Adapt

Existing recordings may be played over a phone bridge, or organizations may want to invest in simple sound-editing equipment to produce realistic recordings that can be used for this purpose.

Attribution

Submitted by Keith Resseau, manager, Learning Technology, Fidelity Information Services, Jacksonville, Florida, USA

Contact: mary.keith.resseau@fnf.com

Trainer-Expert Collaboration

The Big Idea

What

When you have a small training staff delivering a wide range of courses, it's impossible to always have a trainer on hand who is also an expert for all training needs. A collaboration between trainers and experts is an effective solution.

Figure 5.7. Introduction Slide

Source: Keith Resseau

Why

A collaboration between trainers and experts stretches tight training resources and adds depth and additional credibility to your training.

Use It!

How

The synchronous online classroom has great potential for using experts as co-trainers. The trainer provides a good, solid instructional base, making sure that adult learning techniques are applied. The expert can deliver or expand on critical details and answer in-depth questions from the audience.

It's sometimes even possible to get "celebrity" experts to participate in your courses. Fidelity Information Services found that experts who wouldn't agree to teach a face-to-face class were quite agreeable to co-teaching or participating in portions of an online class via conference call. Examples of those who joined their classes (for free) include

- A best-selling author (nine million copies of more than thirty management leadership books) who joined them for a discussion of his latest best-seller

- An award-winning e-learning expert and author

- Executive leaders

Keith Resseau's Tips

- Interview the expert in advance about items you wish him or her to cover and write prescribed questions for the instructor to remind him or her to ask these during the class.

- Practice with the expert ahead of time so he or she understands the technology, or let the trainer do the "driving" and the expert won't have to deal with anything more complicated than dialing into a bridge line.

- Introduce your expert as an honored guest. The more cachet you afford the expert, the more credible the training will be.

- Allow plenty of time for questions and answers between learners and the expert.

Adopt or Adapt

This idea can be adapted for both classroom and asynchronous online instruction. An expert could field questions in the discussion forum or share tips, techniques, and "war stories." Even if experts don't want to be "live" with learners, they are often willing to provide cases and tools to augment instruction.

Attribution

Submitted by Keith Resseau, manager, Learning Technology, Fidelity Information Services, Jacksonville, Florida, USA

Contact: mary.keith.resseau@fnf.com

Pyramid

The Big Idea

What

This activity prompts learners to reflect on and share what was learned during a synchronous online learning event.

Figure 5.8. Pyramid

The Pyramid

Concepts from Leadership Class

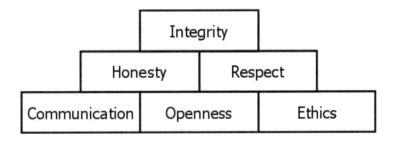

Source: Ken Dobrovolny

Why

Closing activities in a synchronous online classroom can help learners reflect on the experience and what they will take away from it.

Use It!

How

Ask learners to write down one concept they learned in the course. Then have them pair up with someone else, share their concepts, and agree on a ranking so that one concept is first and the other is second in importance. Next, have each pair join two other pairs to form a group of six. This group will share all six concepts (three were ranked first and three were ranked second) and determine an overall ranking from one through six. If there are duplicates, the group should add additional concepts so they have a total of six.

Now ask the group to draw six boxes in the shape of a pyramid (or provide them with a template for this purpose). The highest ranked concept goes in the top box, the second and third ranked concepts go on the second line, and the last three ranked concepts go on the bottom line.

The visual pyramid is intended to show the relationship between the concepts and how they build on one another to form a solid foundation for the course.

This idea is part of a compilation of exercises developed for a session at the National Staff Development and Training Association (NSDTA) national conference.

Adopt or Adapt

This exercise would work well where individuals or groups of learners shared their pyramid with other individuals or groups of learners in a Web conferencing environment. It could also be adapted in other environments, and the pyramids could even be emailed to everyone at the end of or after class.

Attribution

Submitted by Ken Dobrovolny, employee training manager, State of Colorado Department of Human Services, Denver, Colorado, USA

Contact: kenneth.dobrovolny@state.co.us

Before Ninety

The Big Idea

What

This activity helps learners find out something important about other learners during a synchronous online learning event.

Figure 5.9. Before Ninety

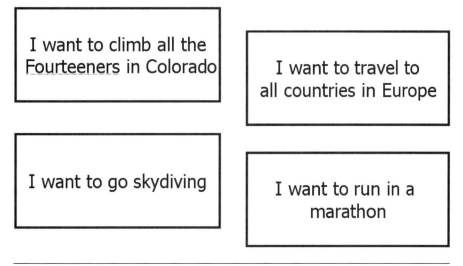

Source: Ken Dobrovolny

Why

Disclosure activities can help learners get to know and appreciate one another. This may be especially important when training intact workgroups or people who will be collaborating in the course.

Use It!

How

Ask learners to think of one important thing they would like to do before they turn ninety years old, something they've always wanted to do but haven't yet accomplished. Have them privately send their one important thing (via private chat function or email) to the instructor. Throughout the course the instructor can read or show one desire and have others guess who it belongs to. The person it belongs to can reveal that it belongs to them whenever they are ready.

This idea is part of a compilation of exercises developed for a session at the NSDTA national conference.

Adopt or Adapt

This exercise could be adapted for classroom-based, blended, and online learning environments as well as synchronous and asynchronous learning environments.

Attribution

Submitted by Ken Dobrovolny, employee training manager, State of Colorado Department of Human Services, Denver, Colorado, USA

Contact: kenneth.dobrovolny@state.co.us

Daring Feats

The Big Idea

What

This activity prompts learners to relate daring feats to what they learned during a synchronous online learning event.

Figure 5.10. Daring Feat

Rodeo Bull-Riding
It's dangerous
It's over very quickly
It has a lot of excitement

My work assignments are often very short-term and challenging and sometimes I have to try different approaches to succeed.

Source: Ken Dobrovolny

Why

This idea can help learners see how things that are difficult can get accomplished.

Use It!

How

Show a slide of a numbered list of daring feats. Ask learners to select the one daring feat they would most like to do or that they have great respect for and input the number of that daring feat in the chat area.

List of Daring Feats

1. Skydiving

2. Bungee jumping

3. Rock climbing

4. Keynote speaking

5. Rodeo bull-riding

6. Crocodile wrestling

Form breakout groups with the people who selected each feat and have each group discuss why members chose that daring feat. Next ask them to determine how the reasons relate to what they learned in the course.

This idea is part of a compilation of exercises developed for a session at the NSDTA national conference.

Adopt or Adapt

This exercise could be adapted for classroom-based, blended, and online learning environments as well as synchronous and asynchronous learning environments.

Attribution

Submitted by Ken Dobrovolny, employee training manager, State of Colorado Department of Human Services, Denver, Colorado, USA

Contact: kenneth.dobrovolny@state.co.us

Spotlights

The Big Idea

What

This activity helps learners review how course concepts relate to each other during a synchronous online learning event.

Figure 5.11. Spotlights

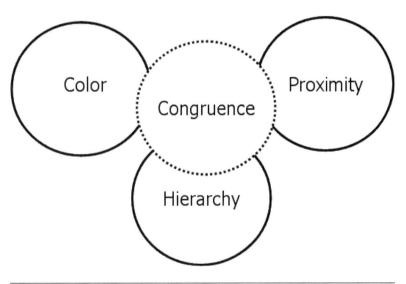

Source: Ken Dobrovolny

Why

This is a good way to review course concepts.

Use It!

How

Ask each learner to list something they learned in today's class in the chat area. Using a slide with the diagram of the four spotlights shown in Figure 5.11, the instructor randomly picks any three items and writes them in the outer three spotlights and then asks someone to say or write what these items have in common. The answer is placed in the center spotlight. This process can be repeated multiple times.

This idea is part of a compilation of exercises developed for a session at the NSDTA national conference.

Adopt or Adapt

This exercise could be adapted for classroom-based, blended, and online learning environments as well as synchronous and asynchronous learning environments.

Attribution

Submitted by Ken Dobrovolny, employee training manager, State of Colorado Department of Human Services, Denver, Colorado, USA

Contact: kenneth.dobrovolny@state.co.us

Vowels

The Big Idea

What

This exercise helps learners review what they have learned.

Figure 5.12. Five Words

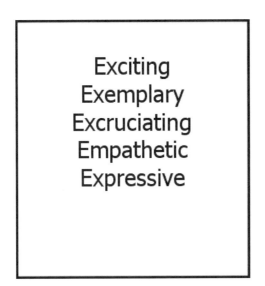

Source: Ken Dobrovolny

Why

This is a very creative way to review what has been learned because it often requires some real thought in order to come up with appropriate words.

Use It!

How

Divide the class into five groups, using the first vowel (A, E, I, O, or U) in each person's last name. Once groups are formed, ask each group to come up with five words starting with their group's vowel that relate to the topic of the class.

Have each group report to the entire class and then discuss the words the groups came up with.

This idea is part of a compilation of exercises developed for a session at the NSDTA national conference.

Adopt or Adapt

This exercise could be adapted for classroom-based, blended, and online learning environments as well as synchronous and asynchronous learning environments.

Attribution

Submitted by Ken Dobrovolny, employee training manager, State of Colorado Department of Human Services, Denver, Colorado, USA

Contact: kenneth.dobrovolny@state.co.us

Gordon Mackenzie–Style Lecture

The Big Idea

What

In synchronous (live or distance) presentations, let learners choose the order in which topics are presented.

Figure 5.13. Main Topics Slide

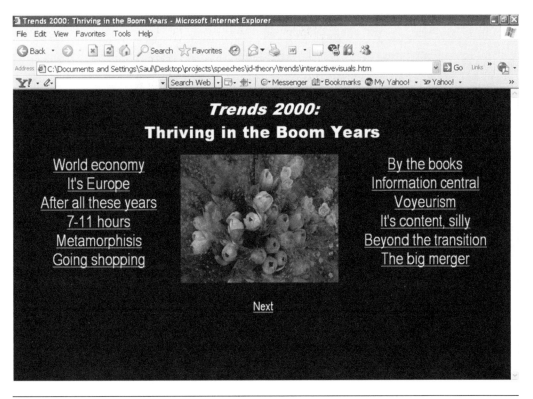

Source: Saul Carliner, http://education.concordia.ca/~scarliner

Figure 5.14. Topic Slide

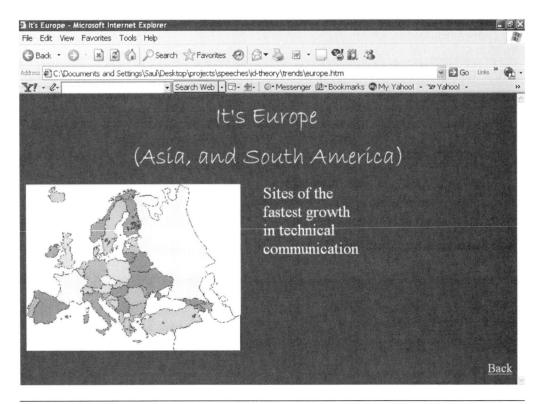

Source: Saul Carliner, http://education.concordia.ca/~scarliner

Why

This is an unexpected and interactive way to give a presentation, useful when the material need not be presented in a linear manner.

Use It!

How

To make synchronous online courses more interactive, the Gordon Mackenzie–style lecture is a natural. The technique is named for the person who Saul Carliner first saw use it, but he acknowledges that someone else may have developed it first. Mackenzie was an executive in the creative area of Hallmark Cards and became a popular speaker after he retired. Although Mackenzie used this technique in live presentations, Carliner has used it in synchronous classes and found it to work well.

The core of the technique is a slide listing several topics. The number varies depending on how many topics are appropriate. A randomly chosen learner is invited to select a topic of interest. Then the topic is presented. When that topic is completed, another randomly chosen learner is invited to select another topic, and so on.

In addition to the main topics, Mackenzie always listed one additional topic—and if a learner called it, the lecture was over. So if Mackenzie had eighteen topics in his lecture, topic nineteen was the one to end it (and was labeled "The End"). Whenever Carliner saw Mackenzie present, he never heard anyone choose the topic to end the presentation until the scheduled time to end the presentation had been reached (and usually a minute or two later).

Carliner's Tips

- The main topics slide lists all of the possible topics.

- Following the main topics slide are slides for each topic. Try to limit the number of slides for a given topic to one.

- Because the slides must be linked so they can be viewed in a somewhat random order, it is easier to develop them as browser pages rather than PowerPoint slides. Or hyperlinks from the main topics slide to the topic slides and back to the main topics slide can be developed in PowerPoint.

- If browser pages rather than PowerPoint slides are used, learners can immediately tell which topics have been discussed (because the links will change color) and which ones are still open.

- Use intriguing titles for topics as a means of enticing learners (and ones that don't give away too much information). For example, the topic "Going shopping" focuses on opportunities in e-commerce and other e-fields for participants in the audience.

- Do not use "The End" (or whatever you choose to call the topic that ends the presentation) in lessons intended for learners who are not likely to be responsible about using it (that is, likely to call for it before the end of the presentation).

Adopt or Adapt

This idea can be adapted for any face-to-face or live distance presentation.

Attribution

Submitted by Saul Carliner, assistant professor of educational technology, Department of Education, Concordia University, Montreal, Quebec, Canada

Contact: saul.carliner@sympatico.ca

URL: http://education.concordia.ca/~scarliner

Vanity License Plate

The Big Idea

What

This activity helps learners and the instructor get acquainted.

Figure 5.15. License Plate Template

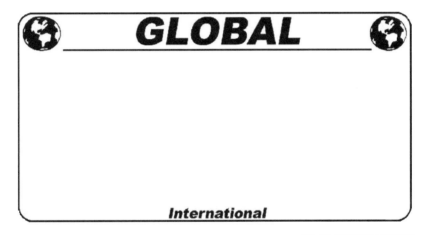

Source: Rosemary Lehman, http://www.uwex.edu/ics/design

Why

Instructors and learners learn about each other in a creative way.

Use It!

How

Rosemary Lehman's team prompts learners to be creative with numbers, letters, short phrases, and symbols while designing a vanity license plate that tells others something about them, their work, their hobbies, or other special interests. Instructors also create license plates. A template is provided to learners for this purpose.

This activity is used during video conferencing and everyone shows their license plate using the document camera. A side benefit is that everyone learns to operate the document camera.

Adopt or Adapt

This idea can be adapted for synchronous or asynchronous learning environments.

Attribution

Submitted by Rosemary Lehman, senior outreach/distance education specialist and manager, Instructional Design Team, Instructional Communications Systems, University of Wisconsin-Extension, Madison, Wisconsin, USA

Contact: lehman@ics.uwex.edu

URL: http://www.uwex.edu/ics/design/

Also involved: Richard A. Berg, instructional design/distance education specialist, and Bruce E. Dewey, outreach/distance education specialist, both from the Instructional Design Team, Instructional Communications Systems, University of Wisconsin-Extension, Madison, Wisconsin, USA

Lighten Up

The Big Idea

What

Help learners get involved early during a Web conferencing session.

Figure 5.16. "Light" Poll

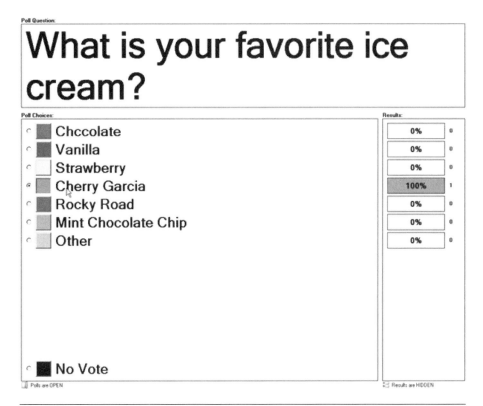

Source: Rosemary Lehman, http://www.uwex.edu/ics/design

Why

Help learners connect and feel comfortable immediately.

Use It!

How

Some attendees can be very intimidated by Web conferencing technology and this can make them passive, which detracts from potential learning. Help them lighten up and get involved early in the session. Use the polling feature to ask a lighthearted question. For example, "What is your favorite ice cream?" "I would like to take a trip to . . ." or "My favorite pizza topping is. . . ."

Adopt or Adapt

This idea can be adapted easily by changing the subject of the poll. It could also be adapted for asynchronous instruction by using polling programs.

Attribution

Submitted by Rosemary Lehman, senior outreach/distance education specialist and manager, Instructional Design Team, Instructional Communications Systems, University of Wisconsin-Extension, Madison, Wisconsin, USA

Contact: lehman@ics.uwex.edu

URL: http://www.uwex.edu/ics/design

Also involved: Richard A. Berg, instructional design/distance education specialist, and Bruce E. Dewey, outreach/distance education specialist, both from the Instructional Design Team, Instructional Communications Systems, University of Wisconsin-Extension, Madison, Wisconsin, USA

Where Are You?

The Big Idea

What

Find out where your Web conferencing attendees are located.

Figure 5.17. Map Marks

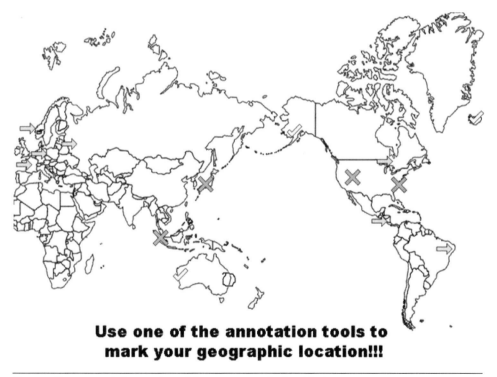

Use one of the annotation tools to mark your geographic location!!!

Source: Rosemary Lehman, http://www.uwex.edu/ics/design

Why

Everyone gets a sense of the geographical spread and gains experience with using the technology.

Use It!

How

Post a map of the state, country, continent, or world on one of your first slides and ask learners to use markup and annotation tools to indicate their location.

Adopt or Adapt

This exercise could be adapted for use in a classroom or other synchronous learning environments. Facilitators could use something other than a map (for example, a four-quadrant table or a list of personal attributes) and have learners use annotation tools to show which apply to them.

Attribution

Submitted by Rosemary Lehman, senior outreach/distance education specialist and manager, Instructional Design Team, Instructional Communications Systems, University of Wisconsin-Extension, Madison, Wisconsin, USA

Contact: lehman@ics.uwex.edu

URL: http://www.uwex.edu/ics/design/

Also involved: Richard A. Berg, instructional design/distance education specialist, and Bruce E. Dewey, outreach/distance education specialist, both from the Instructional Design Team, Instructional Communications Systems, University of Wisconsin-Extension, Madison, Wisconsin, USA

Word Search

The Big Idea

What

Use a custom word search puzzle as a review during synchronous online learning sessions.

Figure 5.18. Word Search

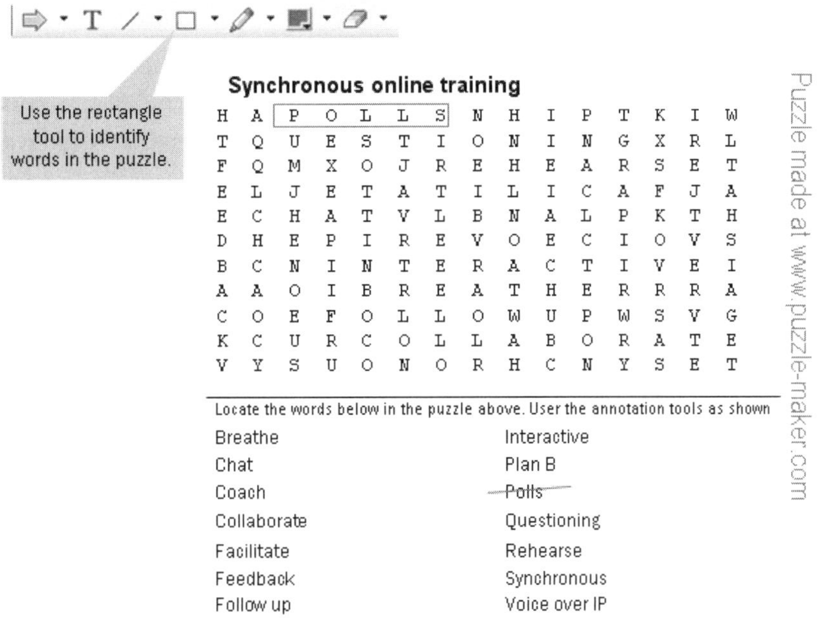

Source: Karen Hyder

Why

This is a fun way to review terms and engage participants.

Use It!

How

A word search is a list of terms that are scrambled into a grid of letters. Learners are asked to locate and, using Web conferencing annotation tools, circle the found words on screen. Software tools such as the one found at http://www.puzzle-maker.com automatically create a grid based on a list of words you provide. The number of words and the size of the grid are adjustable.

Karen Hyder was looking for a way to engage learners who returned early from break and to review vocabulary at the end of sessions. She also keeps extra word searches handy just in case the session is delayed or she needs to fill time.

Hyder's Tips

- Use word search puzzles to encourage learners to review key terms.

- Use them to fill time before the official start of a synchronous online session or when learners are returning from a break.

- Use search puzzles to give learners an activity to do momentarily when you need to troubleshoot.

- Be sure to include instructions on the puzzle screen to eliminate the need to explain the process to each learner as they join.

Adopt or Adapt

Develop a list of keywords or a list of terms and definitions. Then generate a word search. This activity can be adapted for classroom or online (synchronous or asynchronous) instruction.

Attribution

Submitted by Karen Hyder, managing director, Kaleidoscope Training and Consulting, Palmyra, New York, USA

Contact: Karen@karenHyder.com

Also involved: Rachel Rehm, president, Variety Games, Inc., Orem, Utah, USA

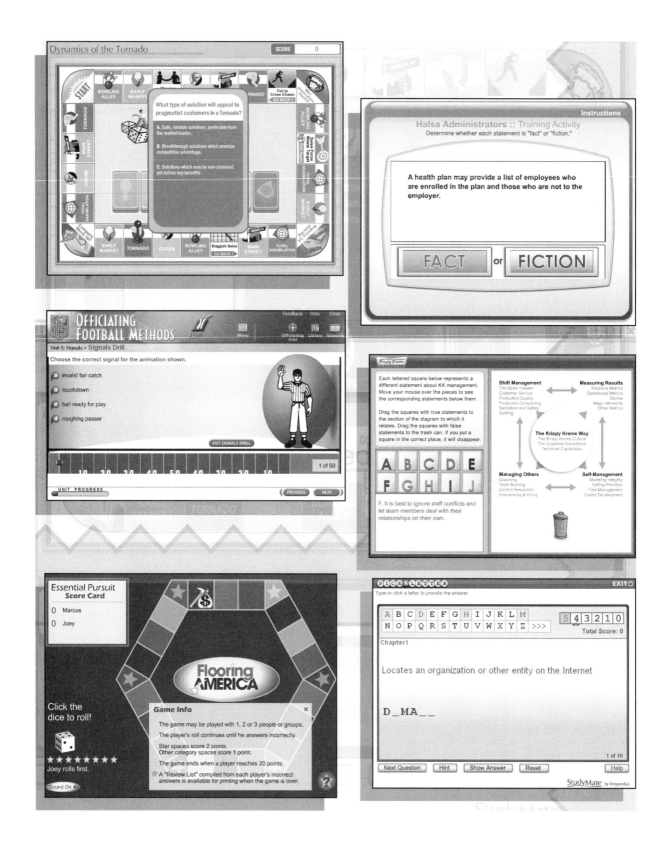

Ideas for Self-Check Activities and Assessments

f you get your teeth examined on an ongoing basis or take your pet to the vet for regular checkups, you already know the value of monitoring. This chapter showcases ideas for activities that help learners monitor their understanding. Self-check activities allow learners to monitor their understanding so they can make needed adjustments. Learning research shows that these types of activities help learners keep an eye on their learning and adjust their efforts, know when to seek help, and stay on track. These actions are important to learning, but are too often not included.

Many instructors and designers use these types of activities throughout the learning process because they know how helpful they are for learning and staying on course. These activities are usually not graded but some instructors provide credit for completing them.

Adapted Classroom Assessment Techniques

The Big Idea

What

Collecting data about teaching and learning as they are occurring helps instructors improve both.

Figure 6.1. CAT in a Discussion Forum

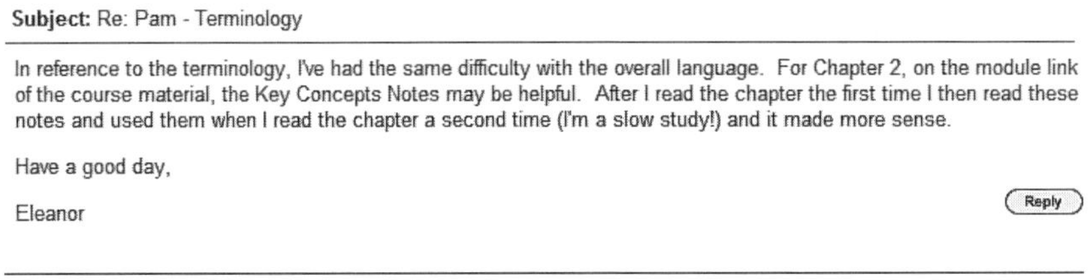

Subject: Re: Pam - Terminology

In reference to the terminology, I've had the same difficulty with the overall language. For Chapter 2, on the module link of the course material, the Key Concepts Notes may be helpful. After I read the chapter the first time I then read these notes and used them when I read the chapter a second time (I'm a slow study!) and it made more sense.

Have a good day,

Eleanor

(Reply)

Source: Terry Morris, http://terrymorris.net

Why

This process empowers both teachers and learners to improve learning immediately and prompts learners to think about what and how they are learning.

Use It!

How

It is helpful for instructors and learners to determine inadequate understandings and misunderstandings so these can be repaired. This idea adapts classroom assessment techniques (CATs) described by Thomas Angelo and K. Patricia Cross in *Classroom Assessment Techniques* (1993).

Anyone who is teaching an online course can adapt CATs for an online learning environment. Example CATs include the following:

- *The Muddiest Point:* Ask learners to describe the most unclear point in the presentation.

- *The One-Sentence Summary:* Ask learners to summarize concisely the who, when, where, how, and why of a given topic.

- *Learner-Generated Test Questions:* Ask learners to generate useful test questions and to answer questions that other learners have posed.

CATs are implemented by giving learners a prompt such as, "Which one point was most unclear or most difficult to understand?" or "In one sentence, summarize the most important points from the reading," or "Create a short-answer question on this topic." (See the URL in the Attribution section for other CATs and example prompts.) Learners read each other's responses and reply (to provide clarification about others' Muddiest Points or answer short-answer questions, for example). The instructor replies and suggests review resources as needed.

CATs can be implemented in an online class using quizzing and survey tools, discussion forums, emails, listservs, or synchronous chats. They can be instituted as either informal or formal (graded) activities.

Adopt or Adapt

CATs work in all subject areas and at many cognitive levels. They would work well in classroom-based, blended, and online learning for academic courses or corporate training. They can assist the instructor in determining what misunderstandings have occurred and help learners assess their understanding.

Attribution

Submitted by Terry Morris, associate professor, William Rainey Harper College, Palatine, Illinois, USA

Contact: tmorris@harpercollege.edu

URL: http://terrymorris.net/cats

Reference

Angelo, T. A., & Cross, K. P. (1993). *Classroom assessment techniques: A handbook for college teachers* (2nd ed.). San Francisco: Jossey-Bass.

Review Puzzles and Games

The Big Idea

What

Have learners use games and puzzles to review their understanding of terms and concepts.

Figure 6.2. Links-to-Course Games

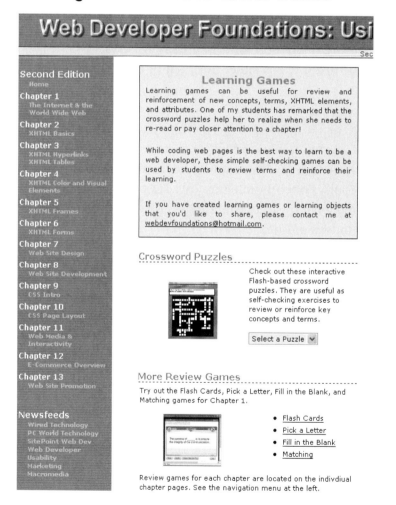

Source: Terry Morris, http://terrymorris.net

Figure 6.3. Fill-in-the-Blank Game

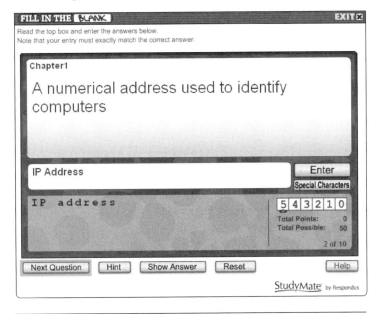

Source: Terry Morris, http://terrymorris.net

Figure 6.4. Pick-a-Letter Game

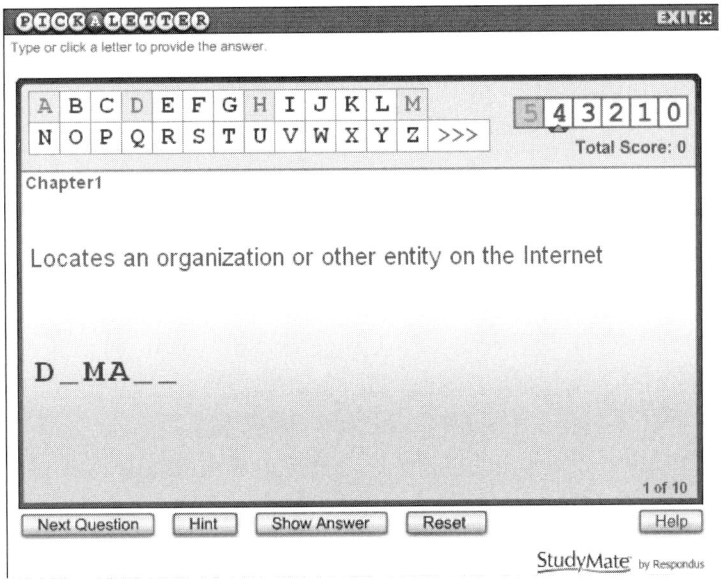

Source: Terry Morris, http://terrymorris.net

Why

This is a fun way to review content and check understanding.

Use It!

How

Learners, in introductory courses especially, often need to review basic terms and concepts. Using games and puzzles for this purpose makes the review more enjoyable. Terry Morris was introduced to Hot Potatoes during a graduate course and found other tools by searching the Web. She decided to try these out to build review activities for her Web site development course and accompanying textbook.

Learners have told her that the games and puzzles are fun, help them remember important terms, and reveal items they may have skimmed over too lightly when doing the reading assignment.

Morris recommends applications such as the following for this purpose:

- Hot Potatoes (http://web.uvic.ca/hrd/hotpot)

- CrossSkins (http://www.learnertools.com/crossskins/crossword.html)

- Respondus StudyMate (http://www.respondus.com/products/studymate.shtml)

Morris has found StudyMate to be a great way to create a variety of puzzles and games in a short amount of time. You need to enter the review material (such as terms and definitions) only once and StudyMate will create a wide range of activities including flash cards, pick a letter, fill in the blank, matching, and crossword puzzles. StudyMate also accepts input from word processing files. The puzzles and games can be published to the Web or to course management systems such as Blackboard and WebCT. Some textbook publishers have already created these files for instructor use.

Adopt or Adapt

Anyone who is teaching a course with terms and definitions can use these exercises to provide quick, fun review activities for learners.

Attribution

Submitted by Terry Morris, associate professor, William Rainey Harper College, Palatine, Illinois, USA

Contact: tmorris@harpercollege.edu

URL: http://webdevfoundations.net/games

Flash Cards

The Big Idea

What

Flash cards can help learners review terms, dates, events, or other declarative knowledge.

Figure 6.5. Flash Card, Definition

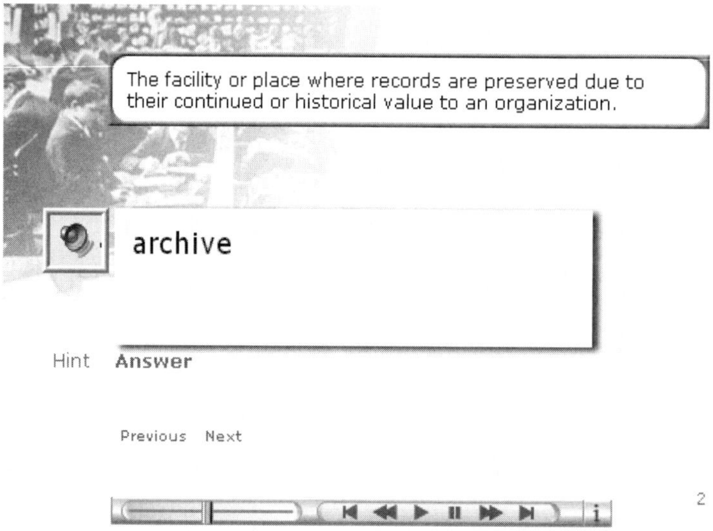

Source: Karen Owen, http://www.karenowen.com

Figure 6.6. Flash Card, Pronunciation

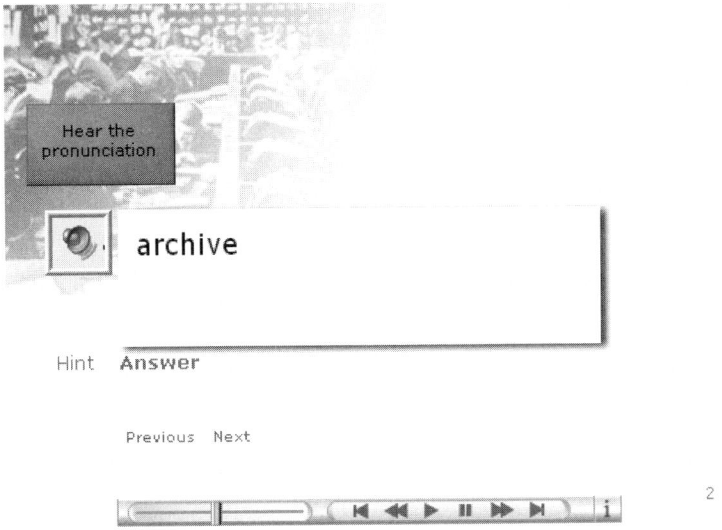

Source: Karen Owen, http://www.karenowen.com

Why

Flash cards can be a fun way to practice.

Use It!

How

Karen Owen created a series of flash cards for her records management course and her other online and classroom-based courses. She wanted to make sure learners knew the correct pronunciation as well as the definition of common vocabulary items. Learners have told her that these flash cards help them remember definitions and pronounce words correctly. They were created with Adobe Captivate and the audio was recorded using the audio capture feature in Captivate.

Adopt or Adapt

> Develop flash cards for knowledge elements that learners need to be able to remember.

Attribution

Submitted by Karen Owen, assistant professor, San Diego Mesa College, San Diego, California, USA

Contact: kowen@cox.net

URL: http://www.karenowen.com/lessons/robodemoMy_Examples.htm

Know Your Flooring

The Big Idea

What

A Flash-based game allows learners to practice and assess their knowledge prior to taking a certification exam.

Figure 6.7. Game Begins, Two Players

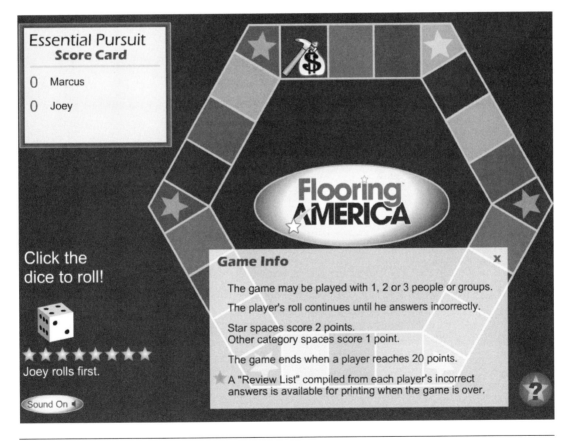

Source: William Gauthier

Figure 6.8. Game Feedback

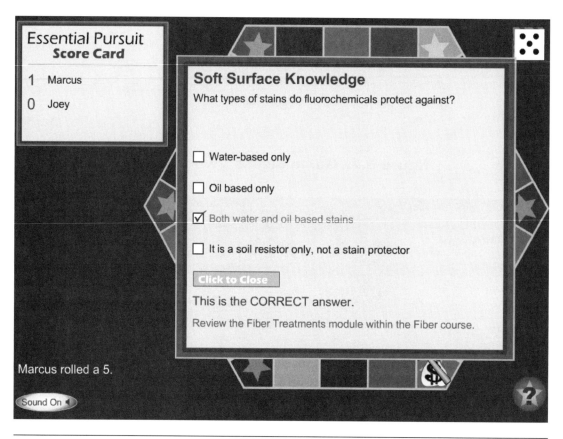

Source: William Gauthier

Figure 6.9. Game Statistics and Review

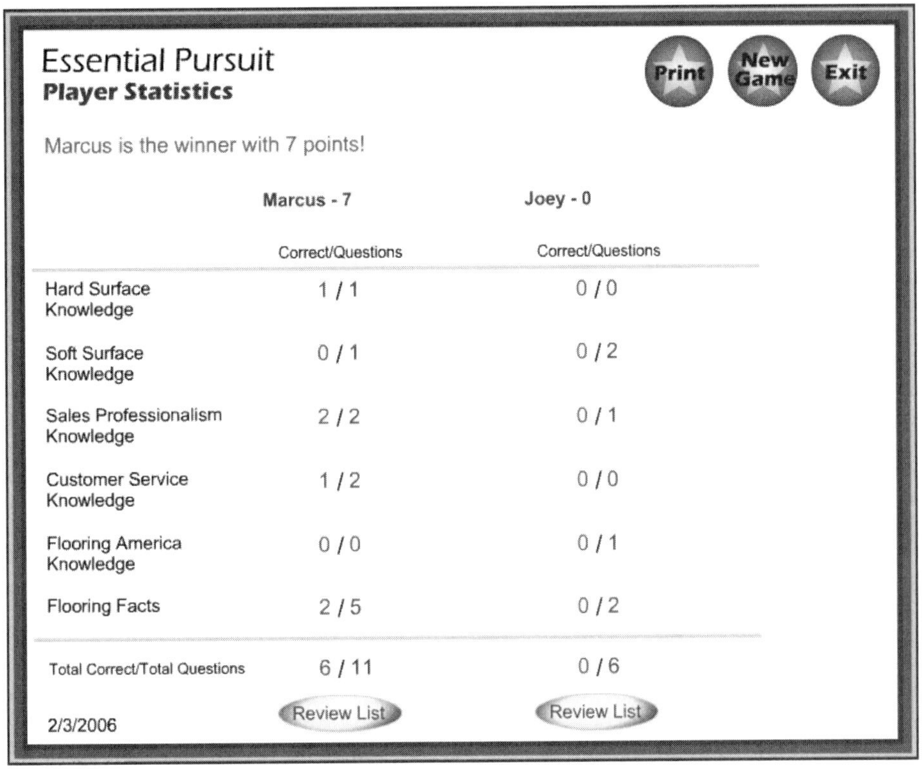

Essential Pursuit
Player Statistics

Print   New Game   Exit

Marcus is the winner with 7 points!

	Marcus - 7	Joey - 0
	Correct/Questions	Correct/Questions
Hard Surface Knowledge	1 / 1	0 / 0
Soft Surface Knowledge	0 / 1	0 / 2
Sales Professionalism Knowledge	2 / 2	0 / 1
Customer Service Knowledge	1 / 2	0 / 0
Flooring America Knowledge	0 / 0	0 / 1
Flooring Facts	2 / 5	0 / 2
Total Correct/Total Questions	6 / 11	0 / 6
2/3/2006	Review List	Review List

Source: William Gauthier

Why

Games can be an engaging and effective way to practice.

Use It!

How

This knowledge game was developed to help learners pass a certification exam. The game gives learners an opportunity to test their knowledge about flooring in a fun and nonthreatening way. In addition, learners can play the game with others and compare scores, which adds impact in the form of a contest. If learners are able to answer the questions, they will be able to pass the certification exam.

At the end of the game, learners see their scores (and the scores of anyone else playing at the same time). They are able to print a report that pinpoints areas where additional study is advised.

Adopt or Adapt

Develop games to help learners practice and pass certification exams, and use them throughout courses to allow learners to assess their knowledge.

Attribution

Submitted by William Gauthier, director of training technology, CCA Global Partners, Manchester, New Hampshire, USA

Contact: wgauthier@ccaglobal.com

Also involved: Kathleen Callahan, project manager, CCA Global Partners, Manchester, New Hampshire, USA; Tanya Bottas, Flash developer/graphic designer, CCA Global Partners, Manchester, New Hampshire, USA; and Bob Hutter, senior director of training, CCA Global Partners, Manchester, New Hampshire, USA

Board Game Self-Check

The Big Idea

What

A board game is an engaging way to test understanding and an alternative to multiple-choice questions.

Figure 6.10. Board Game Question

Source: Option Six, http://www.optionsix.com

Figure 6.11. Board Game Feedback

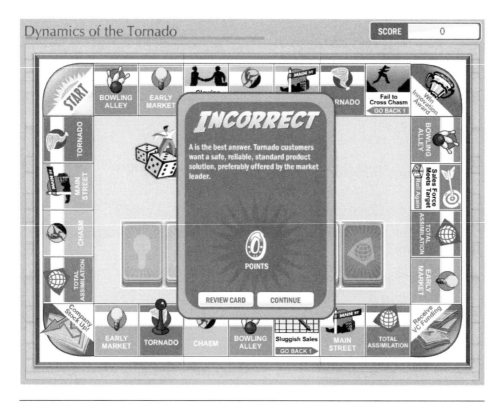

Source: Option Six, http://www.optionsix.com

Why

Games are a fun way for learners to check their understanding.

Use It!

How

Learners can get bored doing the same type of practice activity over and over. The board game approach is one that almost everyone is familiar with so it works well with a wide target audience. It "disguises" multiple-choice questions and makes them more enjoyable.

In a course about marketing in the high-tech industry, for example, the third module was about the dynamics of market development. The module described six development phases in high-tech markets: Early Market, Chasm, Bowling Alley, Tornado, Main Street, and Total Assimilation. These comprised the six parts of the module and at the end of each part there was a practice activity.

Melissa Carter's team at Option Six decided to use a board game format to test learners on the six market phases and market dynamics themes. The object of the game was for the learner to go around the board, correctly answer questions, and accumulate points. Informative feedback reinforced concepts and corrected misunderstandings.

The game was developed in Flash.

Adopt or Adapt

A board game can be used for assessing knowledge in almost any content area. Plus, once a Flash game template and logic are developed, it can be repurposed with different questions for different courses.

Attribution

Submitted by Melissa Carter, vice president, Option Six, Bloomington, Indiana, USA

Also involved: The Option Six Design and Development Team, http://www.optionsix.com; and Mark Cavender, founder and managing director, Chasm Institute, San Mateo, California, USA

Drag-and-Drop Self-Check

The Big Idea

What

Drag-and-drop activities allow learners to match related objects by selecting an object on the screen with the mouse, dragging it to another location on the screen, and releasing the mouse. These activities are good for assessing whether learners understand models, relationships, and classifications.

Figure 6.12. Statements and Model

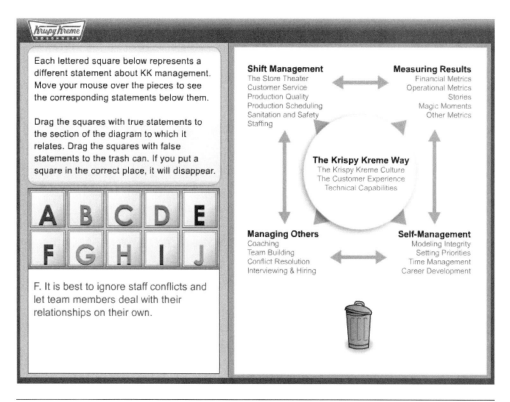

Source: Option Six, http://www.optionsix.com

Why

These types of interactions allow learners to interact with a model or classification scheme and gain immediate feedback about their understanding.

Use It!

How

When learners must demonstrate understanding about how things relate or are classified, or how parts fit into the whole, multiple-choice assessments are often cumbersome or inappropriate. A drag-and-drop assessment can be more appropriate.

Option Six developed a series of courses for Krispy Kreme (KK). One of them, Managing the Krispy Kreme Way, introduced learners to the KK management philosophy and management model. The Option Six team used a drag-and-drop practice activity to help learners assess their understanding of the model. The learner reads a statement and then drags the letter representing the statement to the appropriate place on the model. If the statement is not part of the model, the learner drags it to a trash can. Use of sounds and animation also makes this format fun and engaging for learners.

The game was developed in Flash.

Adopt or Adapt

The format of this drag-and-drop activity could be reused with many other types of models or diagrams for almost any content area.

Attribution

Submitted by Melissa Carter, vice president, Option Six, Bloomington, Indiana, USA

Also involved: The Option Six Design and Development Team, http://www.optionsix.com

Fact-or-Fiction Self-Check

The Big Idea

What

A fact-or-fiction self-check can be an effective activity for dispelling previously held misconceptions and checking learners' knowledge of basic concepts.

Figure 6.13. Fact-or-Fiction Question

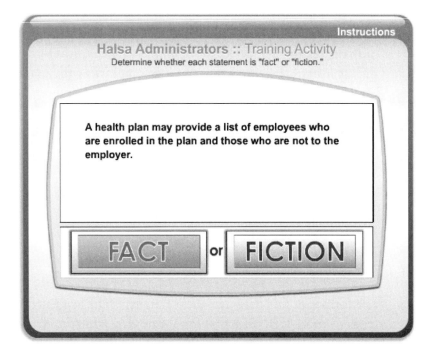

Source: Option Six, http://www.optionsix.com

Figure 6.14. Fact-or-Fiction Feedback

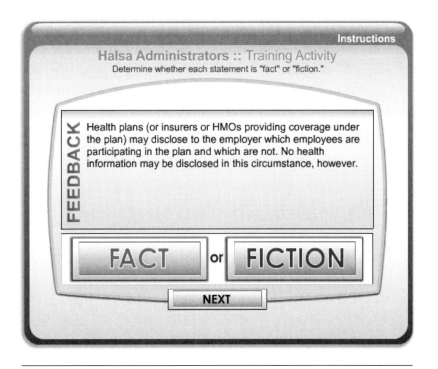

Source: Option Six, http://www.optionsix.com

Why

These self-checks are fast paced and fun!

Use It!

How

The practice activity shown in Figures 6.13 and 6.14 was implemented in a Health Insurance Portability and Accountability Act (HIPAA) course for insurance professionals and used a fact-or-fiction format to check learners' understanding of special rules that apply to employer-sponsored plans. Informative feedback reinforced concepts for learners and corrected misunderstandings.

While multiple-choice items are typically better than true-or-false items for assessing learning, sometimes dichotomous true-or-false assessments are enough for checking knowledge of basic concepts. Melissa Carter's team at Option Six developed a fact-or-fiction game for this purpose. This type of activity is especially useful when trying to dispel previously held misconceptions about a topic. Sounds and animation make the true-or-false format fun and engaging.

The game was developed in Flash.

Adopt or Adapt

The fact-or-fiction self-check is adaptable to almost any content area. It could be called true-or-false instead of fact-or-fiction. Plus, once a Flash game template and logic are developed, they can be repurposed with different questions for different courses.

Attribution

Submitted by Melissa Carter, vice president, Option Six, Bloomington, Indiana, USA

Also involved: The Option Six Design and Development Team, http://www.optionsix.com

Mixed Signals

The Big Idea

What

Animated flash cards let learners match numerous football officiating signals to the name of the signal. Incorrect answers are tested again.

Figure 6.15. Signal 1

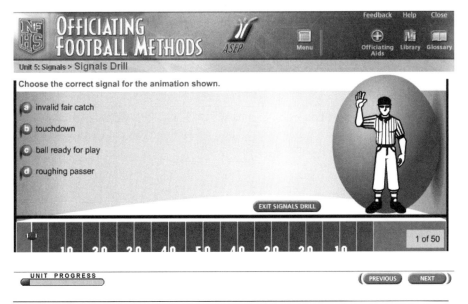

Source: American Sport Education Program, 2005, *NFHS Officiating Football Methods Online.* © 2005 by American Sport Education Program. Reprinted with permission from Human Kinetics (Champaign, IL).

Figure 6.16. Signal 2

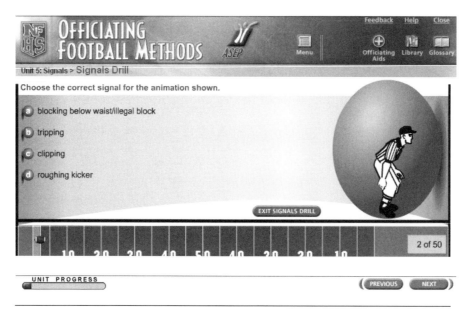

Source: American Sport Education Program, 2005, *NFHS Officiating Football Methods Online.* © 2005 by American Sport Education Program. Reprinted with permission from Human Kinetics (Champaign, IL).

Why

Learners need to remember a multitude of football officiating signal names and this is a fun way to practice.

Use It!

How

In the *NFHS Officiating Football Methods Online* course, the Signals Drill shows approximately fifty animated football officiating signals. As each signal is shown, the learner selects the signal name. Signals identified incorrectly are presented again later.

When a signal is correctly identified, the ball on the progress bar advances down the field. When the ball reaches the end zone, the learner has correctly identified all of the signals. Audio clips are utilized for background music and response feedback.

The course was built with Flash, ActionScript, JavaScript, XML, and HTML. An engine built in ActionScript loads an external XML file that contains all of the relevant information about each question, including the four response options, the correct response, and the associated animation. The ActionScript programming then checks to see if any Shared Objects (SOs) have been set to indicate if any of the questions were answered correctly. Of the remaining unanswered or incorrectly answered questions, the ActionScript programming randomly selects a question to display. If the question is not correctly answered, it is reinserted into the pool of available questions.

Correct answers are accompanied by a short MP3 clip and trigger a Flash animation of a progress bar at the bottom and an update of the question tally at the bottom right.

Adopt or Adapt

This approach could be used for drill and practice in identifying objects, people, terms, and so on. The audio feedback and progress bar can be replaced or eliminated to fit individual project needs.

Attribution

Submitted by Dean Hixson, instructional designer, Human Kinetics, Champaign, Illinois, USA

Contact: deanh@hkusa.com

URL: http://www.hkusa.com

Also involved: Greg George, instructional designer, Susi Huls, associate instructional designer, Stuart Cartwright, senior graphic designer, Jason Mock, course programmer/analyst, and Yury Borukhovich, course programmer/analyst, all from Human Kinetics, Champaign, Illinois, USA

Millionaire Game

The Big Idea

What

A game based on a popular television show allows learners to practice and assess their knowledge.

Figure 6.17. Millionaire Game Begins

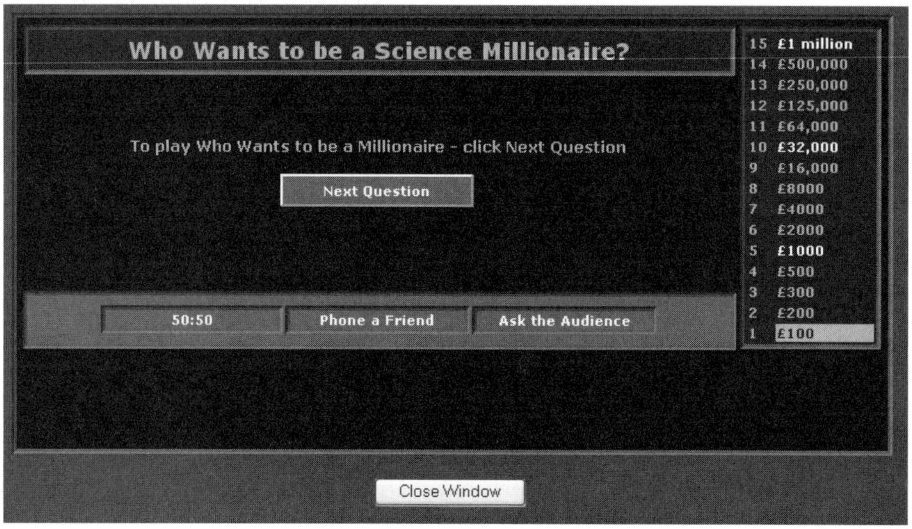

Source: Diane Hawkins, http://www.teachingandlearningresources.co.uk

Figure 6.18. Millionaire Game Question

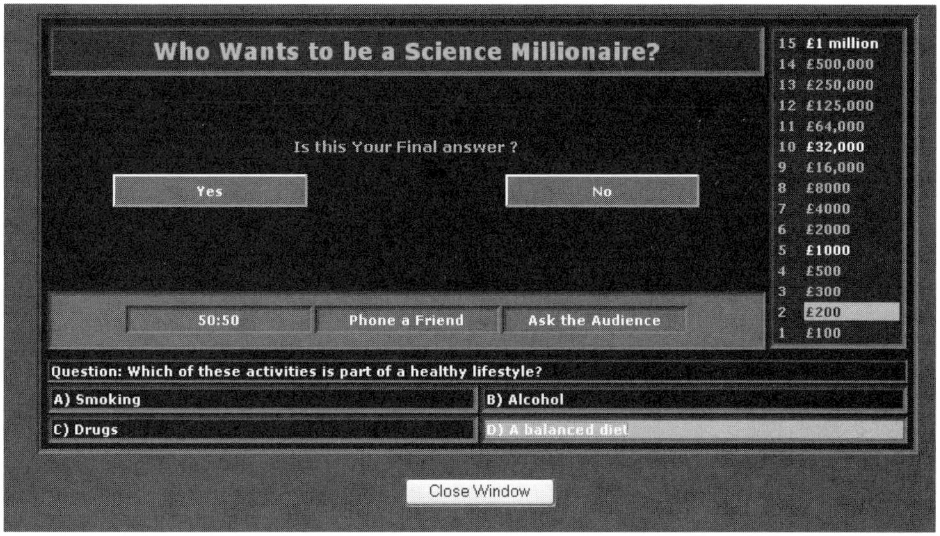

Source: Diane Hawkins, http://www.teachingandlearningresources.co.uk

Figure 6.19. Audience Help

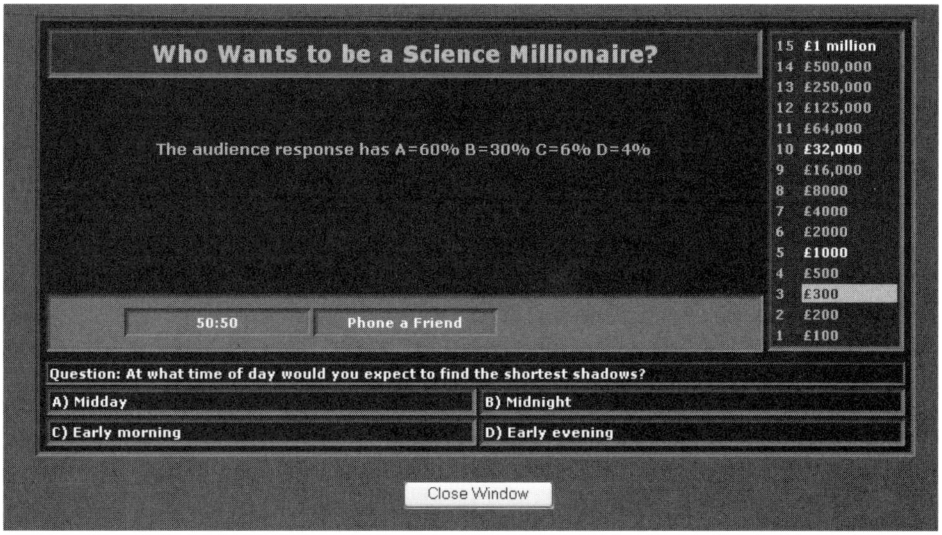

Source: Diane Hawkins, http://www.teachingandlearningresources.co.uk

Why

Games are often an engaging way to check factual knowledge.

Use It!

How

Diane Hawkins is a teacher and developer of online instructional materials. This Millionaire Game was developed for testing science knowledge in grades five and six. Hawkins developed the game using QuizMaster (http://www.cybertrain.info/quizman/qmhome.html), which allows teachers and trainers to create sixteen Web-based quiz games with their own content and feedback.

Adopt or Adapt

Develop games to help learners practice and assess their knowledge.

Attribution

Submitted by Diane Hawkins, Teaching and Learning Resources, Tonyrefail, Mid Glamorgan, Wales, United Kingdom

Contact: webmistress@teachingandlearningresources.co.uk

URL: http://www.teachingandlearningresources.co.uk

Show Training Value

The Big Idea

What

Help learners see the value of their training by using a pre- and post-assessment and by sharing data with learners.

Figure 6.20. Assessment with Confidence Rating

#	Question	Pretraining Response	Post Training Response
6.	All of the following are true about shared households **EXCEPT**: a. If one of the households 'sharing' expenses is the landlord, then the other household(s) cannot be considered sharing but must be looked at as a roomer living arrangement. b. The total shelter costs cannot exceed the actual total expenses. c. Sharing households are each allowed the full SUA if each is contributes to the heat payment. d. If one of the households is not responsible for the heat or utility costs, that household is not allowed the SUA (unless on Fuel).	6. _____ **Confidence Index** +++I'm sure of my answer. ++ I'm somewhat sure. + I'm not very sure.	6. _____ **Confidence Index** +++I'm sure of my answer. ++ I'm somewhat sure. + I'm not very sure.
7.	All of the following describe roomers **EXCEPT**: a. A roomer is an individual residing with others and paying compensation to others for lodging, but not for meals. b. Compensation does not have to be "reasonable"; the landlord can charge any amount. c. Roomers are entitled to a full SUA ONLY if they are living in subsidized housing. d. Your roomrent payments will count as income to the household you're living with if they receive assistance (FS, RU, Health Care).	7. _____ **Confidence Index** +++I'm sure of my answer. ++ I'm somewhat sure. + I'm not very sure.	7. _____ **Confidence Index** +++I'm sure of my answer. ++ I'm somewhat sure. + I'm not very sure.

Source: Terence R. Traut, http://www.unlockit.com

Why

Helping learners see the value of the training they attended can improve commitment and motivation.

Use It!

How

One challenge for those who develop and deliver training is helping learners see the value of their training. This challenge can be addressed by beginning training with a well-designed pre-assessment. Administer the same assessment at the end of the training. Allow learners to compare their post-training responses and scores to the pre-training responses and scores in order to verify that the training was a valuable use of their time.

Terence Traut includes with his assessments a Confidence Index, which asks learners to rate how confident they are about each answer. The Confidence Index allows even the most knowledgeable learners (who may get all of the answers correct) to see how much their confidence increased as a result of the training. Learners realize that they know the correct answer and they know they know.

In addition to providing a gauge for participants, assessment results can provide input for improving instruction.

Adopt or Adapt

This idea can be used in classroom-based, blended, and online instruction and can be especially useful with multiple-choice tests.

Attribution

Submitted by Terence R. Traut, president, Entelechy, Inc., Merrimack, New Hampshire, USA

Contact: ttraut@unlockit.com

URL: http://www.unlockit.com

Instructional Design

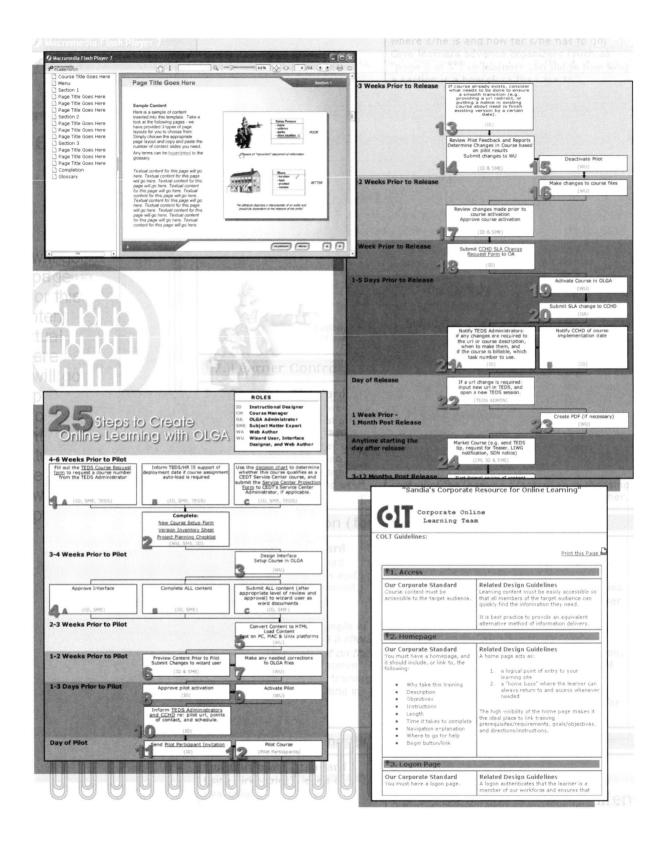

Ideas for the Design and Development Process

This chapter emphasizes ideas that can improve the design and development process, which can make building online learning easier and less frustrating for all involved. Typically, building online learning requires many people and processes, and it's easy to miscommunicate or do other things that necessitate rework (no fun!). The ideas in this chapter can make these processes more efficient and effective so that effort and frustration are reduced.

I'm a strong proponent of good processes and communication. Good processes take time but save more time. Although some may find the ready-fire-aim approach to work okay, I find it exhausting. In the long run, it is extremely worthwhile to spend time and effort building (and updating as needed) good processes with stakeholders and gaining consensus on how those processes will be used.

Process Flowchart

The Big Idea

What

A flowchart describes a standardized process for developing online courses.

Figure 7.1. Process Flowchart

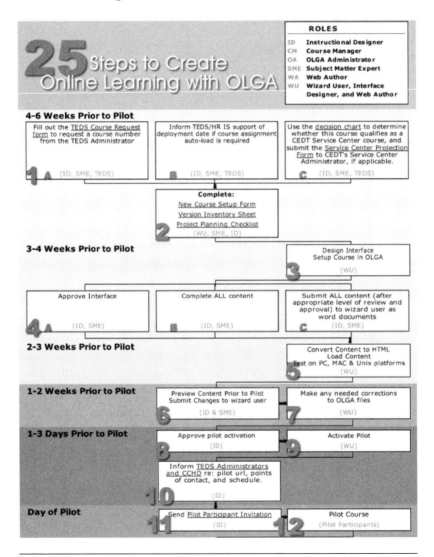

Source: Elsa Glassman

Figure 7.2. Process Flowchart, Continued

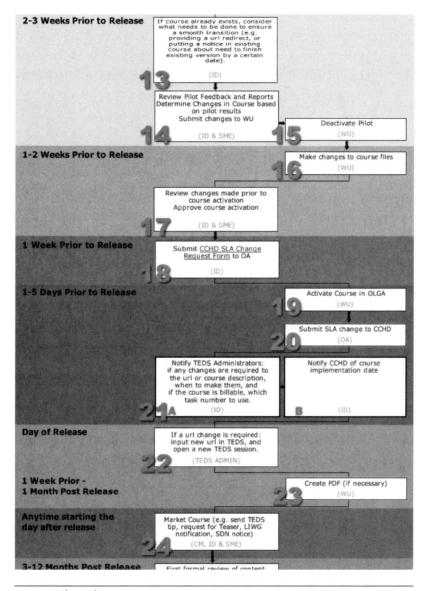

Source: Elsa Glassman

Why

A standardized process helps all stakeholders know what to expect and keeps everyone on track. A flowchart that describes a standardized process for developing online courses is used by course owners, subject matter experts, and the course development design team so everyone is on the same page from start to finish.

Use It!

How

Course owners submit a New Online Course Request to the design team. The design team sets up a meeting with the course owners to scope and schedule the project. At that meeting, content and learning objectives are discussed and the team uses the flowchart to discuss what happens when, roles and responsibilities, and estimated time and cost.

Once a budget is approved, the team meets to complete the Development Project Planning Checklist (a table version of the process flowchart that contains all the steps from the flowchart and provides space for dates and names). An electronic copy of the checklist is sent to all members of the course development team and the master is kept in an online document management system, where team members can access and update it.

Adopt or Adapt

Want to reduce frustrations and misunderstandings among your team and course owners? Adapt the flowchart and process for your own organization. Consider sharing a draft version with all stakeholders for input and revision prior to implementing. Building a flowchart as a team can initiate critical discussions among stakeholders about how things are working and how to make the process more effective and efficient. Then the team can improve it over time.

Attribution

Submitted by Elsa Glassman, corporate Online Learning Team lead, Sandia National Laboratories, Albuquerque, New Mexico, USA

Contact: ejglass@sandia.gov

Also involved: Barbara Lucero, Online Learning Generation Application Functional Project lead, Leslie Gardner, Online Learning Generation Application Technical Project lead, Amanda Saba, Online Learning Generation Application Wizard user, and Jared Pearce, Online Learning Generation Application Wizard user, all from Sandia National Laboratories, Albuquerque, New Mexico, USA

Design Guidelines

The Big Idea

What

It is helpful to develop design standards and guidelines applicable to all online learning projects.

Figure 7.3. Design Guidelines

```
        "Sandia's Corporate Resource for Online Learning"

        COLT        Corporate Online
                    Learning Team

  COLT Guidelines:

                                                      Print this Page ▢

  ⬆1. Access

  Our Corporate Standard       Related Design Guidelines
  Course content must be       Learning content must be easily accessible so
  accessible to the target     that all members of the target audience can
  audience.                    quickly find the information they need.

                               It is best practice to provide an equivalent
                               alternative method of information delivery.

  ⬆2. Homepage

  Our Corporate Standard       Related Design Guidelines
  You must have a homepage, and   A home page acts as:
  it should include, or link to, the
  following:
                                  1.  a logical point of entry to your
                                      learning site
      •  Why take this training   2.  a "home base" where the learner can
      •  Description                  always return to and access whenever
      •  Objectives                   needed
      •  Instructions
      •  Length                  The high visibility of the home page makes it
      •  Time it takes to complete   the ideal place to link training
      •  Navigation explanation   prerequisites/requirements, goals/objectives,
      •  Where to go for help     and directions/instructions.
      •  Begin button/link

  ⬆3. Logon Page

  Our Corporate Standard       Related Design Guidelines
  You must have a logon page.  A logon authenticates that the learner is a
                               member of our workforce and ensures that
```

Source: Elsa Glassman

Figure 7.4. Design Guidelines, Continued

	the learner gets credit for taking the course
↑4. Course Map & Progress Indicator	
Our Corporate Standard You must have a course map and progress indicator if more than one module exists.	**Related Design Guidelines** Always orient the learner and provide a sense of context/direction. It is important that learners know what materials they have accessed, completed, and still need to complete every time they access the course. A course map displays all the modules that are included in the training, and instruction on how they are to be viewed. The user either selects or is assigned a module from the Course Map. A progress indicator identifies which modules are complete.
↑5. Web Pages	
Our Corporate Standard Each web page must include: • Standard/consistent navigation (back/previous, forward/continue, and quit) • Web page number • Last modified date	**Related Design Guidelines** Writing for the web is very different than writing for print. The challenge is to overcome online readers' impatience by keeping things as brief as possible. Reading onscreen text is more difficult and time-consuming, so use less text. Choose a typeface that facilitates reading on screen. Also, don't hinder readability with poor contrast between background and text. Limit scrolling. Place the most important information "above the fold". Make text more easily scannable by chunking information into small units. Shorter is better: use shorter words, sentences, and paragraphs. Let the nature of the content suggest how it should be subdivided and organized. Insert meaningful headings and subheads. Highlight key words and provide adequate white space. Turn any series into bulleted or numbered list. Help learners visualize data by moving data into tables, charts, or graphs. Learners should be able to get to anywhere within a course very quickly (3 clicks or less is ideal). Links or buttons should be present on every page that allow learners to go forward or back. Provide clear and concise descriptions for text links to help users more effectively navigate rather than using "Click here". Learning can occur more rapidly when the user is able to make mental picture of the information in space. This means knowing

Source: Elsa Glassman

Figure 7.5. Design Guidelines, Continued

	where s/he is and how far s/he has to go. Give learners advance organizers (such as "page 8 of 5") so learners can judge how long a section is a how close they are to completing a unit.
⬆6. Interactivity	
Our Corporate Standard You must provide an opportunity for the user to interact.	**Related Design Guidelines** Active participation enhances and facilitates learning. Online training should encourage interaction between the learner and the content, between learners and subject matter experts, and among learners. Feedback to user input should be informative, and positive.
⬆7. Learner Control	
Our Corporate Standard The learner must be allowed some control over the presentation and pace. At a minimum, the learner must be provided with the option to go forward, back and quit (either quit-and-save, or quit-and-start over).	**Related Design Guidelines** Keep in mind that people learn at different speeds and in a variety of ways. A presentation supportive of different learning styles helps maximize learner engagement. User-centered design dictates that users be in control of the learning process, each choosing the approach most comfortable to him or her.
⬆8. Pilot Evaluation (formative)	
Our Corporate Standard Evaluation must be planned during the design process and occur during the development phase via a pilot. A pilot must include a sample of the target audience. Pilot participants must receive credit for completing the training as incentive for participating in the pilot.	**Related Design Guidelines** Quality design demands that learners are tested throughout training cycle. Test your designs on real users. This applies to both the instructional design and the user interface. Pilot evaluation questions are often more detailed than end-of-learning evaluation questions: obtaining feedback on navigation, art work, information sequence, amount of information, accuracy, ease of use, time spent, access, etc. A pilot can be conducted via the web and/or the classroom.
⬆9. End-of-Learning Evaluation (summative)	
Our Corporate Standard Using Kirkpatrick's levels of evaluation:	**Related Design Guidelines** Summative Evaluation takes place after completing the training. A post-implementation evaluation determines

Source: Elsa Glassman

Why

Documenting standards and guidelines improves consistency, reduces design and development time, and makes courses better and pages and sites easier to use.

Use It!

How

The Corporate Online Learning Team developed standards and guidelines based on lessons learned from experience, from reviewing the literature, and from researching best practices. These standards and guidelines are applied to all online courses. They are not tied to a specific content area.

The guidelines reside on the organization's intranet and are linked to from the Corporate Education, Development, and Training homepage; the Corporate Online Learning Team homepage; the Online Learning Generation Application homepage; and Sandia's TechWeb.

Adopt or Adapt

Consider developing standards for the following items:

- Elements to include in every course (such as objectives, references, and help)

- Elements to include on every page (such as help link and course home link)

- Names and formatting for elements (such as Course HOME and <Back, Next>)

- Terminology standards (such as *select* from a menu, *click* on a visible screen element, and *press* a key on the keyboard)

- Reusable text (such as executive welcome and activity instructions)

- Procedures for login, getting help, tracking, design, accessibility, evaluation and assessment, and course maintenance

- Anything else you want to standardize such as screen resolution, browsers, required bandwidth, fonts, formatting, screenshots, use of logos, colors, and so on

Attribution

Submitted by Elsa Glassman, Corporate Online Learning Team lead, Sandia National Laboratories, Albuquerque, New Mexico, USA

Contact: ejglass@sandia.gov

Also involved: Barbara Lucero, Online Learning Generation Application Functional Project lead, Sandia National Laboratories, Albuquerque, New Mexico, USA

Learner Stories

The Big Idea

What

As part of the prototyping phase of a design project, write a story of expected or actual learner experiences with the instruction. This process can reveal rich details of the learning experience, including its practical, aesthetic, and ethical dimensions, and provide a more complete understanding of the potential impact of the design.

Why

Learner empathy is important to good instructional design practice. This type of storytelling elicits imagination and empathy in design. Because it describes one of the ultimate goals of design—a positive user experience—it can be one of the most critical interim products of the design process. Patrick Parrish (2005) has been practicing this approach to design intuitively for years as a way to incorporate his concern for the aesthetic experience of learning. This tactic has been employed in architectural and information technology design processes for some time (see also Lawson, 1997; Löwgren & Stolterman, 2004).

Use It!

How

Instructional design prototyping often consists merely of screen and interaction mockups, sometimes with roughed-out content. Formative evaluation of these prototypes (when it happens) is often focused on understanding the degree to which objectives are met and whether the products demonstrate good usability. However, the final impact of online learning is the result of more than these elements. It depends on all the qualities of the learner experience, including its practical, aesthetic, and ethical dimensions.

A learner story is created in the prototyping phase of the design process—which includes consideration of the job or learning site and learner personalities, motivations, frustrations, constraints, ambitions, and desires—and depicts a typical learner engaged with the designed instruction. Using such stories, instructional designers can develop a richer understanding of the impact a particular instructional design will have on the learner's experience and final learning outcomes. These stories do more than flesh out design solutions; they enact them in dramatic rehearsal.

While writing these stories, the designer can better discern holes and fill in initially unconsidered aspects of the experience that might influence choice of design features. Such stories can be shared with clients as part of a design document to provide a better picture of the design qualities and how they meet criteria set forth in the analysis. The stories can also be shared with experts responsible for providing content as a way of communicating the type and tone of content desired. Like all prototypes, the story is a transition between analysis and design activities because it tests original assumptions about criteria and constraints, and how the design idea meets them. Stories are meant not to replace tangible prototypes and true formative evaluation with representative learners, but to augment them and to help in preparing better materials in advance of formative evaluation or beta tests.

Some guidelines for writing learner stories follow:

1. Write stories during the design phase of a project in order to explore an episode of use of (a) a key or problematic design feature; (b) a complete, coherent learning experience; or (c) an entire learning path.

2. Use analysis details as the backstory.

3. Include sufficient details to establish character and setting.

4. Put the learner in the story as you imagine his or her responses during the learning experience.

5. Improvise and allow yourself to be surprised by the outcome.

6. Write rapidly, almost automatically, to avoid rationalization.

7. Stick to a single idea or question, regardless of how narrow or broad.

8. Give the action immediacy. Use present tense and include learner responses to tangible elements of the design.

9. Explore as many aspects of the learner's experience as possible, including setting, motivations, desires, ambitions, and frustrations.

Learner stories should not just describe interaction with computer interfaces or instructional content in cognitive terms, but should also reveal learner personalities, motivations, ambitions, and desires.

Example from Patrick Parrish's Work

This story describes a complete learning experience with a self-paced product. It was used in a project plan to demonstrate to the client how key concerns were being addressed by the design.

Kim is a weather forecaster taking the Numerical Weather Prediction module as a required training assignment. She has less than a year of experience in the field and feels her education has prepared her in only a limited way. While she is dedicated to perform competently, she is a little skeptical about the need to learn what might be perceived as unnecessary details about numerical models. She is somewhat reluctant to complicate her forecast process, with its already significant time constraints, by including the need to analyze the performance of more than one model.

In the opening section of the module, the first thing Kim encounters is a realistic case, the type a forecaster might experience in the field. She immediately perceives the relevance of the content and becomes engaged with the problem of sorting out the performance discrepancies between the global model and the Weather Research and Forecasting (WRF) model. She attempts the interactions, which she finds challenging because they ask her to think about the implications of the differences between the global model and WRF guidance, with which she is unfamiliar. But because the presentation of the exercises is instructional rather than testlike, she doesn't feel inhibited about making the best guesses she can. What also adds to her comfort level in approaching this new content is that it supports what she already understands about the need to use a forecast funnel—to start with the large scale (including global scale model guidance) and work down to the mesoscale. After reviewing the case, she feels she knows what to expect to learn from the rest of the module.

Kim enters the second section of the module and finds it conveniently divided into four subsections, each addressing a key forecast problem (such as the effects of topography, which she knows frequently makes model forecasts suspect) and how the WRF model offers improved guidance for the problem. The small divisions make it easier for her because she is unsure whether she will get through the module in one sitting. As in the opening section, the first page in the Topography subsection begins with a case example. It provides two model products (one global, one WRF) with widely different depictions of winds and vertical motion in the same region. Identifying the differences is relatively easy, but once again she is asked to consider the further implications for weather impacts, which is not so easy. But she is prepared from the opening case interactions to make just an educated guess and then to learn from the results without embarrassment if she's way off. The next page is a very short continuation of the example, providing a couple of forecast verification products and a brief explanation of why the WRF model forecast was verified over the global model, not just in the details it depicted but in its characterization of the event. The third page is a more traditional instructional presentation about how the WRF model offers a major improvement in numerical weather prediction treatment of issues of topography (the traditional treatment is almost a relief after the previous difficult interactions). Kim begins to feel a growing, deeper understanding about how and when the WRF model will make a difference due to its more realistic depiction of topography. In the final page, her new understanding is confirmed as she reads about a few operational scenarios describing how other forecasters like her might use WRF data in their forecasts.

Adopt or Adapt

> This idea can be applied to any form of instruction, whether classroom, synchronous online learning, or self-paced.

Attribution

Submitted by Patrick Parrish, manager of instructional design and production, The COMET™ Program, University Corporation for Atmospheric Research, Boulder, Colorado, USA

Contact: pparrish@comet.ucar.edu

URL: http://meted.ucar.edu

References

Lawson, B. (1997). *How designers think: The design process demystified* (3rd ed.). Amsterdam: Architectural Press.

Löwgren, J., & Stolterman, E. (2004). *Thoughtful interaction design.* Cambridge, MA: MIT Press.

Parrish, P. E. (2005). Embracing the aesthetics of instructional design. *Educational Technology, 45*(2), 16–25.

Personalized Learning Model

The Big Idea

What

A personalized learning model is utilized to enhance learning outcomes.

Why

Using a personalized learning model can help the designer ensure that his or her designs adhere to current learning research and his or her personal values for teaching and learning.

Use It!

How

Margaret Martinez's research (see http://www.trainingplace.com/source/research/papers.htm) indicates that learners are often better supported by personalizing learning and tapping into emotions to improve learning. Too often designers encourage passivity by building memorization activities, rule-based learning, and one-size-fits-all and sage-on-the-stage instruction. New understandings and technologies challenge us to offer newer approaches that use emotion to fuel motivation, persistence, innovation, and achievement.

Martinez recommends an excellent book by James Zull, *The Art of Changing the Brain* (2002). It discusses recent advances in the neurosciences that highlight the impact of emotions on learning, memory, and performance. Highlighting David Kolb's active learning research, Zull (p. 18) describes the following four-step learning process:

> *Step 1: Concrete Experience.* The learner receives input from the external world through his or her senses.

> *Step 2: Reflective Observation.* The learner experiences and processes the sensory input in the temporal (back) integrative cortex of the brain

and tries to connect what is known and of personal value with new meanings and patterns.

Step 3: Abstract Hypothesis. The learner tries to integrate or synergize new meanings in the frontal integrative cortex (working memory) to create and test new ideas and solve problems.

Step 4: Active Testing. The learner executes the new ideas to perform and evaluate new actions (active learning) and acquires new knowledge and ability.

Martinez uses the "emotional brain" and her learning orientation research to create learner-centered instructional design models that personalize learning with objectives and strategies that tap into the individual's power of emotion to encourage self-motivation, self-direction, and autonomy for improved learning and performance.

Adopt or Adapt

Others can use this model or one that includes the strategies and components they feel are most important.

Attribution

Submitted by Margaret Martinez, president, The Training Place, Inc., Oro Valley, Arizona, USA

Contact: mmartinez@trainingplace.com

URL: http://www.trainingplace.com

Reference

Zull, J. E. (2002). *The art of changing the brain: Enriching teaching by exploring the biology of learning.* Sterling, VA: Stylus Publishing.

Content Templates

The Big Idea

What

Use a template to tell content experts exactly what content is needed in order to rapidly design online learning content.

Why

Templates can help content experts organize their expertise in a manner that quickly produces usable instructional content. The instructional designer then has well-organized content to work with. Templates can greatly reduce time and frustration in developing usable content, facilitating quicker design and development.

Use It!

How

Laura Summers worked with K–12 professional development content experts who are great face-to-face facilitators. When asked to translate what they do in front of an audience into online learning, they had a hard time, and Summers did not have the time to attend all of their face-to-face workshops to extract the content she needed.

The template helped the content experts organize their expertise with minimal instructional design guidance. The results provided good course content that incorporated real-life application and best practices into the classroom.

Once the content expert fills in the template, an instructional designer uses it to develop the module in Web pages. The pages are put into a learning management system that contains a discussion board, a blog, and a tracking system.

Laura Summers's Example of Content Template

This is an adapted version of Summers's template. A description of the needed content is in the left column. The content expert fills in the content in the right column.

Content Description	Write Content Here
Introduction	
Topic sentence: What is this course about? Write three reasons why this course is important. Keep in mind the new teacher!	
Objectives: Describe, in specific, measurable, and observable terms, the skills participants are expected to exhibit.	Participants in this course will. . . . [Verb based on Bloom's taxonomy]
Course Organization: Describe the organization of the course/module.	This [course/module] is made up of four parts: *Introduction.* Participants learn what the course is about and what is expected of them. *Part One.* Participants view a video presentation that highlights several applets (small computer programs) that can be used to enhance students' understanding of algebra concepts. *Part Two.* Participants conduct explorations of ideas and other applets, in search of those that will address specific classroom needs. *Part Three.* Participants complete a closing reflection and a course evaluation survey. [Insert standard navigation instructions here.]
Blog instructions: Describe the purpose of the blog and how to use it.	During this course you will be supported by a facilitator who will interact with you at assigned times during the course. This will be done through a blog. [Insert blog instructions here.]
Video	
Video and handout instructions: Describe the video, how to watch it, and where to get handouts.	In this part of the course, you will view a thirty-minute video presentation produced by [insert source] about [insert topic]. The presenter is [insert bio information about the presenter from site].

Content Description	Write Content Here
	Before you begin, download and print out the handouts posted below so you can follow the presentation. Since the presentation will include actual Web sites, you will find it helpful to open two separate screens on your computer, one on which you will view the video, the other on which you can go to the Web sites as they are demonstrated.
	When you have completed viewing the video, close the video window, return to the online course, and go on to the next page. There you will be given the opportunity to explore more deeply.
	[Insert standard video instructions here.]
Video reflection question: Write a question that helps participants consider the concepts presented in the video.	Go to the blog and respond to the following question about the video. [Add reflection question here.]
Activities	
Article: Supply a link to an online article that provides additional information. Provide a list of questions to consider while reading the article.	*URL:* [Add concise annotation.] *Questions to consider while reading this article:*
Application: Provide an activity that prompts participants to reflect on the concepts in the video. Example: Think about what you have read about how students learn mathematics. How do the applets you viewed in the video or the one you used with your class align with the ideas discussed in the chapter about student learning? Go to the blog and record your thoughts.	[Add activity here.]

Content Description	Write Content Here
Closing	
Closing Reflection: Write a question that helps participants reflect on the learning experience. Example: Go to the blog and reflect on this learning experience by addressing the following questions: In what way(s) was this course helpful to you as a professional? What tools did you find that you plan to use in the future?	Go to the blog and respond to the following question about the [course/module]. [Add reflection question here.]
Assessment: Describe assessment, if an assessment will be used.	
Survey	[Insert standard instructions for accessing survey here.]

Source: Laura Summers

Adopt or Adapt

Anyone who works with content experts can build content templates in order to facilitate better and more rapid content development. You may need to do some brief training or coaching so content experts know how best to fill in these templates. The process should also reduce the frustration that many content experts feel when working with instructional designers because the templates make clear what is needed.

Attribution

Submitted by Laura Summers, online learning team specialist, Centennial BOCES and University of Northern Colorado, Longmont, Colorado, USA

Contact: DrLSummers@SummersAlliance.com

Also involved: Dana Selzer, former director of learning services, Centennial BOCES, Longmont, Colorado, USA

Fast E-Learning Templates

The Big Idea

What

Create an e-learning content template with different page types (home, main menu, section introduction, section content, and so on) in Microsoft PowerPoint and add hyperlinks for menu navigation, URLs, references, and so on. Publish to FlashPaper to create cheap, fast, and easy Flash e-learning content with navigation and links.

Figure 7.6. PowerPoint E-Learning Template for Menu Page

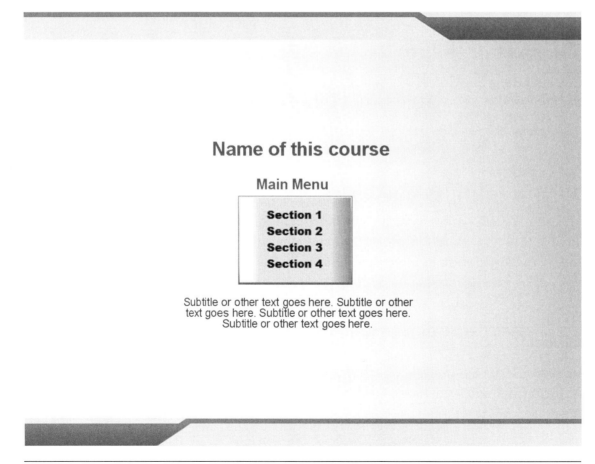

Source: Paul Clothier, http://www.learnhost.com

Figure 7.7. FlashPaper Menu Page

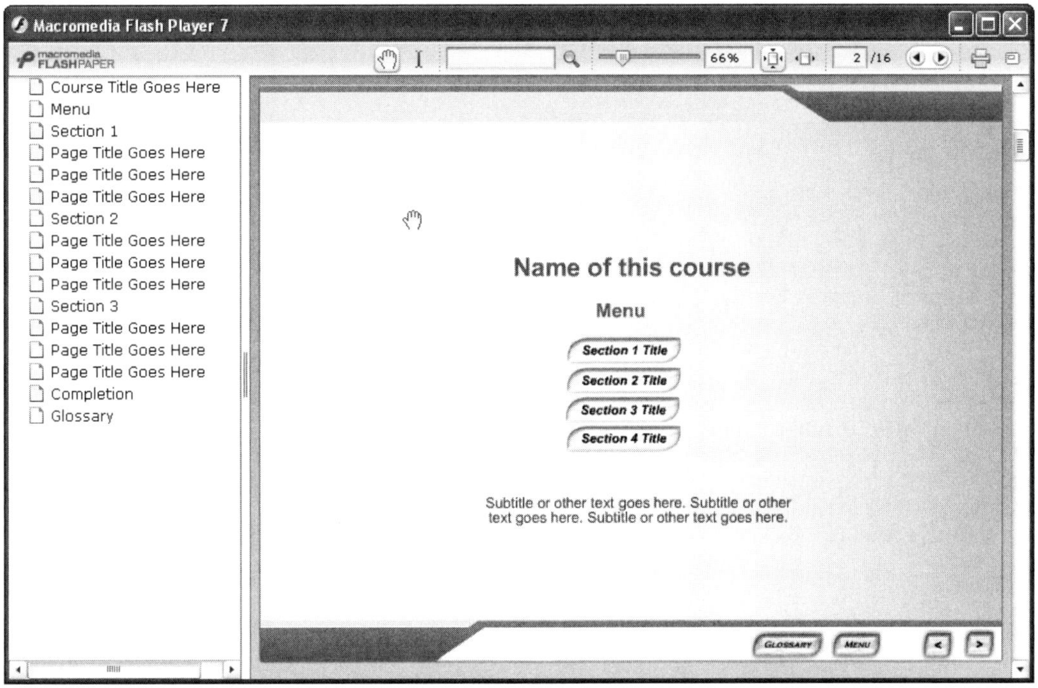

Source: Paul Clothier, http://www.learnhost.com

Figure 7.8. PowerPoint E-Learning Template for Content Page

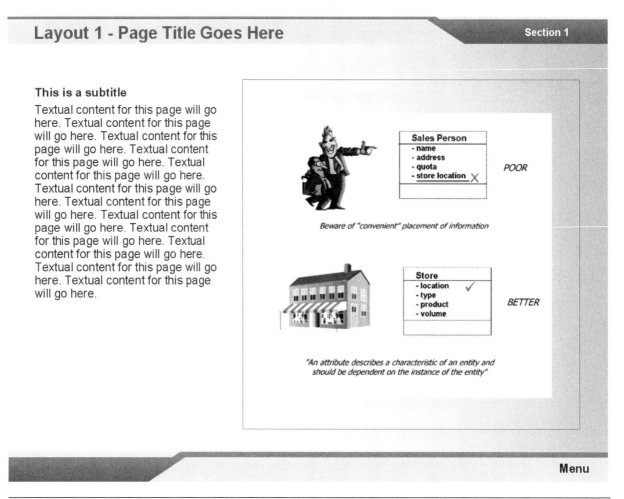

Source: Paul Clothier, http://www.learnhost.com

Figure 7.9. FlashPaper Content Page

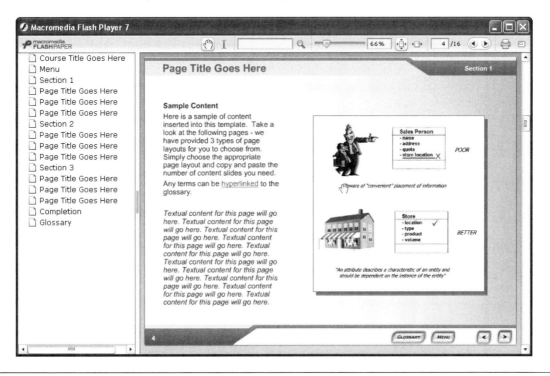

Source: Paul Clothier, http://www.learnhost.com

Why

This development method is extremely simple and inexpensive and lends itself to very rapid e-learning development for simple informational content.

Use It!

How

The desired template pages were developed in Microsoft PowerPoint, and FlashPaper was used to convert them to a Flash object. FlashPaper allows anyone to convert printable files easily into Flash documents. Create Flash documents that are immediately available cross-platform on any Web browser. These documents open within a Web page, eliminating the need for a separate viewer application.

Adopt or Adapt

Build PowerPoint template pages to which you or others can add simple informational content. Then add content and use FlashPaper to convert these pages to Flash objects. There are many other authoring tools that facilitate conversion of PowerPoint to Flash (for example, Articulate Presenter, Adobe Captivate, and Tech Smith Camtasia), so this idea could be adapted for use with other tools.

Attribution

Submitted by Paul Clothier, learning specialist, Sausalito, California, USA

Contact: paulc@learnhost.com

URL: http://www.learnhost.com

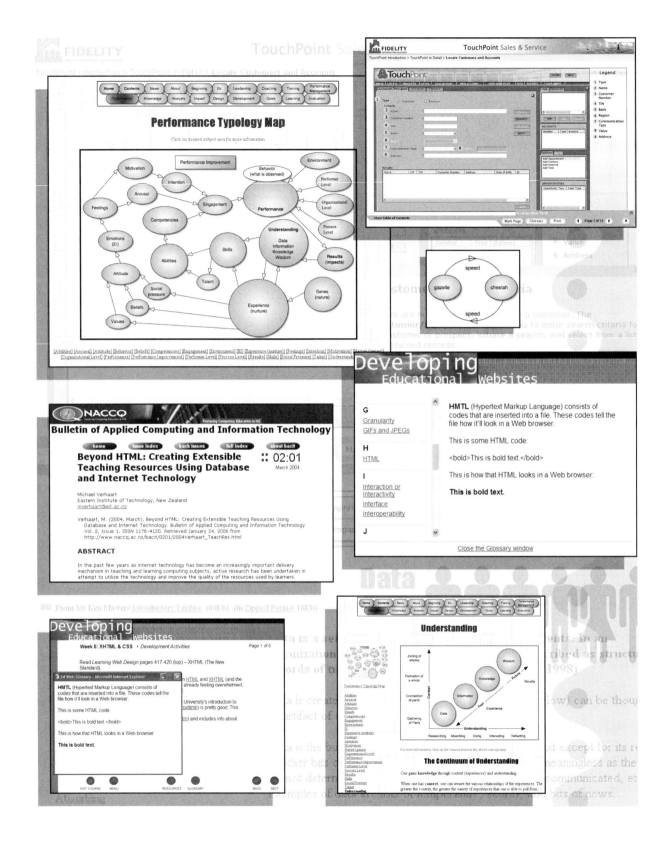

CHAPTER 8

Ideas for Navigation and Usability

T his chapter presents ideas that can augment navigation and usability. The Web is a relatively new medium for learning and doesn't work like print materials or video or other media. We need to consider ways to use it well and to help learners meet their goals without requiring unnecessary effort.

It's sometimes hard to remember, when building instructional materials, that form and function go hand in hand. If an object needs to perform a certain function, design should support that function. When people are learning online, they are there primarily to learn, not to be dazzled (which for learners is often spelled f-r-u-s-t-r-a-t-i-o-n). They have a lot to contend with on the computer screen alone: the browser, the navigational elements on the page, text, graphics, multimedia, branching, and so on. It's a lot to handle and users are overwhelmed more regularly than we realize.

Concept Maps and Causal Loops for Navigation

The Big Idea

What

When faced with a large domain of complex content, learners can be greatly assisted by seeing visual representations of how the smaller pieces relate to and affect each other. These visual representations are a good way to navigate complex content.

Figure 8.1. Top Level: Performance Map

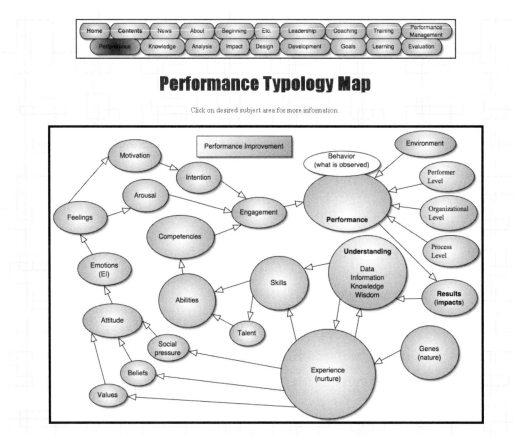

Source: Donald Clark, http://www.nwlink.com/~donclark

Figure 8.2. Understanding Map and Content

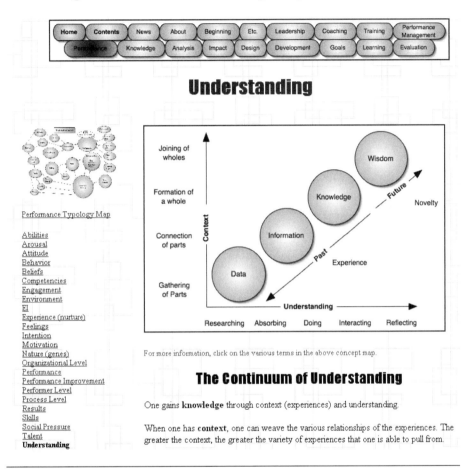

The Continuum of Understanding

One gains **knowledge** through context (experiences) and understanding.

When one has **context**, one can weave the various relationships of the experiences. The greater the context, the greater the variety of experiences that one is able to pull from.

Source: Donald Clark, http://www.nwlink.com/~donclark

Figure 8.3. Data Content

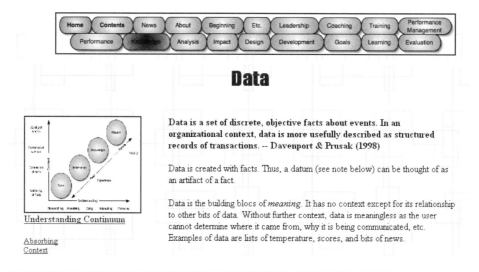

Source: Donald Clark, http://www.nwlink.com/~donclark

Why

When models are complex, this type of navigation can help users understand the big picture and the relationships among smaller parts that make up the big picture.

Use It!

How

Causal loop diagrams illustrate how variables are interconnected in dynamic ways. A causal loop diagram uses arrows that show how one variable affects another over time. For example, the casual loop in Figure 8.4 shows that cheetahs hunt gazelles, which in turn puts selection pressure on gazelles for running speed. As they evolve to be faster, pressure is in turn put back on the cheetahs to be faster.

Figure 8.4. Simple Causal Loop

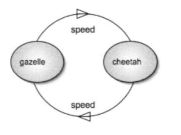

Source: Donald Clark, http://www.nwlink.com/~donclark

Concept maps are a graphical two-dimensional display of a knowledge domain. They comprise nodes connected by lines that indicate relationships. The maps shown in Figures 8.1, 8.2, and 8.3 illustrate how the individual variables involved in performance are related to and affect each other. Each of the variables is a hyperlink, so clicking on any of the variables drills down to content about that variable (and in some cases, an additional map with additional hyperlinks).

Most diagramming and charting software, such as Visio, SmartDraw, Omnigraffle, ConceptDraw, and Inspiration allow you to save a chart you have created as an HTML image map, to which hyperlinks can be added.

Adopt or Adapt

This approach can make navigation and understanding of any complex Web content easier. It can also be adapted for use in paper-based instructional materials by substituting page numbers or references in lieu of hyperlinks.

Attribution

Submitted by Donald Clark, Starbucks Coffee Corporation, Edmonds, Washington, USA

Contact: donclark@nwlink.com

URL: http://www.nwlink.com/~donclark

Collapsible and Movable Text Layer

The Big Idea

What

When the screen real estate doesn't allow enough space for needed text to explain a complex graphic, the text can be placed on a collapsible and movable layer that the learner can open and close or move. (See Figures 8.5 and 8.6.)

Figure 8.5. Text Layer Closed

Source: Patti Shank, http://www.learningpeaks.com

Figure 8.6. Text Layer Opened

Source: Patti Shank, http://www.learningpeaks.com

Why

Complex graphics that need to take up the entire screen (such as detailed screenshots) often require additional explanation. By putting that text on a collapsible and movable layer, learners can either look at the explanation and collapse it to see the entire graphic or move it elsewhere on the screen.

Use It!

How

Patti Shank's team developed a training program that includes many complex screenshots. For learners to see the screenshots at maximum size, the screenshots needed to take up most of the screen area, with just enough space for a legend.

Instancy, the developers who built the training from the team's design, used Macromedia Dreamweaver's Drag Layer action to provide a collapsible layer for explanatory text. Dreamweaver's Drag Layer functionality can specify the direction in which the layer can be dragged, where the layer snaps to, and more. First a layer is drawn (Insert > Layer) and then the Behaviors panel is used to select functionality. This functionality is available for most 5.x+ browsers.

Adopt or Adapt

This functionality is useful when the screen size doesn't allow enough space for explanatory text. It could also be used to create collapsible elements that will be used regularly, such as a table of contents, glossary, or references.

Attribution

Submitted by Patti Shank, president, Learning Peaks, LLC, Centennial, Colorado, USA

Contact: info@learningpeaks.com

URL: http://www.learningpeaks.com

Also involved: Eric Replinger, Flambeau Productions, Inc., Centennial, Colorado; Kunal Thakkar, project manager, Instancy, Inc., Cary, North Carolina, USA; and Scott Berrett, e-learning specialist, Fidelity Information Services, Little Rock, Arkansas, USA

Automated Back and Next Buttons and Page Numbering

The Big Idea

What

The links for Back and Next buttons on each page are often manually coded as are page numbers (for example, page 1 of 5). So if you add a page, remove a page, or change the order of pages, you have to edit the links and page numbers manually on all the affected pages. This idea automates both Back and Next button links and page numbering with JavaScript, eliminating the hassle of making changes.

Figure 8.7. Automated Back, Next, and Page Numbering

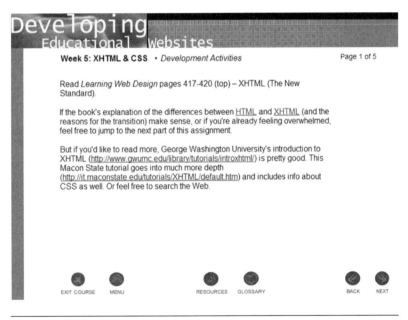

Source: Eric Replinger

Why

This idea saves time and effort in that if you make a change, all you have to change is the list of pages in the JavaScript array; you don't have to edit any of the links. The same list of pages that make the Back and Next buttons work also automate the page numbering.

Use It!

How

The original code for this idea is from Ken Ward's JavaScript Tutorial site (http://www.trans4mind.com/personal_development/JavaScript/Back ForwardNew.htm), but Eric Replinger made two enhancements to the original idea.

1. The original code uses alerts to tell the user if they try to go back from the first page or forward from the last page. Replinger added the lesson menu page to the beginning and end of the list of file names so that if users click back from the first page, they go to the menu; if they click forward from the last page, they go to the menu. No more annoying alert boxes, just nice clean navigation.

2. Adding the line "n=NumberOfFiles-1;" in the JavaScript code made it easy to automate the page numbering. Here's how the page number code looks in the lesson page:

```
<script language="JavaScript"
type="text/javascript">document.write("Page " + ThisPageNumber +
" of " + (n-1));
</script>
```

Adopt or Adapt

This idea can be used in any Web materials where automating the Back and Next buttons and page numbering makes sense.

Attribution

Submitted by Eric Replinger, Flambeau Productions, Centennial, Colorado, USA

Double Use Glossary

The Big Idea

What

If you have terms that are new to learners, it is beneficial to provide definitions both from the pages in the course and from a common glossary that contains all the definitions in the course.

Figure 8.8. Definitions from Course Page

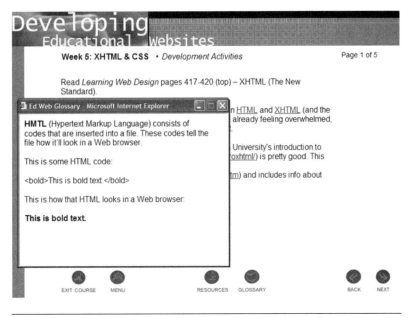

Source: Eric Replinger

Figure 8.9. Definitions from Glossary

Source: Eric Replinger

Why

This idea allows learners to get definitions by clicking on term links within course pages and by opening the glossary and searching for the term. Populating both from the same HTML file saves time and makes maintenance easier.

Use It!

How

The first step was to create each definition in a separate HTML page. To display the definition from a link on a page in the course, Replinger used Dreamweaver's Open Browser Window behavior. To display the definitions in the glossary window, Replinger created a page with two iframes. The left iframe contains the table of contents for the glossary. Then, when you click a glossary term, the definition is displayed in the right iframe.

Here's what the HTML looks like on the page:

```
<p> If the book's explanation of the differences between <a
href="javascript:;"
onclick="MM_openBrWindow('./glossary/html.htm','','scrollbars=yes,width=
420,height=296')">HTML</a> and <a href="javascript:;"
onclick="MM_openBrWindow('./glossary/xhtml.htm','','scrollbars=yes,width
=420,height=296')">XHTML</a> (and the reasons for the transition) make
sense, or if you're already feeling overwhelmed, feel free to jump to the next
part of this assignment.</p>
```

Within the iframe (actually, within the toc.htm document that opens in the left iframe), the target attribute in the anchor tag forces the html.htm definition to open in the right iframe (named "iframecontent" as opposed to the left iframe, which is named "iframetoc") and looks like this:

```
<li><a href="html.htm" target="iframecontent">HTML</a></li>
```

Adopt or Adapt

This idea can be used in Web materials when it would be beneficial to have links to definitions on pages and a glossary that is maintained from the same file. This same idea might also be useful for maintaining other files that appear in two places, such as tips and hints.

Attribution

Submitted by Eric Replinger, Flambeau Productions, Centennial, Colorado, USA

Automated Reference

The Big Idea

What

> Academic authors often supply reference text for online materials so a
> reader can use it to properly reference the materials. The automated refer-
> ence code automatically adds the Date Retrieved (the current date) and the
> URL (the current location) to the reference.

Figure 8.10. Automated Date and URL for Reference

Source: Michael Verhaart, http://is-research.massey.ac.nz/verhaart

Why

> This idea helps those citing your work to cite it correctly (no small feat!),
> and if you move your work to another location, it automatically grabs the
> new URL.

Use It!

How

The following code when added to a page produces a one-paragraph reference where the Date Retrieved (current date) and the URL (current location) are automatically created. The following JavaScript goes in the head section:

```
<script language="JavaScript">
var monthName = new Array();
monthName[0]="January";monthName[1]="February";
monthName[2]="March";monthName[3]="April";
monthName[4]="May";monthName[5]="June";
monthName[6]="July";monthName[7]="August";
monthName[8]="September";monthName[9]="October";
monthName[10]="November";monthName[11]="December";
</script>
```

The following combination of HTML and JavaScript goes where you want the reference to appear:

```
<p>Verhaart, M. (2004, March), Beyond HTML: Creating Extensible Teaching
Resources Using Database and Internet Technology. Bulletin of Applied Comput-
ing and Information Technology, Vol. 2, Issue 1. ISSN 1176–4120. Retrieved
<script>var now=new Date();document.write(monthName[now.getMonth()] +
" " + now.getDate() +", " + now.getFullYear())</script> from <script>document.
write(window.location)</script> </p>
```

which gives a reference in the form:

Verhaart, M. (2004, March), Beyond HTML: Creating Extensible Teaching Resources Using Database and Internet Technology. Bulletin of Applied Computing and Information Technology, Vol. 2, Issue 1. ISSN 1176–4120. Retrieved January 24, 2006 from http://www.naccq.ac.nz/bacit/0201/2004Verhaart_TeachRes.html

Adopt or Adapt

If you are putting academic materials on the Web, it's valuable to make it easy for others to reference them correctly. This idea makes it easier for readers to cite your materials with the correct date retrieved and URL.

Attribution

Submitted by Michael Verhaart, principal lecturer, Eastern Institute of Technology, Hawke's Bay, Taradale, New Zealand

Contact: mverhaart@eit.ac.nz

URL: http://is-research.massey.ac.nz/verhaart

Here's What's New

The Big Idea

What

When new information is regularly posted to an instructional site, it's often hard for learners to find what's new. Better organization of content and files is commonly needed but may not be enough. An automated graphic that indicates what is new but that disappears at a specified time can help learners find new information quickly.

Figure 8.11. Automated "New" Graphic

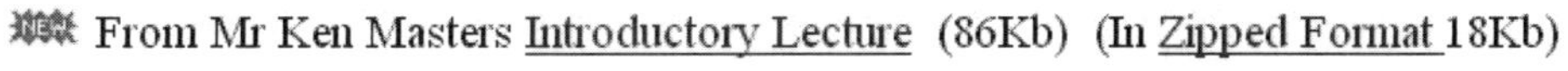

From Mr Ken Masters <u>Introductory Lecture</u> (86Kb) (In <u>Zipped Format </u>18Kb)

Source: Ken Masters

Why

In combination with other organizational strategies, this idea saves learners time and frustration.

Use It!

How

This solution combines a "new" graphic placed next to the new information, and JavaScript that sets the date that the "new" graphic expires (and therefore disappears). This allows learners to check periodically for new information by looking for the "new" graphic.

This code was adapted from Nic's JavaScript Page http://www.javascript-page.com/expnew.html.

In the head section place the following code:

```
<HEAD>
<SCRIPT LANGUAGE="JavaScript">
<!—
// please keep these lines on when you copy the source
// made by: Nicolas—http://www.javascript-page.com
var image = "images/new.gif"
function expnew(when) {
when = new Date(when)
date = new Date()
if (when.getTime() > date.getTime()) {
document.write("<img src="+image+">")
}
}
//—>
</SCRIPT>
```

In the body section, place the following code before the item to be tagged as new (for example, in a bulleted list of files):

```
<LI><SCRIPT language="Javascript">
<!—expnew("01/16/2008")
//—>
</SCRIPT>
From Mr. Ken Masters <A HREF= [link to materials]. . .>Introductory Lecture
</A>
```

The date input here indicates that the gif will expire on January 16, 2008.

You will also need to find or develop an animated or nonanimated graphic that appears when the script is called. In the script just provided, the image new.gif was placed inside an images folder (images/new.gif); this is the image that is called up by the script.

Adopt or Adapt

Build or find a "new" graphic and then use this script to call it up (and then expire). This approach could also be used with the same script but another graphic to point out other important information (such as Start here!) on a site.

Attribution

Submitted by Ken Masters, University of Cape Town, Cape Town, Western Cape Province, South Africa

Contact: kam@its.uct.ac.za

Well, it does really, doesn't it?

CHAPTER 9

Ideas for Creative Design

Although instructional design is generally seen as a structured process, it's called instructional *design* for a reason. *Design* implies using creativity and innovation, within the bounds of foundational principles, to solve a problem or achieve a goal. Consider how an interior or landscape designer comes up with his or her plans or how a graphic designer determines the look of a business card and you'll understand the nature of design work.

This chapter showcases ideas for creative design. Some designers have a background in instructional design, but a lot of online instruction is designed by people with all sorts of backgrounds. That's actually a good thing because different views can increase creativity. So this chapter is for everyone who designs instruction, no matter what background they have.

Many designers (like other people in other jobs) have a more-or-less typical way of designing instruction and too often their instructional materials begin to have a cookie cutter look and feel. Great for cookies, bad for instruction.

One myth about creativity and design is that creative equals expensive. Not so (or not always so). In fact, it can take extra creativity to design well with fewer resources.

Funny Stats

The Big Idea

What

A humorous and engaging storyline can help learners understand difficult concepts and lessen anxiety.

Figure 9.1. Squirrel Intelligence

Source: Kognito Solutions, http://www.kognito.net

Figure 9.2. Analyzing Payout Claims

Source: Kognito Solutions, http://www.kognito.net

Why

It can be easier to understand difficult or intimidating concepts when they are embedded in an entertaining story.

Use It!

How

The Kognito team developed Adventures in Statistics (http://www.kognito.net/stat) to help learners taking introductory statistics courses understand topics that many learners struggle with. The interactive supplement to statistics textbooks and courses utilizes humorous cartoon characters, animations, and stories to reduce the all-too-typical statistics anxiety that can interfere with learning.

The five modules explain and illustrate common introductory statistics topics such as normal distribution, standard deviation, confidence intervals, hypothesis testing, and common statistical tests. The first module, for example, uses a story about determining typical (mean) squirrel IQ scores and variability (variance). The third module follows an investigative journalist who is attempting to analyze a gambling company's claims about their payout levels (hypothesis testing). Additional resources include a study guide, assignments, and quiz questions.

The course was built using Flash and XML.

Adopt or Adapt

This idea could be adapted anywhere a humorous approach to a difficult or intimidating concept is appropriate. For example, new employee orientation could be embedded in a company scavenger hunt storyline. Training on departmental budgeting could employ a financial superhero storyline. It may not be appropriate to take a humorous approach to some topics, so caution is advised.

Attribution

Submitted by Ralph Vacca, director of learning technology, Kognito Solutions, LLC, New York, New York, USA

Contact: info@kognito.net

URL: http://www.kognito.net

Take the Metro

The Big Idea

What

When the learning objectives include knowing what questions to ask and what path to take on the basis of the answers, a Metro (subway) map navigation makes lots of sense.

Figure 9.3. Metro Stop

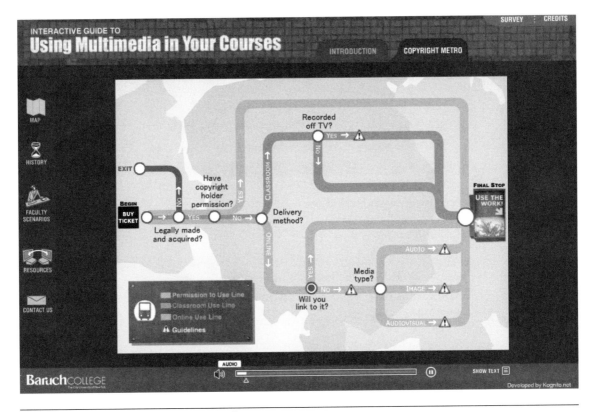

Source: Kognito Solutions, http://www.kognito.net

Figure 9.4. Question

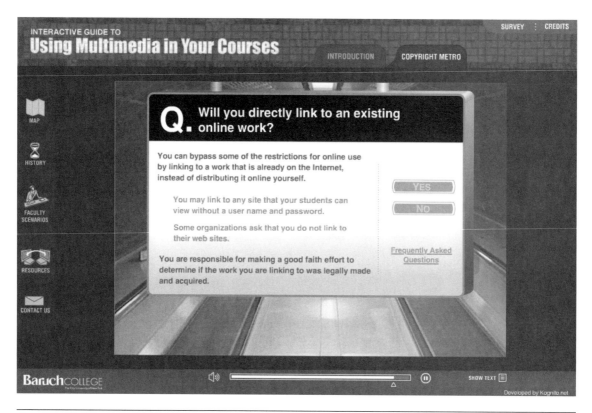

Source: Kognito Solutions, http://www.kognito.net

Why

The Metro map navigation metaphor makes the questions and paths clear to the learner.

Use It!

How

Baruch College's *Interactive Guide to Using Copyrighted Media in Your Courses* (http://www.baruch.cuny.edu/tutorials/copyright) helps faculty determine what copyright guidelines they need to follow when using different types

Figure 9.5. Printable Summary

A Baruch faculty member or adjunct professor **may link to copyrighted media** that is already on the Internet under the following conditions:

1. The link will only be given to students enrolled in his or her class.
2. His or her class must be part of Baruch's regular credit-bearing offerings.
3. The link will only be transmitted through a secure, password-protected system like Blackboard.
4. The media on the site is directly relevant to the teaching content of the course – it is not for entertainment or research.
5. If no copyright notice appears on the site, students will be informed that the work may be copyright protected.
6. The media on the site has been legally made and acquired.
7. The site does not require users to enter a user name and password.
8. The site does not restrict linking (e.g. in its "Terms of Use" section).

Source: Kognito Solutions, http://www.kognito.net

of copyrighted media in their courses. The Kognito team developed this course to help faculty determine when they can use copyrighted media, so they won't find themselves in a situation where they may infringe on copyright law.

The path of the tutorial takes the learner from the ticket booth on the left to the final stop on the right (see Figure 9.3). At each stop, learners are asked a specific question about a specific work they wish to use, and their answers determine which path they will take and the next stop/question and so on until they get to the final stop. Arrival at the final stop means the media can be used. A summary of the guidelines to follow for the path they took (for example, linking to a work in an online course) is made available at the end for printing.

The course was built using Flash and XML.

Adopt or Adapt

A similar approach would work well for instruction where it is important for learners to recognize and follow the path that should be taken under different circumstances.

Attribution

Submitted by Ralph Vacca, director of learning technology, Kognito Solutions, LLC, New York, New York, USA

Contact: info@kognito.net

URL: http://www.kognito.net

Metaphors to Aid Learning

The Big Idea

What

Unfamiliar or confusing concepts can be made easier to understand by using a good metaphor.

Why

Metaphors help learners see how unfamiliar or confusing content is like something they already know. Well-chosen metaphors can also improve motivation and fun.

Use It!

How

John MacCarfrae, based in Liverpool, England, builds classroom, blended, and online workshops that use one of the world's most successful teams, the Beatles, as a metaphor. Course names begin with "All You Need Is" to further enhance the metaphor. The Beatles were renowned musicians and one can apply their particular critical success factors—including teamwork, collaboration, communication, marketing, branding, selling, and personal development, to name but a few—to other situations.

Using the Beatles character styles in this way is purely a metaphor and does not necessarily represent the actual Beatles characters themselves.

Adopt or Adapt

Consider what types of metaphors might be useful for making your content clearer. For example, a complex process might have similarities to planning an event, or a new application might work like a well-known online store. There are a few caveats when using this approach. Make sure not to select metaphors that may be offensive or worn-out (sports metaphors feel this way to many) and be sure to make clear how the new concept is different from the metaphor so learners don't expect them to act or work exactly the same.

Attribution

Submitted by John MacCarfrae, director, Maverick, Liverpool, United Kingdom

Contact: info@maverickelearningplace.com

URL: www.mavericktraining.co.uk

Stories to Understand the Big Picture

The Big Idea

What

Online stories help novices build industry knowledge and understand roles, responsibilities, and work processes.

Figure 9.6. Health Care Industry Basics Course

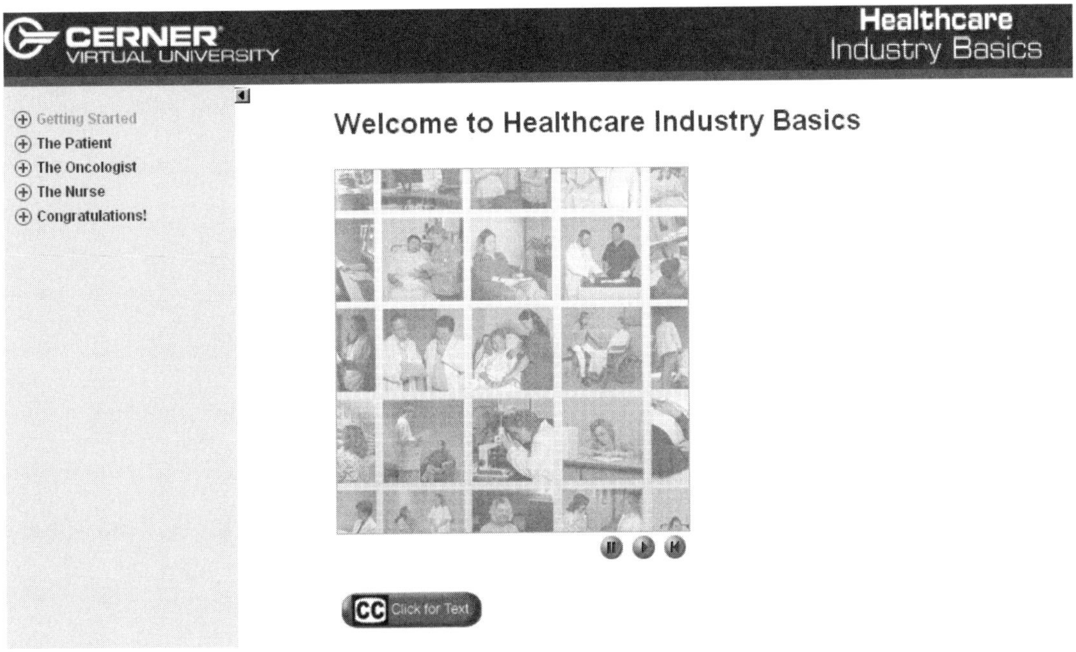

Source: Cerner Corporation, http://www.cerner.com

Figure 9.7. Terry, Patient

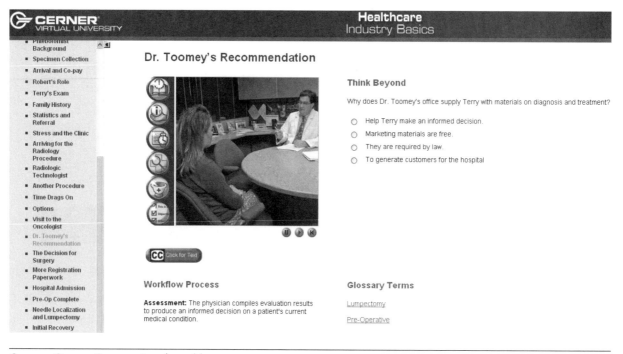

Source: Cerner Corporation, http://www.cerner.com

Why

Stories are a powerful and engaging way to learn. They help learners see the big picture in a meaningful way.

Use It!

How

Stories can help people new to a field better understand how that field works, including key terminology, important facts, key concepts, rules and procedures, people and roles, and important principles. The story behind Figures 9.6, 9.7, and 9.8 contains a main character, supporting characters,

Figure 9.8. Scenario: Nurse

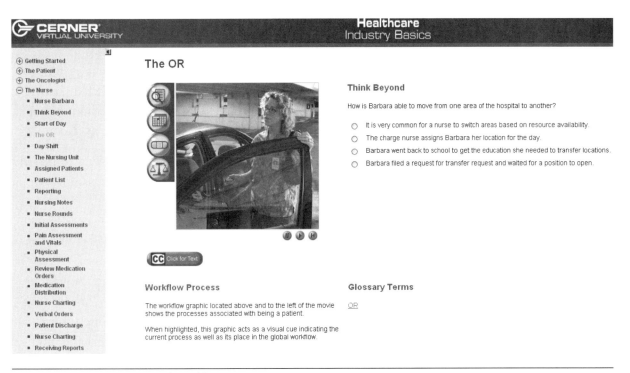

Source: Cerner Corporation, http://www.cerner.com

dramatic conflicts, and emotional content. It is presented in integrated chapters that contain scenarios depicting a specific health care industry experience.

The story was created for a self-paced online course in which the learner follows a patient, nurse, oncologist, radiologist, medical technologist, pharmacist, patient accounts manager, and physician office manager through integrated scenarios. In the patient scenario, the learner follows the main character, Terry, who is diagnosed with cancer, and watches him interact with a primary care physician, a physician specialist, nurses, and other clinicians. The nurse scenario tells the story from the nurse's perspective, the oncologist scenario tells the story from the perspective of the oncologist, and so on. The scenarios introduce the learner to health care terminology and processes, key players and tasks, key drivers, and health care regulatory and government agencies affecting each role, department, or process.

Learners are asked throughout the scenarios to respond to questions intended to help them reflect on what they are seeing and how it applies to them. Questions are not scored but detailed feedback is provided. Learners say that they relate to the stories and that the questions help them better understand their work environment and the people working in it.

The course was developed in HTML and Flash for delivery over a standard Internet connection. It primarily uses pictures and audio (a narrator) to tell the story.

Adopt or Adapt

This approach would be valuable for foundational big-picture knowledge, like understanding roles and responsibilities, processes, and workflow. A story approach could be used to facilitate an experience in which the learner becomes emotionally involved with the content, improving attention and learning of concepts and domains.

Attribution

Submitted by Stephen Smith, senior learning architect, Cerner Corporation, Kansas City, Missouri, USA

Contact: Ssmith2@Cerner.com

URL: http://www.foleyworks.com/HCB_Demo/index.htm

Also involved: Shawn Foley, learning strategist, Cerner Virtual University, Cerner Corporation, Kansas City, Missouri, USA

Virtual Coach

The Big Idea

What

Use multiple virtual experts to let learners hear a range of opinions.

Figure 9.9. Virtual Coaches' Answers, Question 1

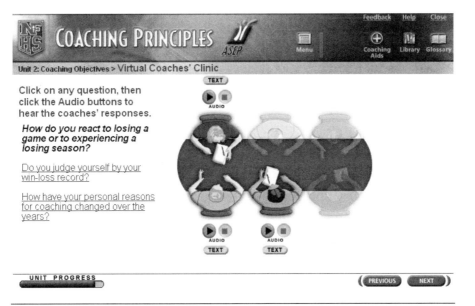

Source: American Sport Education Program, 2004, Coaching Principles Online.
© 2004 by American Sport Education Program. Reprinted with permission from
Human Kinetics, Champaign, Illinois.

Figure 9.10. Virtual Coaches' Answers, Question 2

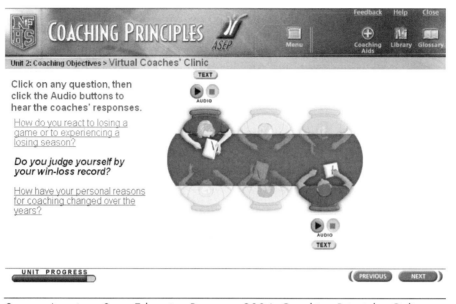

Source: American Sport Education Program, 2004, Coaching Principles Online.
© 2004 by American Sport Education Program. Reprinted with permission from
Human Kinetics, Champaign, Illinois.

Why

Some situations have more than one right answer. In those situations, it's
important for learners to be exposed to multiple perspectives.

Use It!

How

At the end of each unit in the Coaching Principles Online course, the
learner enters the Virtual Coaches Clinic. Six virtual coaches are seated at a
table, as if they are in roundtable discussion. For each listed question, the
learner uses a mouse to roll over each coach to get detailed information

about that coach and then clicks on the audio or transcript controls to listen to or read that coach's answer to the question. By listening to all opinions, the learner is exposed to a range of approaches and opinions.

Dean Hixson and his team at Human Kinetics wanted to introduce learners—novice sport coaches—to some of the questions and challenges they would face in the field, but these questions did not have one correct answer. Virtual coaches become a window into the culture of sport coaching; the right answer was situational at best and was derived from the oral tradition of coaches' education, in which novices learn from the anecdotes and advice of mentors. The objective, then, was for learners to seek the opinions and expertise of trusted peers. The answers for these questions were gathered and in some cases passed along verbatim from interviews with respected coaches, who were then fictionalized in an audio-based roundtable discussion simulation.

The course was built using HTML, JavaScript, CSS, and Flash. Clicking on a coach's image displays a close-up of that coach via JavaScript and CSS. Clicking on a text link displays a transcript of the associated audio via JavaScript and CSS. The Play button is a Flash element programmed to play a referenced external MP3 file.

Adopt or Adapt

This approach would work well wherever it is important for learners to see that there are varying answers and opinions.

Attribution

Submitted by Dean Hixson, instructional designer, Human Kinetics, Champaign, Illinois, USA

Contact: deanh@hkusa.com

URL: http://www.hkusa.com

Also involved: Stuart Cartwright, senior graphic designer, and Michael Wichlin, course production specialist, both from Human Kinetics, Champaign, Illinois, USA

Field Clinic

The Big Idea

What

Multiple scenarios provide a realistic way to let learners practice assessing and responding to injuries.

Figure 9.11. Field Clinic

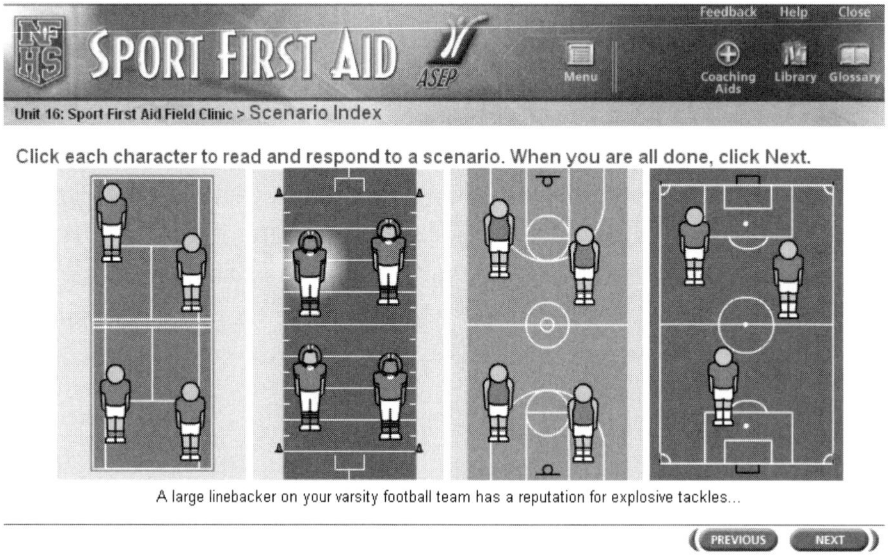

Source: American Sport Education Program, 2004, Coaching Principles Online. © 2004 by American Sport Education Program. Reprinted with permission from Human Kinetics, Champaign, Illinois.

Figure 9.12. Field Clinic, Tennis Player

Source: American Sport Education Program, 2004, Coaching Principles Online. © 2004 by American Sport Education Program. Reprinted with permission from Human Kinetics, Champaign, Illinois.

Why

Learners gain a wide range of realistic practice.

Use It!

How

In the Sport First Aid Online course, the Field Clinic activity presents four sports venues (tennis court, football field, basketball court, and soccer field). Learners select virtual athletes in each of these venues and see a textual overview of their injuries. Learners answer a series of questions and gain feedback.

Figure 9.13. Field Clinic, Tennis Player, Response

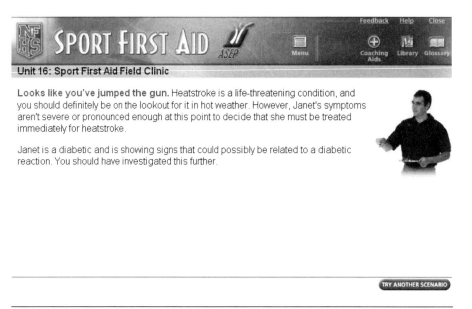

Dean Hixson's team at Human Kinetics wanted to provide a summative activity where the learner would be challenged to recognize the type of injury that had likely occurred in a given scenario and identify the correct first-aid response. Earlier units of the course required learners to demonstrate comprehension of first-aid procedures for various categories of injuries, but learners also needed to know what to do when they didn't know the exact type or severity of an athlete's injury, which is typical. They also wanted to provide an engaging, challenging, gamelike activity that would motivate learners to practice their skills in a realistic way.

The course was built using Flash, ActionScript, HTML, JavaScript, and CSS. It relies on Flash Shared Objects (SOs) as the data-storage device instead of cookies or a database. Each question page in the activity sets a value in an SO (via a home-grown JavaScript-to-Flash communication method) depending on whether the learner correctly answers the question. The front Flash-driven menu page then reads the values of the SOs and changes the icon displayed next to each clickable player image accordingly.

Adopt or Adapt

This course provides opportunities for learners to practice in the range of potential situations in which they will find themselves in real life.

Attribution

Submitted by Dean Hixson, instructional designer, Human Kinetics, Champaign, Illinois, USA

Contact: deanh@hkusa.com

URL: http://www.hkusa.com

Also involved: Greg George, instructional designer, Kevin Wright, instructional designer, Stuart Cartwright, senior graphic designer, Jason Mock, course programmer-analyst, and Yury Borukhovich, course programmer-analyst, all from Human Kinetics, Champaign, Illinois, USA

Outrageous Nonexamples

The Big Idea

What

Outrageous but clear nonexamples help learners recognize what *not* to do.

Figure 9.14. Abused Apostrophes Home

The Language LIVE Home for Abused Apostrophes

<u>Abused Apostrophes</u> | <u>Contracted Words</u> | <u>Ownership</u> | <u>It's and its</u> |
<u>Sad examples</u>

The rural beauty of Cornwall is the ideal setting for sanctuary. Donkeys flourish in the Donkey Rest Home near Bodmin, and seals down at Gweek.

The Home for Abused Apostrophes in Truro is a haven for little punctuation marks which have been cruelly misused by greengrocers and other uncaring notice-writers. Here they may be cosseted and coddled by a punctuation-enthusiast; allowed to mix with other survivors of apostrophe-abuse; perhaps one day returned to the community to do useful work <u>in contracted words</u> or <u>to show ownership</u>.

Click to visit

- <u>a tragically misplaced apostrophe</u>
- <u>a "greeting's" card</u>
- <u>numerical challenge in the supermarket</u>
- <u>the fallen apostrophes of Cambridge</u>
- <u>Texan doubles</u>
- <u>visitor's to high places</u>
- <u>a sad case of hubri's</u>

Source: Sue Palmer, http://www.suepalmer.co.uk

Figure 9.15. Apostrophe Misuse Example 1

Well, it does really, doesn't it?

Source: Sue Palmer, http://www.suepalmer.co.uk

Figure 9.16. Apostrophe Misuse Example 2

All God's children get Easter Eggs, but only one of God's adolescents. Perhaps this helps account for their general churlishness.

Source: Sue Palmer, http://www.suepalmer.co.uk

Why

Humor can be loads of fun and have exceptional impact.

Use It!

How

Sue Palmer is an independent literacy specialist who facilitates courses on how to teach writing, grammar, and spelling, and writes books and educational television programs on literacy, children's poems, stories, and nonfiction.

Palmer describes the part of her Web site that she calls "The Language LIVE Home for Abused Apostrophes" as "a haven for little punctuation marks that have been cruelly misused by greengrocers and other uncaring notice-writers. Here they may be cosseted and coddled by a punctuation-enthusiast; allowed to mix with other survivors of apostrophe-abuse; perhaps one day returned to the community to do useful work in contracted words or to show ownership." In other words, it's a place to learn how to use apostrophes correctly.

This part of Palmer's site is exceptionally humorous and combines very clear nonexamples taken from real life (along with her humorous commentary) with advice on how to use apostrophes so they don't need to end up at her "home."

Adopt or Adapt

Humor can be applied to many types of content and instruction. Using it to illustrate nonexamples is a natural. This is the point at which I am supposed to warn you to use humor judiciously, but I've decided to let you worry about that yourself.

Attribution

Submitted by Sue Palmer, educational writer, Truro, Cornwall, United Kingdom

URL: http://www.suepalmer.co.uk

What I Really Think

The Big Idea

What

Simple media can effectively tell a dramatic story. Add lots of drama and the sky is the limit.

Figure 9.17. Incoming Email

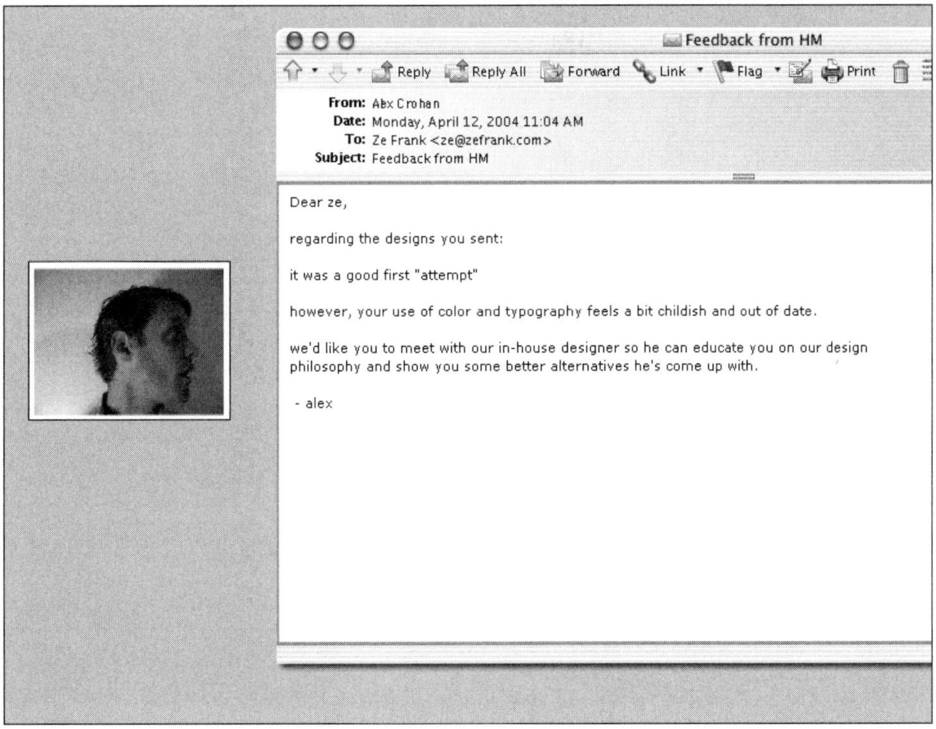

Source: Ze Frank, http://www.zefrank.com

Figure 9.18. Response I Want to Send

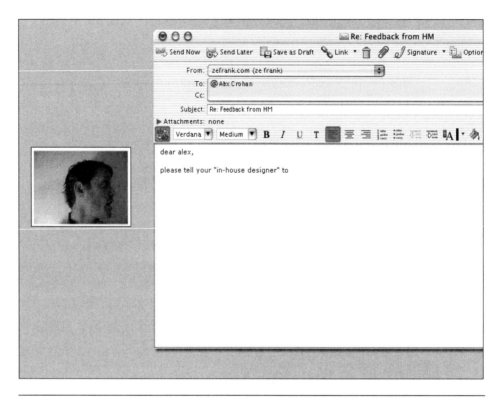

Source: Ze Frank, http://www.zefrank.com

Why

Simple media elements can deliver a message with a lot of impact. Humor elements can be very effective, but what's appropriate will vary.

Use It!

How

Ze Frank is a humorous writer, speaker, and graphic artist with an exceptionally funny Web site. While skimming it one day I found his Punctua-

Figure 9.19. Response I Actually Send

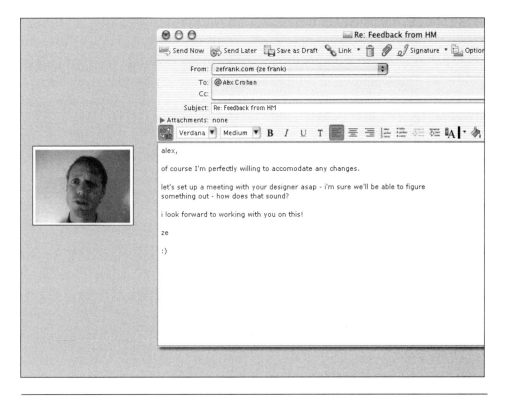

Source: Ze Frank, http://www.zefrank.com

tion Substitution video and found myself laughing because it was very effective at making a dramatic point by using simple media (video, audio, screen captures). Frank dramatizes how people send you emails you wish you could respond rudely to but can't (or shouldn't, even if you could). (Warning: Some people will likely find this offensive. Don't say I didn't warn you.)

Check out the other educational videos and gamelike pages on his site for more inspiration on how to use simple media to amuse, annoy, and demonstrate.

This site was developed with a digital camera, Apple iMovie, and Flash.

Adopt or Adapt

This idea shows how a message with a great deal of impact can be delivered with very simple media elements. It clearly shows the humor in not saying what you really mean in emails. This kind of approach (perhaps implemented in a more sensitive manner) could be used to make a strong point or show behind-the-scenes feelings in cases used for learning.

Attribution

Submitted by Ze Frank, zefrank productions, Brooklyn, New York, USA

Contact: ze@zefrank.com

URL: http://www.zefrank.com

Virtual Campus

The Big Idea

What

Develop a virtual campus with amusing tutorials for distance learners to help them get off to a good start.

Figure 9.20. Main Menu

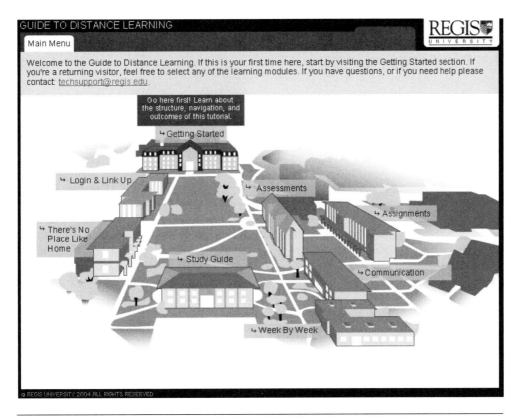

Source: Distance Learning, Regis University, School for Professional Studies, http://www.regis.edu/sps.htm

Figure 9.21. Guide to Distance Learning

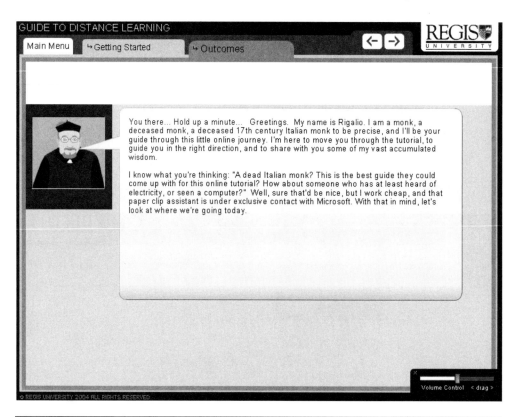

Source: Distance Learning, Regis University, School for Professional Studies,
http://www.regis.edu/sps.htm

Why

A virtual campus graphical interface with embedded tutorials helps distance learners "visit," connect, and get onboard.

Use It!

How

Regis University's Distance Learning Team developed the Guide to Distance Learning tutorial with a graphical interface of a virtual campus in

Figure 9.22. Assignments Overview

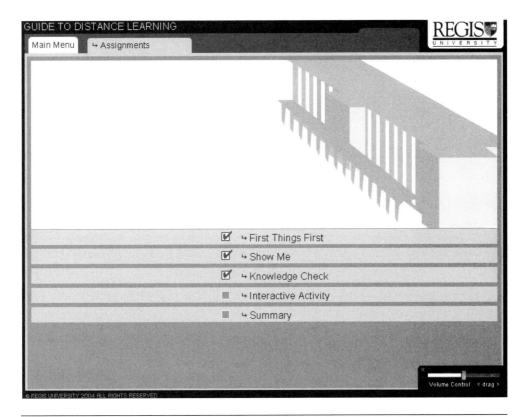

Source: Distance Learning, Regis University, School for Professional Studies, http://www.regis.edu/sps.htm

order to prepare distance learners for a successful distance learning experience. The main menu shows numerous buildings, each of which corresponds to a module within the tutorial. The tutorial includes modules that help learners use the tutorial, discover how to get into their online courses, find and use the course syllabus and other course resources, use course management system elements, complete and submit course assignments, and communicate with the instructor and other participants. When the learner places the mouse over any of the buildings, a description of that module is displayed. Click on any building and that module starts with an overview. As each element in the module is completed, it is checked off.

Figure 9.23. Assignments Demo

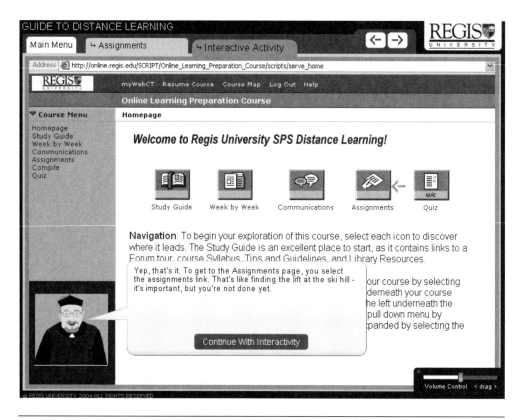

Source: Distance Learning, Regis University, School for Professional Studies, http://www.regis.edu/sps.htm

The tutorial contains numerous interactive elements, including interactive demos of online course components and quiz questions with feedback. One humorous aspect of the tutorial is the guide, Rigalio, a deceased seventeenth-century Italian monk (Regis University is a Jesuit higher education institution). He speaks and provides feedback throughout the tutorial in a Brooklyn accent.

This tutorial was developed in Flash.

Adopt or Adapt

Providing support to new distance learners helps them become successful quickly. This idea can be adapted for introducing new online learners to any type of online program.

Attribution

Submitted by Ellen Waterman, director of distance learning, Regis University, School for Professional Studies, Denver, Colorado, USA

URL: http://support.regis.edu/GTDL/Regis_eTutorial.html

Also involved: Maureen Hencemann, instructional designer, Regis University, School for Professional Studies, Denver, Colorado, USA; Kevin Himmel, director of performance consulting, Regis Learning Solutions, Golden, Colorado, USA; Alex Benedict, Web developer, Regis University, School for Professional Studies, Denver, Colorado, USA; Blenda Crawford, faculty chair, Communication, Psychology, and Sociology, Regis University, School for Professional Studies, Denver, Colorado, USA; and Fr. Don Highberger, undergraduate faculty, Regis University, School for Professional Studies, Denver, Colorado, USA

Visual Ideas

The Big Idea

What

Visual representations show how course concepts relate to one another.

Figure 9.24. Technê Graphic

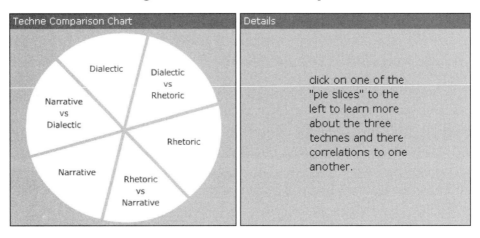

Source: Shawn Foley, http://www.foleyworks.com

Figure 9.25. Technê Graphic Rollover

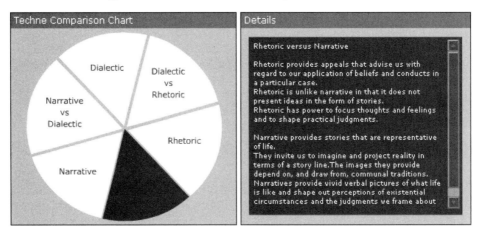

Source: Shawn Foley, http://www.foleyworks.com

Why

Making ideas visual helps make difficult concepts easier to understand and aids in building effective mental models.

Use It!

How

The graphic in Figure 9.24 is used in an Introduction to Rhetorical Theory course that uses visual representations to show connections between course topics and as the basis of learner activities. In addition, learners develop concept maps in order to understand interconnections between the core tenants of rhetorical theory. Learners exchange maps with one another, discuss their individual understandings, and compare their interpretations with the instructor's explanation and understanding.

Visual reflections aid understanding and create an active and collaborative learning community to support one another's learning throughout the course. Mapmaking discussions allow learners to "see" (in the double sense of "I see what you are saying" and visually) and understand course concepts.

Adopt or Adapt

Showing concepts visually and having learners develop and share visual representations aids understanding and helps learners build effective mental models. Conceptual graphics and concept maps could be adapted for use in many different types of courses.

Attribution

Submitted by Shawn Foley, learning strategist, Cerner Virtual University, Cerner Corporation, Kansas City, Missouri, USA

Contact: Shawn.Foley@cerner.com

URL: http://www.foleyworks.com

Also involved: Jane Sutton, associate professor of communication arts and sciences, The Pennsylvania State University, York, Pennsylvania, USA

Ideas for Creative Media

This chapter is a continuation of the creativity theme started in Chapter Nine and presents additional ideas for creative uses of media in online instruction. Although media can be used for the wrong reasons (gratuitous clip art or eye-candy animations, for example) and can actually detract from learning, media can also be instrumental for learning. The cliché "a picture is worth a thousand words" certainly applies whenever a picture, model, illustration, animation, or other media explains, elucidates, illuminates, or guides attention. As the ideas in this chapter show, the right media can truly make ideas come alive.

Show Me

The Big Idea

What

Graphics can be used to help people with limited reading skills or whose native language is other than the language in which the material is presented.

Figure 10.1. Version 1: How to Make a Cup of Hot Chocolate

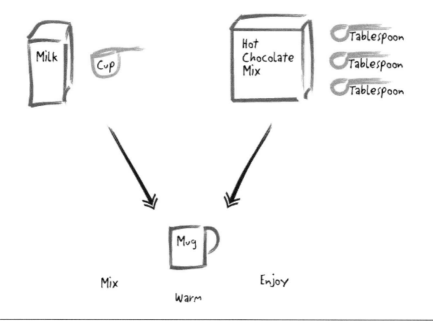

Source: Linda Lohr, http://www.unco.edu/coe/EdTech/LindaLohr

Figure 10.2. Version 2: How to Make a Cup of Hot Chocolate

Source: Linda Lohr, http://www.unco.edu/coe/EdTech/LindaLohr

Why

Graphics are an effective tool for communicating information, despite reading or language barriers.

Use It!

How

Linda Lohr gave learners in her Advanced Design of Instructional Materials course an assignment to use graphics to create instructions for making a cup of hot chocolate for an audience with limited English reading skills. The learners interpreted the assignment in different ways, taking numerous effective approaches to using graphics for this purpose. Lohr's book, *Creating Graphics for Learning and Performance,* shows other excellent examples of applying graphics to learning.

Adopt or Adapt

Consider how graphics can be used to convey information to an audience with limited reading skills. Also consider how to use the strategy of having learners complete an assignment in different ways.

Attribution

Submitted by Linda Lohr, associate professor, University of Northern Colorado, Greely, Colorado, USA

Contact: Linda.lohr@unco.edu

URL: http://www.unco.edu/coe/EdTech/LindaLohr

Reference

Lohr, L. (2002). *Creating graphics for learning and performance.* Columbus, OH: Merrill.

Slow or Fast Images

The Big Idea

What

Complex physical skills are demonstrated through a series of still images that can be viewed one at a time or in rapid succession.

Figure 10.3. Top Moves

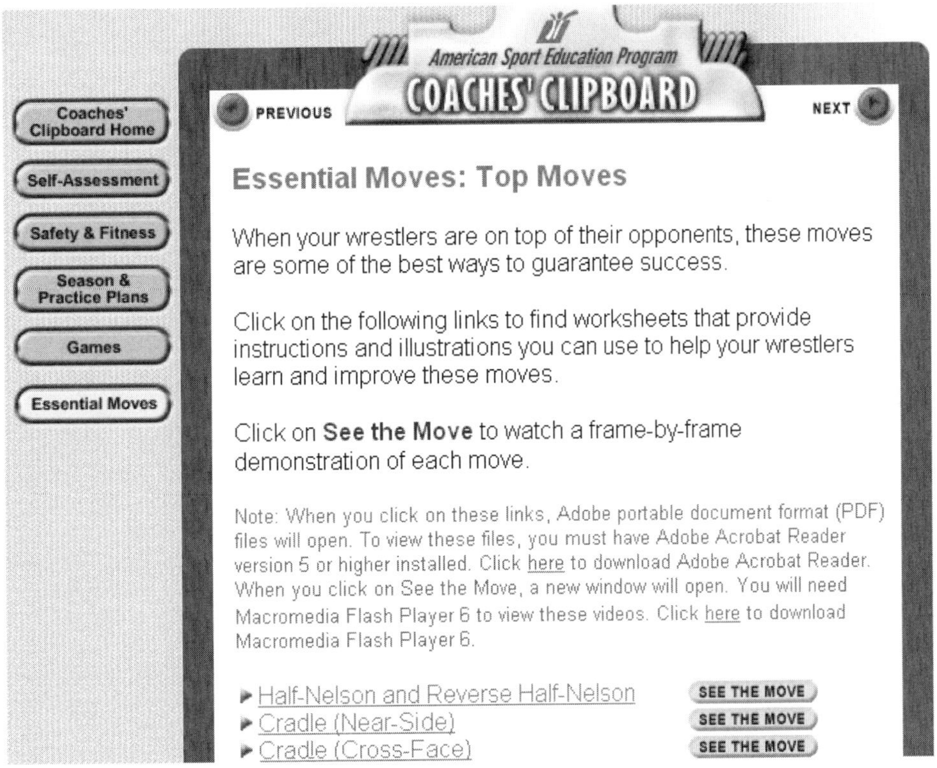

Source: From American Sport Education Program, 2003, Coaching Youth Wrestling Online. © 2003 by American Sport Education Program. Reprinted with permission from Human Kinetics, Champaign, Illinois.

Figure 10.4. The Moves

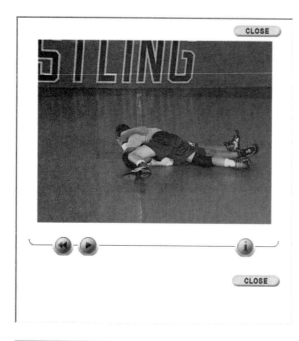

Why

Being able to see the skills slowly and quickly helps learners see the skills used one skill at a time or together as a whole.

Use It!

How

In the Coaching Youth Wrestling Online course, a subject-matter expert identified thirty-one "essential moves" that were universally taught by effective wrestling coaches. The challenge was to introduce each of these moves to learners, to provide specific coaching tips for each step of each move, and to provide learners with a printable job aid to which they could refer while teaching and coaching the moves to their young athletes.

The still images were obtained by shooting well-lit digital video (controlling motion blur through proper exposure and other settings and generally locking the camera down to keep a stable background).

The course was built with HTML, Flash, JavaScript, and Acrobat (job aids). Flash loads a series of images and is programmed to step or play through them in sequence. Each image changes the destination of the "i" link, where additional information about the image is presented in an HTML page.

Adopt or Adapt

It is extremely helpful to be able to step through a demonstration of a physical performance. Any step-by-step performance skill that can be taught with a series of photos can use this idea.

Attribution

Submitted by Dean Hixson, instructional designer, Human Kinetics, Champaign, Illinois, USA

Contact: deanh@hkusa.com

URL: http://www.hkusa.com

Also involved: Stuart Cartwright, senior graphic designer, Human Kinetics, Champaign, Illinois, USA

Energy Balance

The Big Idea

What

> An animated balance scale helps learners visualize how complex concepts (food intake, physical activity, and weight management) are connected.

Figure 10.5. Energy Balance Concept

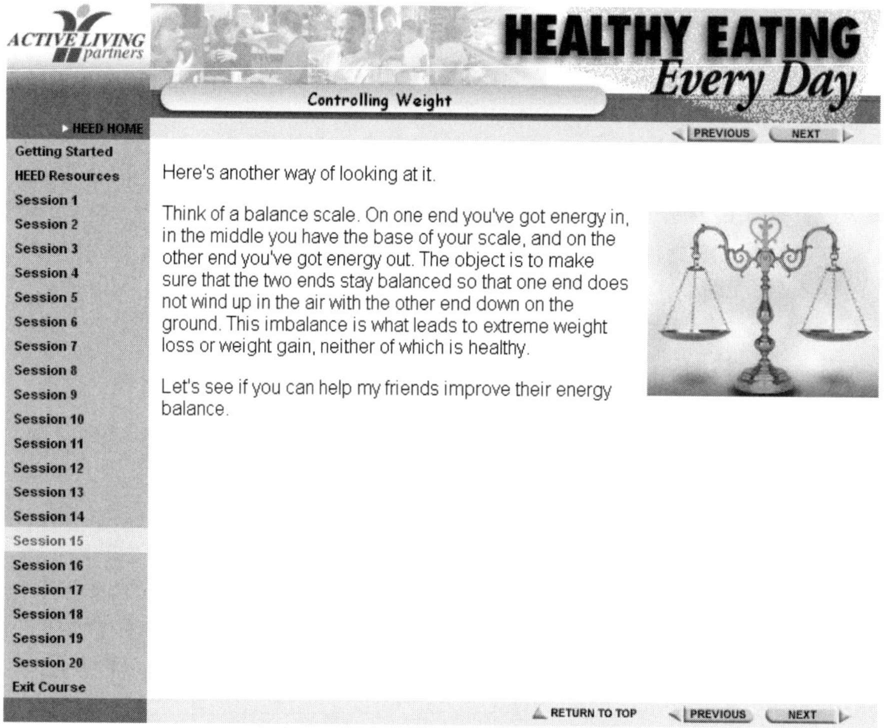

Figure 10.6. Linda's Energy Balance

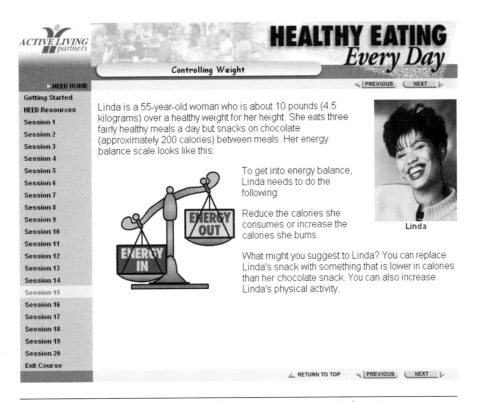

Source: Cooper Institute, 2005, Healthy Eating Every Day Online Participant Course. © 2005 by Cooper Institute. Reprinted with permission from Human Kinetics, Champaign, Illinois.

Figure 10.7. Physical Activity Impact on Linda's Energy Balance

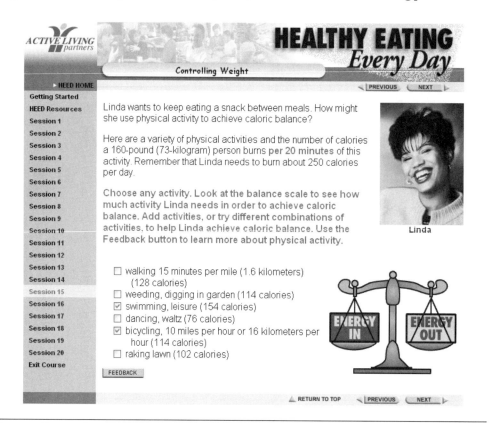

Source: Cooper Institute, 2005, Healthy Eating Every Day Online Participant Course.
© 2005 by Cooper Institute. Reprinted with permission from Human Kinetics, Champaign, Illinois.

Why

Visualizing the relationship between the concepts helps learners know how to manipulate them individually or together.

Use It!

How

In the Healthy Eating Every Day Online course, an animated balance scale helps learners see how losing weight is affected by decreasing the amount of energy in (food intake) or by increasing the amount of energy out (physical activity). The scale adjusts to show the resulting energy balance when the learner makes different choices.

The course was built with Flash, ActionScript, JavaScript, and HTML. As the learner checks or unchecks a checkbox, JavaScript calculates a total value based on numbers associated with each box. JavaScript then tells the Flash-based scale image to change and ActionScript animates the transition.

Adopt or Adapt

Graphical analogies like a scale can be used to illustrate other concepts that are correlated or have a causal relationship.

Attribution

Submitted by Susan Zahn, instructional designer, Human Kinetics, Champaign, Illinois, USA

Contact: susanz@hkusa.com

URL: http://www.hkusa.com

Also involved: Stuart Cartwright, senior graphic designer, Jason Mock, course programmer-analyst, and Yury Borukhovich, course programmer-analyst, all from Human Kinetics, Champaign, Illinois, USA

Interactive History

The Big Idea

What

An interactive multidimensional timeline lets learners see when and where events took place and helps them obtain additional information.

Figure 10.8. The United States in 1686

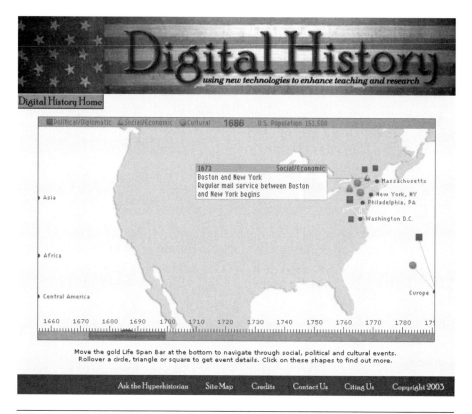

Source: Steven Mintz, http://www.digitalhistory.uh.edu

Figure 10.9. The United States in 1807

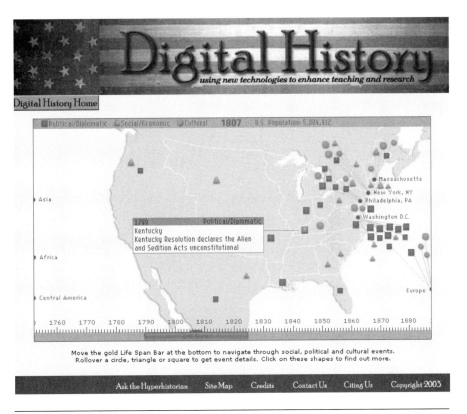

Source: Steven Mintz, http://www.digitalhistory.uh.edu

Figure 10.10. The United States in 1952

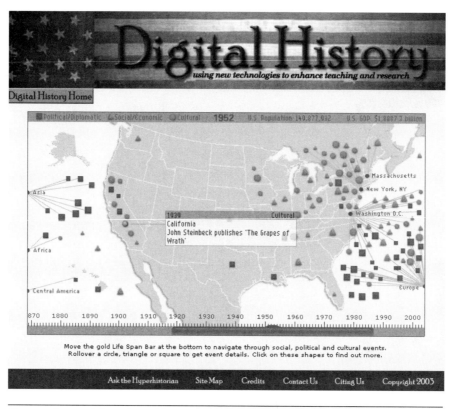

Source: Steven Mintz, http://www.digitalhistory.uh.edu

Why

A multidimensional timeline provides a great deal of information in a compact space and affords multiple connections.

Use It!

How

The Digital History site was developed to support the teaching of American history in K–12 schools and colleges and is supported by the Department of History and the College of Education at the University of Houston. It is an interactive, multimedia history of the United States from the American Revolution to the present. The site has three goals: to provide teachers and learners with a comprehensive collection of high-quality historical resources, to facilitate the potential of the Internet for history learning and research, and to offer valuable exercises that can transform learners and teachers into historians.

Steven Mintz wanted learners to be able to think about history multi-dimensionally. The timeline (http://www.digitalhistory.uh.edu/timeline/ timelineO.cfm) shown in Figures 10.8, 10.9, and 10.10 helps learners visualize and situate political and diplomatic, social and economic, and cultural events both in the years when they occurred and in the part of the country where they occurred. Many of us recall the clear overlays found in encyclopedias—for example, the human body overlays—that helped us think in visual layers of information. Mintz's timeline represents an updated version of that earlier idea—but one that provides much greater opportunity for interactivity.

The slider beneath the timeline changes the year and events shown. Rolling the mouse over any event provides a brief description, and clicking on it opens a page with an in-depth description. The timeline was developed with Flash.

Adopt or Adapt

A multidimensional timeline can be extremely useful when trying to convey multiple events in time and space. For example, this approach could be used to show company events over time for new hire orientation, or events leading up to modern word processing in a computer applications course.

Attribution

Submitted by Steven Mintz, Moores Professor of History, University of Houston, Texas, USA

URL: http://www.digitalhistory.uh.edu

Interactive Physics

The Big Idea

What

Graphics can clearly show a hierarchy of physical structures in the world.

Figure 10.11. Overview of NSF's Interactive Physics Web Site

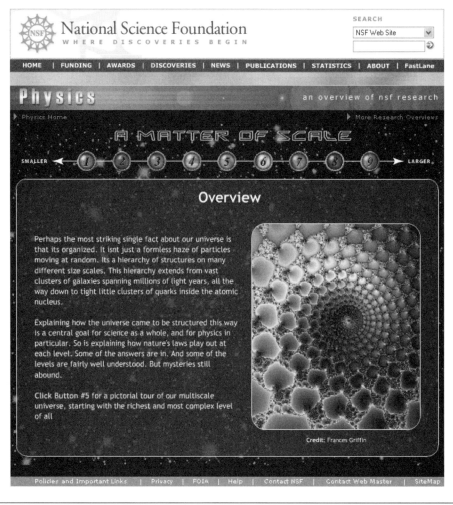

Source: National Science Foundation, http://nsf.gov

Figure 10.12. Quarks, Leptons, and Nuclei

Source: National Science Foundation, http://nsf.gov

Figure 10.13. The Human Scale

Source: National Science Foundation, http://nsf.gov

Figure 10.14. Galaxies and Clusters

Source: National Science Foundation, http://nsf.gov

Why

Graphics can illustrate scale more clearly than a text explanation alone.

Use It!

How

The National Science Foundation's interactive physics site (http://nsf.gov/ news/overviews/physics/interactive/interactive.jsp#Scene_1) provides a magnificent, scaled tour of our universe. The online exhibit shows, at different levels of scale, how the universe is organized: from strings, the smallest level that physicists are attempting to understand, to the human scale, which is what our eyes perceive, to galaxies, clusters, and the cosmos.

The site was compiled from photographs and simple animations. These were catalogued in an XML document. A Flash interface was built that could pull in files and information associated with the XML-catalogued assets.

Adopt or Adapt

Graphics effectively show changes in size or scale and illustrate unseeable concepts. This idea could be adapted for many concepts where seeing changes in size or scale would be beneficial, such as growth stages, building phases, macro- and microviews of volcanoes, and so on.

Attribution

Submitted by Nicolle Rager Fuller, science illustrator, Dynamics Research Corporation, National Science Foundation, Arlington, Virginia, USA

Contact: rager@sayo-art.com

URL: http://www.sayo-art.com

Also involved: Zina Deretsky, science illustrator, Dynamics Research Corporation, National Science Foundation, Arlington, Virginia, USA; Mitch Waldrop, lead writer, media officer, National Science Foundation, Arlington, Virginia, USA; Branden Hall, programmer and action scripter, owner, Department of Notations, Hyattsville, Maryland, USA; Curt Suplee, director, National Science Foundation, Arlington, Virginia, USA; and Phillip Lippel, former media officer, National Science Foundation, Arlington, Virginia, USA

Inside a Cell

The Big Idea

What

Graphics allow visualization of structures that are too small to see with the human eye.

Figure 10.15. Inside the Cell

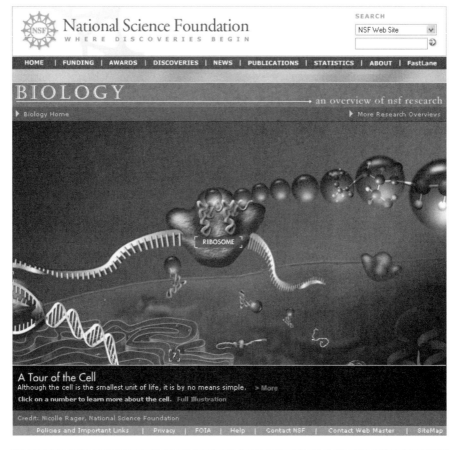

Source: National Science Foundation, http://nsf.gov

Figure 10.16. Ribosome

Source: National Science Foundation, http://nsf.gov

Why

Being able to visualize something that can't be seen with the human eye makes it easier to understand.

Use It!

How

The National Science Foundation's Tour of the Cell site (http://nsf.gov/news/overviews/biology/interactive.jsp) makes visualizing the structures inside a cell possible. The online exhibit allows users to click on a particular structure, which opens a page with more information about that structure.

Adopt or Adapt

Graphics can make processes that are invisible (to the human eye) or almost invisible easier to visualize and understand. This approach could be used to explain and show other concepts like digestion, evaporation, sublimation (when a frozen substance changes to gaseous form), and so on.

Attribution

Submitted by Nicolle Rager Fuller, science illustrator, Dynamics Research Corporation, National Science Foundation, Arlington, Virginia, USA

Contact: nrager@nsf.gov

URL: http://www.sayo-art.com

Sea Vents

The Big Idea

What

Graphics allow visualization of structures that are in places that humans rarely visit.

Figure 10.17. Sea Vents

Source: National Science Foundation, http://nsf.gov

Figure 10.18. Tubeworms

Source: National Science Foundation, http://nsf.gov

Why

Being able to visualize something rarely seen makes that object easier to understand.

Use It!

How

The National Science Foundation's Sea Vent Viewer site (http://nsf.gov/news/overviews/earth-environ/interactive.jsp) makes it possible to visualize the structures on the ocean floor, which thrive in the absence of sunlight. The online exhibit allows users to click on a particular structure, which opens a page with more information about that structure.

A series of underwater photographs was manipulated in Adobe Photoshop and then animated using Flash.

Adopt or Adapt

This approach could be used to explain and show other concepts such as volcano eruptions, solar flares, glaciers, and so on.

Attribution

Submitted by Nicolle Rager Fuller, science illustrator, Dynamics Research Corporation, National Science Foundation, Arlington, Virginia, USA

Contact: rager@sayo-art.com

URL: http://www.sayo-art.com

Tsunami

The Big Idea

What

Media and graphics allow visualization of events and concepts that are complex and multifaceted.

Figure 10.19. Introduction to NSF's After the Tsunami Web Site

Source: National Science Foundation, http://nsf.gov

Figure 10.20. What Causes Tsunamis

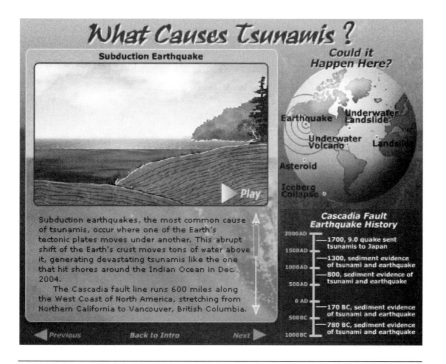

Source: National Science Foundation, http://nsf.gov

Why

Being able to visualize complex, multifaceted events or concepts makes them more understandable.

Use It!

How

The National Science Foundation's After the Tsunami site (http://nsf.gov/news/special_reports/tsunami/index.jsp) explains and illustrates the devastating 2005 Indian Ocean tsunami. Animations, audio, video, and interactive graphics explain what happened. Learners can drill down for more information about many of the events and organizations involved.

Figure 10.21. Preparation for Disaster

Source: National Science Foundation, http://nsf.gov

Detailed information about tsunami detection efforts is described and shown. The online exhibit allows users to investigate what happened; current research; and detection, response, and emergency preparation efforts.

The storyboard was developed with pencil and paper. The graphics were then developed in Illustrator, exported as .swf files, and animated in Flash.

Adopt or Adapt

Graphics and media help complex concepts and events become more understandable. A multimedia approach allows learners to get additional information about the topic at hand.

Attribution

Submitted by Zina Deretsky, science illustrator, Dynamics Research Corporation, National Science Foundation, Arlington, Virginia, USA

Contact: Deretsky_zina@hotmail.com

URL: http://www.zina-studio.com

Movement Sensors

The Big Idea

What

> Graphics and media allow visualization of tiny structures and better understanding of complex concepts.

Figure 10.22. Overview of NSF's Sensor Revolution Web Site

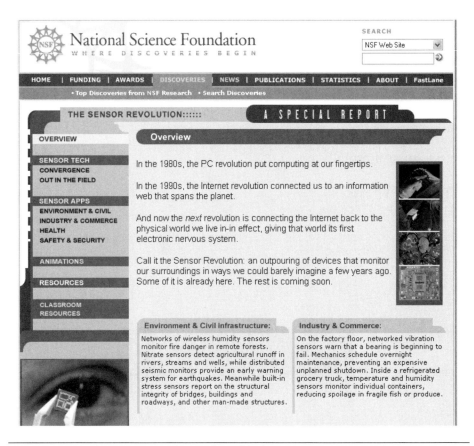

Source: National Science Foundation, http://nsf.gov

Figure 10.23. About Sensors

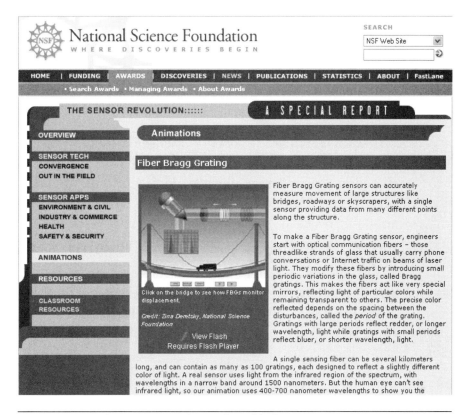

Source: National Science Foundation, http://nsf.gov

Figure 10.24. Micro-Cantilever Animation

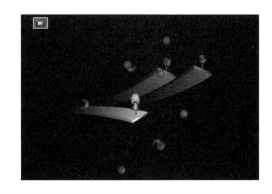

Source: National Science Foundation, http://nsf.gov

Why

Being able to visualize something tiny and complex makes it easier to understand.

Use It!

How

The National Science Foundation's Sensor Revolution site (http://nsf.gov/news/special_reports/sensor/animations.jsp) uses graphics and animations to explore sensor devices that can monitor our surroundings, including accurate movement measurement for large structures like bridges and skyscrapers. The site explains and illustrates how these sen-sors work, the engineering and physical concepts involved, and how they are used and may be applied in the future.

The graphics on this site were initially developed in Illustrator, and then were exported as .swf files, and animated in Flash.

Adopt or Adapt

Graphics and media can make small and complex concepts easier to visualize and understand. Animations are especially valuable for explaining things that are too small to see.

Attribution

Submitted by Zina Deretsky, science illustrator, Dynamics Research Corporation, National Science Foundation, Arlington, Virginia, USA

Contact: Deretsky_zina@hotmail.com

URL: http://www.zina-studio.com

Also involved: Mitch Waldrop, lead writer, media officer, National Science Foundation, Arlington, Virginia, USA; Nicolle Rager Fuller, science illustrator, Dynamics Research Corporation, National Science Foundation, Arlington, Virginia, USA; Curt Suplee, director, National Science Foundation, Arlington, Virginia, USA; Phillip Lippel, former media officer, National Science Foundation, Arlington, Virginia, USA

Genome Timeline

The Big Idea

What

An interactive timeline lets learners see how events unfold over time and recognize active and inactive periods.

Why

Visualizing events on an interactive timeline makes the sequence of historical events more obvious.

Use It!

How

Bang Wong developed this idea for an online biochemistry textbook. When information like this is presented in a tabular format (see Figure 10.25), the elapsed time between one event and the next is not readily

Figure 10.25. Biochemistry Timeline Data

Year	Event
1885	Theodor Escherich isolates a microbe from the colon that is later given the name *Escherichia coli* in his honor. This microbe later becomes the workhorse of molecular biology.
1897	Edward Buchner helps launch the field of enzymology by developing a cell extract from yeast that is able to ferment sugar to alcohol.
1952	Salvador Luria and Mary Human, and independently Jean Weigle, describe sensitivity in bacteriophage imposed by the host on which it was grown. The viruses are restricted to grow well only on specific strains of bacteria. This later leads to the study of bacterial systems of restriction and modification, and eventually the discovery of restriction enzymes.
1959	O. Sawada and others demonstrate that antibiotic resistance can be transferred between *Shigella* strains and *Escherichia coli* strains by plasmids.

Source: Bang Wong, http://virtualtext.jbpub.com

Figure 10.26. Biochemistry Event in 1885

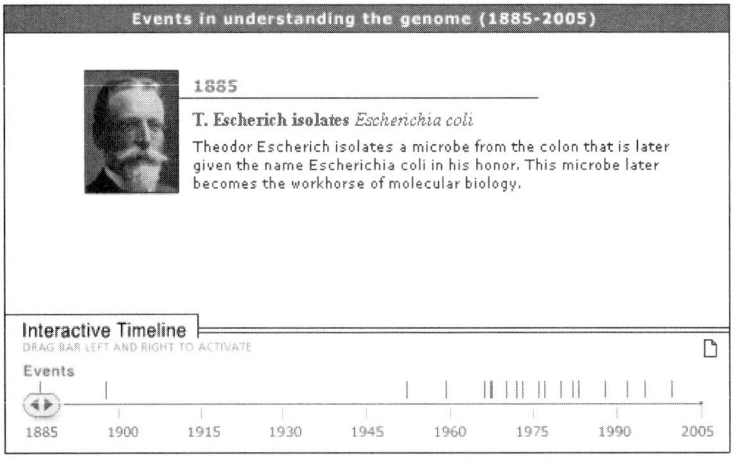

Source: Bang Wong, http://virtualtext.jbpub.com

Figure 10.27. Biochemistry Event in 1988

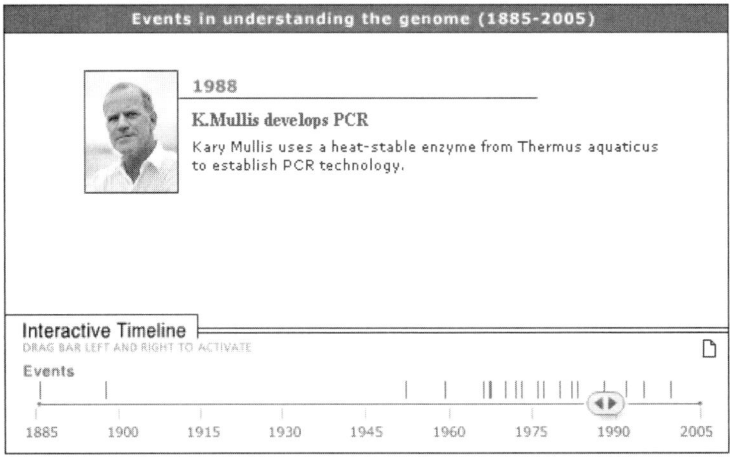

Source: Bang Wong, http://virtualtext.jbpub.com

apparent. The timeline explorer makes active and inactive periods of history much more obvious.

The idea was produced with Flash and a small amount of ActionScript. Text is dynamically loaded from an external plain text file so the artist and author can work simultaneously. Revision or reuse for production of other timelines is also facilitated.

Adopt or Adapt

There are many potential uses for an interactive timeline, including historical, company, business, and personal events, and so on. Because the interface and logic are reusable, they can be developed once and reused over and over.

Attribution

Submitted by Bang Wong, art director, Jones and Bartlett Publishers, Cambridge, Massachusetts, USA

Contact: info@jbpub.com

URL: http://virtualtext.jbpub.com

Also involved: Andrew Tang, scientific illustrator, Jones and Bartlett Publishers, Cambridge, Massachusetts, USA

DNA Sliding Clamp

The Big Idea

What

Building an interactive module to simulate 3D permits visualization from many angles while keeping file size small and easily viewable by all.

Figure 10.28. DNA Sliding Clamp

Source: Bang Wong, http://virtualtext.jbpub.com

Figure 10.29. DNA Sliding Clamp, with Text Information

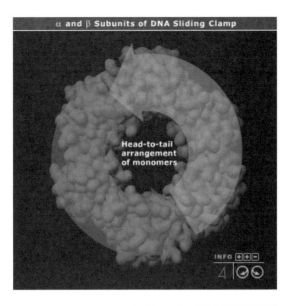

Source: Bang Wong, http://virtualtext.jbpub.com

Figure 10.30. DNA Sliding Clamp, Turned

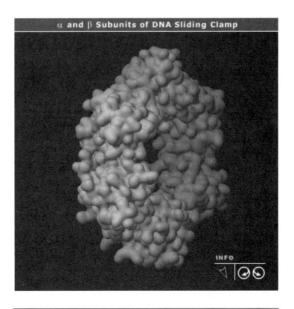

Source: Bang Wong, http://virtualtext.jbpub.com

Why

Visualizing objects in 3D helps learners understand structural elements that may not be obvious otherwise.

Use It!

How

The discovery of the DNA sliding clamp was a major breakthrough in understanding DNA replication. The clamp wraps itself around the DNA strand and allows the bound polymerase to stay on track. It is very difficult to appreciate the structure of this protein by seeing it from any one side. As an analogy, a doughnut viewed on end doesn't give any clues to the hole that is at its center.

Bang Wong needed to present the structure in 3D but did not want to require learners to download an obscure plug-in to view it. Plus, 3D images commonly require extremely large file sizes. His solution was to select predefined views and stitch them together to provide a good sense of the three-dimensionality of the protein while keeping the file size small and viewable using the ubiquitous Flash Player. The learner moves through the predefined views using the arrows, and a text overlay (obtained by clicking on the + sign) adds descriptions to some views.

Adopt or Adapt

Simulating 3D by stitching together images and allowing the learner to move through them could be useful for visualizing any object that needs to be seen from many angles while keeping file size small.

Attribution

Submitted by Bang Wong, art director, Jones and Bartlett Publishers, Cambridge, Massachusetts, USA

Contact: info@jbpub.com

URL: http://virtualtext.jbpub.com

DNA Sequence Explorer

The Big Idea

What

Animation allows learners to visualize minute details of a small portion of the sequence at a time, or to see it in its entirety.

Figure 10.31. DNA Sequence Portion 1

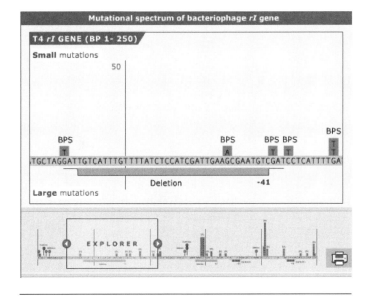

Source: Bang Wong, http://virtualtext.jbpub.com

Figure 10.32. DNA Sequence Portion 2

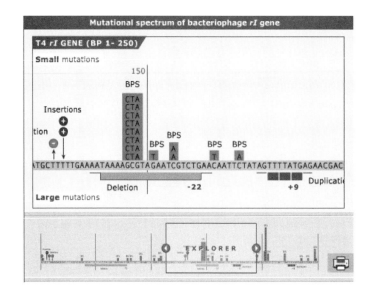

Source: Bang Wong, http://virtualtext.jbpub.com

Why

The ability to view both micro- and macroviews can aid understanding.

Use It!

How

Bang Wong developed this idea for an online genetics textbook. He developed an animation that allows learners to study the DNA sequence in all its detail while not sacrificing the ability to be able to see the entire sequence at once. Learners can use the slider to view a small portion at a time, or they can print all the information on one sheet of paper (using the printer icon).

The idea was produced with Flash and a small amount of ActionScript.

Adopt or Adapt

There are many situations in which being able to visualize a micro- and macroview would be beneficial. For example, learners could toggle between the big picture and detailed views of maps, processes, and the like.

Attribution

Submitted by Bang Wong, art director, Jones and Bartlett Publishers, Cambridge, Massachusetts, USA

Contact: info@jbpub.com

URL: http://virtualtext.jbpub.com

Also involved: Andrew Tang, scientific illustrator, Jones and Bartlett Publishers, Cambridge, Massachusetts, USA

Build Your Own Instructional Game

The Big Idea

What

This idea allows content experts to design learning games without programming knowledge. Content experts enter information into XML documents that populate the game.

Figure 10.33. Portion of XML Document

```xml
<scene id="DressingRoom">
  <documentation>The barn is used as a dressing room. There are lockers containing
    personal items and hangers with safety clothing. In the middle of the room there is a
    pair of safety boots specifically designed to work with electricity. Jose must grab here
    all the safety clothing required to start working.</documentation>
  <resources>
    <asset type="background" uri="assets/dressing.jpg" />
    <asset type="bg-music" uri="assets/sounds/construction-muffled.mp3" />
  </resources>
  <exits>
    <exit x="600" y="300" width="5" height="10">
      <documentation>Barn door: Leads back to "Site Access"</documentation>
      <next-scene idTarget="SiteAccess" />
    </exit>
  </exits>
  <objects>
    <object-ref idTarget="SafetyBoots" x="300" y="400">
      <documentation>Safety boots for electricity.</documentation>
    </object-ref>
    <object-ref idTarget="SafetyClothes" x="400" y="250">
      <documentation>Safety clothing.</documentation>
    </object-ref>
  </objects>
</scene>
```

Source: Pablo Moreno-Ger, http://www.moreno-ger.com

Figure 10.34. Game Screen Populated by XML

Source: Pablo Moreno-Ger, http://www.moreno-ger.com

Why

This approach can save time and programming resources, allowing content experts to build valuable interactive instructional elements.

Use It!

How

Game-based learning can be fun and meaningful, but games can also be time-consuming and difficult to program. The <e-Game> project addresses this problem by offering an authoring environment for educational adventure games that does not require heavy programming skills. After the game shell has been designed by programmers, content experts can adapt it for their own uses by entering text that describes the contents of the game.

The game is made up of a group of "scenes." There are several <scene> elements in the XML file, each one describing one scene in the game. A <scene> element contains a <documentation> element, which is an optional human-readable description of the scene and what goes into it. This element is ignored by the game engine.

The scene contains an <environment> element (not shown in the screen capture in Figure 10.34) that includes references to the different art assets related to the scene. In Figure 10.33, the dressing.jpg file is the room graphic you see in Figure 10.34 but without the boots, the safety clothing, and the main character. Similarly, the construction-muffled.mp3 file is the music that plays in the background.

Scenes are populated by objects and characters. Objects are defined using <object> elements. Objects include a <documentation> element, a <resources> element referring to assets required by the object, and the descriptions of the object. Objects may include markup describing the different actions that can be performed with the object (such as use them with another object, grab them, give them to a character, and so on). Scenes are connected with the <exit> elements, that indicate the regions of the screen that, when clicked, will take the player to the next scene.

The content expert uses a simple text editor to input text into these XML documents. The interpreter, built with Java technologies, reads the XML files and launches and manages the game. The content expert writes everything that is needed for the game in these documents, which are then fed to a compiler that generates the game.

The game creation process is documented in a short, easy-to-understand tutorial that includes a brief introduction to text editors and a tutorial about the interpreter and its syntax.

There are future plans to develop a graphical user interface for inputting text into the documents, eliminating the need for the content expert to deal with the XML documents themselves.

Previous approaches required a high degree of technical knowledge. They were aimed at decreasing development times, but the target audience was developers, not content experts. By reducing the scope and power of the game compiler, very simple game design could be accomplished with little technical knowledge. This approach allows content experts easy entrance into building game-based learning.

Adopt or Adapt

Given the fun factor and interactivity offered by games, this approach could be useful to many educators. Adapting this approach requires significant programming expertise on the front end but reduces the time and resources required to build interactive elements. Pablo Moreno-Ger's project is fascinating and worth watching for additional insights. It is hoped that authoring vendors will consider developing tools like this for the general public as well. This is already starting to occur.

Attribution

Submitted by Pablo Moreno-Ger, professor, Universidad Complutense de Madrid (Facultad de Informática), Madrid, Spain

Contact: pablom@fdi.ucm.es

URL: http://www.moreno-ger.com/egame

Also involved: Baltasar Fernández-Manjón, professor, Universidad Complutense de Madrid (Facultad de Informática), Madrid, Spain; Iván Martínez-Ortiz, professor, Centro de Estudios Superiores Felipe II, Madrid, Spain

IT'S NOT NINETY-FIVE

The Big Idea

What

If you're a perfectionist or analytical or both, you may be wondering why the cover of the book says there are ninety-five ideas but the book contains more than ninety-five ideas. Cool that you noticed. (I probably wouldn't have.)

Why

Surprises in your instructional materials can be an effective tool for turning off learners' autopilot and increasing enjoyment.

Use It!

How

One of my former students, Alexander Bolla, a professor of law at Cumberland School of Law at Samford University, includes hidden rollovers in his online courses and I think this is a really fun thing to do. A colleague, Todd Gibson, taught an online PHP hypertext preprocessor (PHP) course (that I struggled through because I don't like semi-colons and you simply cannot write usable PHP code without them) using a science-fiction metaphor. Somewhere during the course, someone figured out that Todd's picture could be seen if you put your mouse over the picture of the alien. Ha!

Adopt or Adapt

Surprise folks, but try hard not to frustrate them. Technology is quite frustrating enough. Perhaps you can hide some interesting facts about the content in unexpected places or hide answers in the text (which might help people read more carefully). Perhaps in each lesson there's an incentive for finding the hidden answer to a certain question. Make it fun!

Attribution

Submitted by Patti Shank, president, Learning Peaks, LLC, Centennial, Colorado, USA

URL: http://www.learningpeaks.com

f you are new to using technology for learning, some terms in this book may be unfamiliar to you. This glossary will help you make sense of some of the most commonly used terms. In addition (in the realm of "shameless plug"), my first book, *Making Sense of Online Learning* (Wiley, 2004), written with Amy Sitze, should be very helpful to people new to this field as well because it was written just for you.

Asynchronous

Asynchronous, as it relates to online learning, means events that are not time coordinated. It means that learners are using the materials and communicating at different times from other learners. Examples: email, threaded discussion, most higher-education online courses, self-paced online courses. Each learner can use, read, and respond at a time of his or her own choosing.

Blended learning

Blended learning refers to a combination of learning methods (including but not limited to online and face-to-face instruction). The advantage of blended learning is that it can employ the best features of each delivery method—for example, the immediate feedback that happens in classroom learning and the self-paced exploration that's possible in asynchronous online learning.

Blog

Blog is short for weblog. A blog is a group of personal journal entries posted in chronological order to a Web page. Many require no programming skills. Some blog hosts provide a Web-page interface that allows users simply to type a text entry and click on the submit button to publish their blog entry. Blogs are typically updated on a regular basis.

Chatbot or chatterbot

A chatbot or chatterbot is a virtual person who can simulate a conversation via audio or text. Chatbots are programmed to appear to be interpreting human input, but most scan for keywords and word patterns and reply from a database of responses.

CSS (Cascading Style Sheets)

CSS are used to describe the presentation of Web pages. They can be used to define text and heading styles, table borders, positions of objects on Web pages, and other formatting attributes. Instead of defining the style of each block of text within a page's HTML, styles can be defined once in a CSS document. These styles can then be applied to any page that references that CSS file.

DTD (Document Type Definition)

A DTD lists the grammar rules for an XML document. It lists the elements, attributes, comments, notes, and entities contained in the XML document and their relationships to one another.

HTML (Hypertext Markup Language)

HTML consists of codes (also called markup tags) that are inserted into a text file. These codes describe how the text should appear in a Web browser.

JavaScript

JavaScript is a Web programming language that allows Web programmers to program items like pop-up messages, new browser windows, feedback when users click on a button, and images (often buttons) that change when users roll their mouse over them. JavaScript is often embedded in the programming of a Web page along with HTML codes.

LMS (Learning Management System)

An LMS, or learning management system, is an application that handles learning administrative tasks such as creating course catalogs, registering users, tracking users within courses, recording data (like test scores) about learners, and providing reports.

Multimedia

Multimedia is a combination of digital media, such as text, images, sound, and video, into an integrated presentation in which the combination of media provides greater benefits than the media elements by themselves.

Plug-in or plugin

A plug-in is a browser extension program used to play supplementary file types. Typical plug-ins used for learning include Flash, QuickTime, Real Media, Windows Media Player, and PDF.

RSS (Really Simple Syndication)

RSS is a mechanism for syndicating and sharing Web content. Content providers can provide a portion or all of their content via RSS text files. RSS aggregators combine RSS content from multiple places.

Synchronous

Synchronous, as it relates to online learning, refers to events that are time coordinated or simultaneous. It means people are "attending" and using the materials at the same time as others, even though they may be in different locations. Examples: chat, instant messaging, Web conferencing.

Usability

Usability refers to how easily the medium can be used to accomplish the goals of the user. Some factors that are considered in determining usability are ease-of-use and capacity to accomplish specific tasks.

Web conferencing

Web conferencing is a method for holding a meeting or course synchronously with multiple participants. It may involve sharing slides, desktop applications, polling, talking (by the presenter, participants, or both), synchronous text discussions, and more. Examples of Web conferencing tools include WebEx, Elluminate, and Connect.

Web form

A Web form contains text boxes, boxes, or buttons that allow a user to enter and submit data. Submitted data can be sent to a file, a database, or an email address.

Wiki

A wiki is a Web site that allows users to collaboratively add and update content using a Web browser without having to know any Web programming. A wiki application that runs on the Web server makes this possible.

XML (Xtensible Markup Language)

XML is a way to share data across dissimilar formats. Both XML and HTML contain symbols (otherwise known as markup tags) that describe aspects of a document. XML describes what the data is. *Extensible* means it is possible to add new markup tags as needed. HTML, conversely, is not extensible; the available markup tags are already specified.

ant to share great ideas, help others, and gain recognition? This book may be updated with new ideas in the future. Here are the factors we are looking for when we review ideas and determine which ones to include:

1. Creative!

2. Can be adopted or adapted by others

3. Proven in the online portion of classroom, blended, or online instruction, either instructor-led or self-directed, synchronous or asynchronous

4. Applicable to a wide variety of content and settings

5. Fairly easy to implement using available industry-standard tools and technologies

6. Easy for the editor to review (publicly available on the Web or submitter can provide easy access) and screen captures are easily taken from it for use in the published volume

7. Few if any hassles to gain permission for publishing (with attribution) the idea and screen captures

Interested? Get more information and submit your idea here: http://www.learningpeaks.com/ideabook

Patti Shank is the owner of Learning Peaks, LLC, an internationally recognized instructional technology and instructional design consulting group best known for helping organizations optimize online and distance education outcomes by focusing on instructional effectiveness. She is well known for her independent and systems-oriented approaches to training, learning, and technology.

Shank is listed in *Who's Who in Instructional Technology*. She is an often-requested speaker and workshop leader at training and instructional technology conferences and is quoted frequently in training publications. She has contributed numerous chapters to training and instructional technology books and coauthored *Making Sense of Online Learning* (2004) with Amy Sitze and *The E-Learning Handbook: Past Promises, Present Challenges* (in press) with Saul Carliner. Both books are published by Pfeiffer/Wiley.

Shank was an award-winning contributing editor for *Online Learning Magazine* and is regularly quoted in training trade journals. Her articles are regularly found in eLearning Guild publications, Macromedia's *eLearning* and *Training Solutions*, Adobe's *Resource Center*, Magna Publications' *Online Classroom*, and elsewhere. She has taught graduate instructional technology courses for George Washington University and the University of Colorado at Denver.

Shank completed her doctoral degree at the University of Colorado at Denver and received the prestigious Certified Performance Technologist designation from the International Society for Performance Improvement. Her research on views of new online learners won an EDMEDIA best research paper award.

In addition to work, some of Patti's favorite things include yoga, hiking, black licorice, Phish Food™, *24* (the TV drama), Stephen King's *Dark Towers* book series, hanging out with friends and family, laughing, and new ideas.

Pfeiffer Publications Guide

This guide is designed to familiarize you with the various types of Pfeiffer publications. The formats section describes the various types of products that we publish; the methodologies section describes the many different ways that content might be provided within a product. We also provide a list of the topic areas in which we publish.

FORMATS

In addition to its extensive book-publishing program, Pfeiffer offers content in an array of formats, from fieldbooks for the practitioner to complete, ready-to-use training packages that support group learning.

FIELDBOOK Designed to provide information and guidance to practitioners in the midst of action. Most fieldbooks are companions to another, sometimes earlier, work, from which its ideas are derived; the fieldbook makes practical what was theoretical in the original text. Fieldbooks can certainly be read from cover to cover. More likely, though, you'll find yourself bouncing around following a particular theme, or dipping in as the mood, and the situation, dictate.

HANDBOOK A contributed volume of work on a single topic, comprising an eclectic mix of ideas, case studies, and best practices sourced by practitioners and experts in the field.

An editor or team of editors usually is appointed to seek out contributors and to evaluate content for relevance to the topic. Think of a handbook not as a ready-to-eat meal, but as a cookbook of ingredients that enables you to create the most fitting experience for the occasion.

RESOURCE Materials designed to support group learning. They come in many forms: a complete, ready-to-use exercise (such as a game); a comprehensive resource on one topic (such as conflict management) containing a variety of methods and approaches; or a collection of like-minded activities (such as icebreakers) on multiple subjects and situations.

TRAINING PACKAGE An entire, ready-to-use learning program that focuses on a particular topic or skill. All packages comprise a guide for the facilitator/trainer and a workbook for the participants. Some packages are supported with additional media—such as video—or learning aids, instruments, or other devices to help participants understand concepts or practice and develop skills.

- *Facilitator/trainer's guide* Contains an introduction to the program, advice on how to organize and facilitate the learning event, and step-by-step instructor notes. The guide also contains copies of presentation materials—handouts, presentations, and overhead designs, for example—used in the program.

- *Participant's workbook* Contains exercises and reading materials that support the learning goal and serves as a valuable reference and support guide for participants in the weeks and months that follow the learning event. Typically, each participant will require his or her own workbook.

ELECTRONIC CD-ROMs and web-based products transform static Pfeiffer content into dynamic, interactive experiences. Designed to take advantage of the searchability, automation, and ease-of-use that technology provides, our e-products bring convenience and immediate accessibility to your workspace.

METHODOLOGIES

CASE STUDY A presentation, in narrative form, of an actual event that has occurred inside an organization. Case studies are not prescriptive, nor are they used to prove a point; they are designed to develop critical analysis and decision-making skills. A case study has a specific time frame, specifies a sequence of events, is narrative in structure, and contains a plot structure—an issue (what should be/have been done?). Use case studies when the goal is to enable participants to apply previously learned theories to the circumstances in the case, decide what is pertinent, identify the real issues, decide what should have been done, and develop a plan of action.

ENERGIZER A short activity that develops readiness for the next session or learning event. Energizers are most commonly used after a break or lunch to stimulate or refocus the group. Many involve some form of physical activity, so they are a useful way to counter post-lunch lethargy. Other uses include transitioning from one topic to another, where "mental" distancing is important.

EXPERIENTIAL LEARNING ACTIVITY (ELA) A facilitator-led intervention that moves participants through the learning cycle from experience to application (also known as a Structured Experience). ELAs are carefully thought-out designs in which there is a definite learning purpose and intended outcome. Each step—everything that participants do during the activity—facilitates the accomplishment of the stated goal. Each ELA includes complete instructions for facilitating the intervention and a clear statement of goals, suggested group size and timing, materials required, an explanation of the process, and, where appropriate, possible variations to the activity. (For more detail on Experiential Learning Activities, see the Introduction to the *Reference Guide to Handbooks and Annuals*, 1999 edition, Pfeiffer, San Francisco.)

GAME A group activity that has the purpose of fostering team spirit and togetherness in addition to the achievement of a pre-stated goal. Usually contrived—undertaking a desert expedition, for example—this type of learning method offers an engaging means for participants to demonstrate and practice business and interpersonal skills. Games are effective for team building and personal development mainly because the goal is subordinate to the process—the means through which participants reach decisions, collaborate, communicate, and generate trust and understanding. Games often engage teams in "friendly" competition.

ICEBREAKER A (usually) short activity designed to help participants overcome initial anxiety in a training session and/or to acquaint the participants with one another. An icebreaker can be a fun activity or can be tied to specific topics or training goals. While a useful tool in itself, the icebreaker comes into its own in situations where tension or resistance exists within a group.

INSTRUMENT A device used to assess, appraise, evaluate, describe, classify, and summarize various aspects of human behavior. The term used to describe an instrument depends primarily on its format and purpose. These terms include survey, questionnaire, inventory, diagnostic, survey, and poll. Some uses of instruments include providing instrumental feedback to group members, studying here-and-now processes or functioning within a group, manipulating group composition, and evaluating outcomes of training and other interventions.

Instruments are popular in the training and HR field because, in general, more growth can occur if an individual is provided with a method for focusing specifically on his or her own behavior. Instruments also are used to obtain information that will serve as a basis for change and to assist in workforce planning efforts.

Paper-and-pencil tests still dominate the instrument landscape with a typical package comprising a facilitator's guide, which offers advice on administering the instrument and interpreting the collected data, and an initial set of instruments. Additional instruments are available separately. Pfeiffer, though, is investing heavily in e-instruments. Electronic instrumentation provides effortless distribution and, for larger groups particularly, offers advantages over paper-and-pencil tests in the time it takes to analyze data and provide feedback.

LECTURETTE A short talk that provides an explanation of a principle, model, or process that is pertinent to the participants' current learning needs. A lecturette is intended to establish a common language bond between the trainer and the participants by providing a mutual frame of reference. Use a lecturette as an introduction to a group activity or event, as an interjection during an event, or as a handout.

MODEL A graphic depiction of a system or process and the relationship among its elements. Models provide a frame of reference and something more tangible, and more easily remembered, than a verbal explanation. They also give participants something to "go on," enabling them to track their own progress as they experience the dynamics, processes, and relationships being depicted in the model.

ROLE PLAY A technique in which people assume a role in a situation/scenario: a customer service rep in an angry-customer exchange, for example. The way in which the role is approached is then discussed and feedback is offered. The role play is often repeated using a different approach and/or incorporating changes made based on feedback received. In other words, role playing is a spontaneous interaction involving realistic behavior under artificial (and safe) conditions.

SIMULATION A methodology for understanding the interrelationships among components of a system or process. Simulations differ from games in that they test or use a model that depicts or mirrors some aspect of reality in form, if not necessarily in content. Learning occurs by studying the effects of change on one or more factors of the model. Simulations are commonly used to test hypotheses about what happens in a system—often referred to as "what if?" analysis—or to examine best-case/worst-case scenarios.

THEORY A presentation of an idea from a conjectural perspective. Theories are useful because they encourage us to examine behavior and phenomena through a different lens.

TOPICS

The twin goals of providing effective and practical solutions for workforce training and organization development and meeting the educational needs of training and human resource professionals shape Pfeiffer's publishing program. Core topics include the following:

Leadership & Management

Communication & Presentation

Coaching & Mentoring

Training & Development

E-Learning

Teams & Collaboration

OD & Strategic Planning

Human Resources

Consulting

What will you find on pfeiffer.com?

- The best in workplace performance solutions for training and HR professionals

- Downloadable training tools, exercises, and content

- Web-exclusive offers

- Training tips, articles, and news

- Seamless on-line ordering

- Author guidelines, information on becoming a Pfeiffer Affiliate, and much more

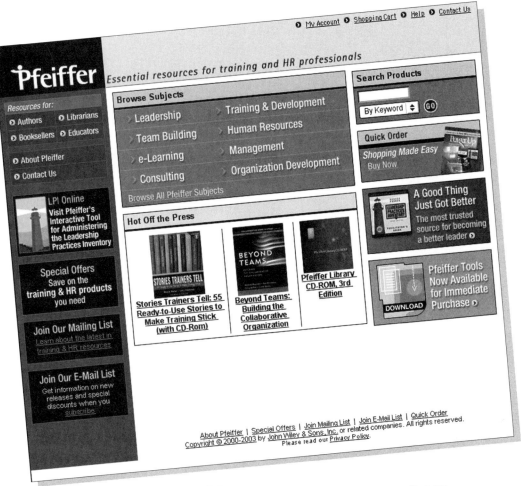

Discover more at www.pfeiffer.com